Hoyt Wilhelm

ALSO BY LEW FREEDMAN
AND FROM MCFARLAND

Chuckin' Charlie Conerly and the New York Football Giants (2023)

Johnny Mize: A Biography of Baseball's "Big Cat" (2022)

*Caught by Don Hutson!: A Biography of
Pro Football's First Modern Receiver* (2022)

*Lightning Strikes Twice: Johnny Vander Meer
and the Cincinnati Reds* (2021)

*Buffalo Bill Cody: The Man Who
Shaped the Wild West Legend* (2020)

Cy Young: The Baseball Life and Career (2020)

Ernie Banks: The Life and Career of "Mr. Cub" (2019)

*Connie Mack's First Dynasty:
The Philadelphia Athletics, 1910–1914* (2017)

*Baseball's Funnymen: Twenty-Four Jokers,
Screwballs, Pranksters and Storytellers* (2017)

The Boyer Brothers of Baseball (2015)

Joe Louis: The Life of a Heavyweight (2013)

*George Altman: My Baseball Journey from the Negro Leagues to the
Majors and Beyond* (by George Altman with Lew Freedman, 2013)

DiMaggio's Yankees: A History of the 1936–1944 Dynasty (2011)

*The Day All the Stars Came Out: Major League
Baseball's First All-Star Game, 1933* (2010)

Hard-Luck Harvey Haddix and the Greatest Game Ever Lost (2009)

Early Wynn, the Go-Go White Sox and the 1959 World Series (2009)

Hoyt Wilhelm
Life of a Knuckleballer

LEW FREEDMAN

McFarland & Company, Inc., Publishers
Jefferson, North Carolina

ISBN (print) 978-1-4766-9206-7
ISBN (ebook) 978-1-4766-5100-2

LIBRARY OF CONGRESS AND BRITISH LIBRARY
CATALOGUING DATA ARE AVAILABLE

Library of Congress Control Number 2023057958

© 2024 Lew Freedman. All rights reserved

No part of this book may be reproduced or transmitted in any form or by any means, electronic or mechanical, including photocopying or recording, or by any information storage and retrieval system, without permission in writing from the publisher.

Front cover: New York Giants pitcher Hoyt Wilhelm
(National Baseball Hall of Fame Library, Cooperstown, N.Y.)

Printed in the United States of America

*McFarland & Company, Inc., Publishers
Box 611, Jefferson, North Carolina 28640
www.mcfarlandpub.com*

Table of Contents

Preface	1
Introduction	3
1. A North Carolina Guy	7
2. From North Carolina to North Carolina	16
3. War	23
4. Starting Over	29
5. Minneapolis: Make It or Break It	35
6. The Majors at Last	42
7. A Hot Commodity	51
8. The World Series	60
9. Entrenched with New York	73
10. On to Other Teams	80
11. Lightning Strikes	88
12. Rebirth with Orioles	98
13. Trying to Make Sense of It	108
14. Out of Control	116
15. Hanging Tough with the Orioles	125
16. Good Company	134
17. Wilbur and Hoyt	143
18. White Sox and Still Going	155

Table of Contents

19. A Thousand Games	165
20. Running Out of Teams	173
21. A Call from the Hall	181
Epilogue	189
Notes	195
Bibliography	203
Index	205

Preface

Hoyt Wilhelm experienced a Major League Baseball career unlike anyone else. His long adventure was as twisting and winding as a rural mountain road, full of slow-motion development, high-speed turns, unexpected trades, and glittering accomplishments.

One of the sport's greatest practitioners of one of its most esoteric weapons—the knuckleball—Wilhelm defied the odds, outlasted a long list of doubters, and became one of the most esteemed pitchers of his era and, through his inclusion in the Hall of Fame, one of the most esteemed of all time.

Born in 1922, Wilhelm was a native of North Carolina who on his own acquired an affinity for the odd knuckleball pitch as a youth. Then for years he suffered in the obscurity of the minor leagues with an inability to convince big-league teams he was the real deal.

A rookie at age 29, Wilhelm somehow stayed active in the majors for almost two decades after that, retiring at age 49 as one of the oldest big leaguers in history.

His knuckleball flummoxed batters, managers and coaches, baseball fans and writers, none of whom could figure out how a man who might regularly hurl pitches to the plate at less than 70 miles per hour could be so successful. The answer? His pitches broke dramatically, seeming to dance or dart as they made their way to the plate. Batters swung and whiffed, but catchers—men on his side—also whiffed, paralyzed when a ball they expected to zig instead zagged. They thrust their mitts out into the air in desperation, only to be left scrambling toward the backstop to retrieve a missed throw. Catchers who might otherwise be All-Stars were sometimes driven to distraction trying to field Wilhelm's tosses, and they were charged with record numbers of passed balls, to their great frustration.

While he represented other franchises that either gave up on him as he aged or worried excessively about his impact on the catching

Preface

corps, Wilhelm is most often identified with three teams: the New York Giants, the Baltimore Orioles and the Chicago White Sox.

Over a stretch of 21 seasons, Wilhelm won 143 Major League games. During an era when the role of the relief pitcher was very different from that of today's closer and set-up men, Wilhelm generally pitched multiple innings in each appearance. He compiled 228 saves.

An eight-time All-Star, Wilhelm compiled a lifetime earned run average of 2.52—or a stellar 147 ERA+—capturing two league ERA titles along the way. The right-hander also twice led the National League in games pitched and twice in winning percentage. Wilhelm won as many as 15 games in a season, quite a number for someone who was predominantly a relief pitcher. (He did, however, spend chunks of time as a starter for different clubs.)

A baseball lifer, Wilhelm didn't really want to retire when he stepped away as an active player in 1972. Instead of seeking a new line of work, he remained in the game for many more years as a minor league manager and coach.

Those who threw the knuckleball in the majors represent a small fraternity of pitchers. Not even the best of them, Wilhelm included, ever declared that they understood exactly why their favorite pitch performed the tricks they asked it to when they most needed it.

Those knuckleballers did consider themselves to be a fraternity of sorts, too. Often over the years, if one of them lost his form and became desperate, he turned to a fellow knuckleball twirler for advice and assistance. Few of these pitchers had full faith in their own professional pitching coaches, who had been fastball and curveball pitchers.

What Wilhelm produced during his journey through the majors was sustained bafflement. No matter how long he stuck around he could still confuse batters with his knuckleball. For the finest hitters, it was an insult of sorts. How could a pitcher throwing at just beyond Little League speed make them appear foolish while they swung their bats? Even worse, from their view, was Wilhelm's continued success—how could the old man keep beating them with that ridiculous pitch?

Fellow Hall of Famer Phil Niekro, the winningest knuckleball pitcher with 318 victories, had an answer for them: "Wilhelm, to me, was the best."[1]

Introduction

The knuckleball, the pitch that defined Hoyt Wilhelm's baseball career, has always been shrouded in mystery. Although there are hints and suggestions, it is not 100 percent certain who invented it. As a weapon, it is not completely clear how something that approaches through the air somewhat like a balloon should be so difficult to hit. And above all, it is not exactly known why the knuckler is so hard to control. It may be that when everything is scientifically evaluated, the most accurate words are "Search me."

If there is such a pitch that can be described as being the dead opposite of the fastball, it is the knuckleball. By its own identifying description, a fastball comes at a batter fast. No pitch leaves the pitcher's hand and floats to the plate slower than a knuckleball. Rather than the typical 95–100 mph speed of a fastball, a knuckler may travel at 65 mph.

The fastball, when thrown inside, may be called "a purpose pitch," thrown with intimidation and intended to move a batter off the plate. A knuckler is meant to fool a hitter, even if he thinks he follows it all the way in, because it changes direction erratically. A hitter may become angry at a pitcher if he feels a high-speed pitch came too close to his head because he worries about getting hurt. A hitter may become angry at a pitcher if he swings and misses at a knuckler because he fears being humiliated.

There are 100 or more times as many successful fastball pitchers throughout Major League Baseball history as there are successful knuckleball pitchers. Throwing at high velocity garners more attention than at batting cage or high school velocity. After all, winners reaching speeds of 230 mph in the Indianapolis 500 are feted. Those who motor along at the speed limit don't make the field.

Legendary umpire and humorist Ron Luciano applied his fertile mind to analyzing the knuckleball and once said, "Like some cult religion that barely survives, there has always been at least one, but no more than five or six devotees throwing the knuckleball in the big leagues. Not only can't pitchers control it, hitters can't hit it, catchers can't catch it, coaches can't coach it, and most pitchers can't learn it. The perfect pitch."[1]

Luciano, who wrote light-hearted books about his experiences umpiring, probably did laugh at a few batters who flailed at knucklers right before his very eyes. However, most of what he said many years ago is still on the money about the knuckleball. Those who relied on it would likely prefer having their club characterized as a brotherhood than a club, but the number of practitioners has dwindled even further to zero in the majors over the last couple of years. Still, one never can predict when a newfound knuckleball artist will arise on the scene. Most hitters, catchers and coaches have always been members of the "can't" group Luciano talked about.

Thomas Edison may have invented the light bulb and the phonograph and received something on the order of 1,000 patents, but he did not invent the knuckleball. Who did is somewhat murky. Different researchers point to different a-ha moments.

Toad Ramsey, throwing for the Louisville Colonels and St. Louis Browns in the American Association between 1885 and 1890 when it was a recognized major league, may have been the guy. Nap Rucker of the Brooklyn Dodgers could have been the one when he pitched during the first decade of the 1900s, or Ed Cicotte, who began using it around 1908, could have been the originator. Cicotte was more infamous than famous because he played a key role in fixing the 1919 World Series when he was the No. 1 starter for the Chicago White Sox. Cicotte was a tremendous pitcher who retreated into seclusion in shame after the Black Sox scandal. Cicotte won 209 games with a lifetime 2.38 earned run average, but he is basically remembered for cheating instead of creating the knuckler.

Phil Niekro, who won 318 games with the knuckleball as his primary pitch, once said he didn't know much about Cicotte as a hurler "other than he was one of the original guys."[2]

In the 2020s, fans listening to a baseball broadcast on radio or watching one on television will inevitably be inundated by analysis of a pitcher's stuff based on his spin rate. The knuckleball is notable for its lack of spin. The combination of being thrown at low speed and with a lack of spin fools batters. The rare twirler who excels with its use baffles hitters, who practically never see it otherwise during their games.

Perhaps only a few dozen big-league pitchers have ever relied on

Introduction

the knuckler with any success, some for only a short time, rarely for long-term success. For the small minority who did not attach themselves to the knuckler as youths and make do throughout their careers, they turned to the pitch in desperation to save their careers. Sometimes they discovered the fastball of their past didn't cut it in the big-time anymore. Sometimes they suffered an injury and grasped for a solution to allow them to make a comeback.

As Luciano elucidated, few coaches are expert enough to teach the knuckler. Several pitchers were self-taught or sought assistance from established knuckleball throwers who could instruct them and offer advice. Many knuckleballers were truly self-made men. They also knew they mostly had to rely on their own judgment if things went askew.

Knuckleballers do not all grip the ball the same way. Contrary to popular thought, they do not all involve their knuckles in the manner in which they hold the ball but more commonly they use their fingertips. Whatever works.

Given that the beginning of the National League in 1876 is the recognized beginning of Major League Baseball, the list of true, accomplished knuckleballers is a short one, though the list of players who had short-term success with it or who gave it a try pads the participation list.

Jim Bouton, better known for writing the best-selling book *Ball Four*, was once a speedster success with the New York Yankees in the early 1960s, but he reinvented himself as a knuckleballer for a comeback in the late 1970s.

Gene Bearden burst on the big-league scene and helped carry the Cleveland (then) Indians to their last World Series championship in 1948, but his career was shortened by injury.

Those who assuredly stand out for counting on the knuckler, with both some longevity and achievement, include Cicotte, Tom Candiotti, R.A. Dickey (a Cy Young award winner), Eddie Fisher, Hall of Famers Jesse Haines and Ted Lyons, Dutch Leonard, Ed Rommel (one of the earliest knuckleballers), Tim Wakefield (who, with 186 victories, won nearly as many games for the Boston Red Sox as Cy Young and Roger Clemens who had 192 each), Charlie Hough, Wilbur Wood, and Phil Niekro and his brother Joe. The Niekros learned how to throw the pitch in their backyard in Ohio from their father, Phil Sr., then combined for a record 539 victories (Joe, the non–Hall of Famer, contributed 221).

And, of course, there was Hoyt Wilhelm, who outdid most of them in most ways or, at least, partially paved a path for his modern knuckleball brethren. Wilhelm was one of the men of the mound who brought

Hoyt Wilhelm

the knuckleball with him to the majors. He did not come to its use as an add-on to his arsenal to replace a too-slow fastball or to supplement what he already had to put himself over the top. Wilhelm became aware of and fascinated by the knuckleball as a youth. Once he became good enough to use it in games against live batters, he rode it for the rest of his career.

1

A North Carolina Guy

Somewhere along the way, James Hoyt Wilhelm's birthdate got messed up. Throughout his long baseball career his DOB was given as July 26, 1923. Much later, it leaked out that Wilhelm was actually born on the same date but in 1922. He never bothered correcting anyone like newspaper reporters because, well, who wouldn't want a free year of life?

Wilhelm's place of birth was Huntersville, North Carolina. It was farm country, though given its proximity to Charlotte, the largest city in the Carolinas, roughly 15 miles to the south, not as rural as might be thought.

Wilhelm, who was around the middle of the pack, was one of 11 children born to John and Ethel. The family resided on a farm and Wilhelm's dad worked the land but also worked in a textile mill. There were four boys in the herd, one older than Hoyt and two younger than him. But they did not gravitate to baseball with anything like the seriousness Hoyt did. It was not a wealthy family but one that got by financially.

Viki Hager, the youngest of the siblings, described herself as "the baby" and said she was the last of the brood still living. In the fall of 2022, she recalled her father as "a tenant farmer. We didn't stay at the same place all the time."[1] Crops grown where he worked were corn and cotton, she said.

Approximately 18 years younger than Hoyt, Hager did not have many memories of childhood that revolved around him in his youth. It was as if they were of different generations. An odd headline, accompanied by no story, can be stumbled upon through the Internet. It says simply: "The Most Famous Person Born in Huntersville, North Carolina, Is Hoyt Wilhelm." The way Viki Hager describes the Huntersville of her youth, it does not sound as if the competition for greatest fame would have been that great.

"It was a nice, small town," said Hager, who still lives in North Carolina. "Everyone's address was basically route 20 Huntersville."[2]

Hoyt Wilhelm

Hoyt Wilhelm (right) shakes hands with New York Yankees pitcher Whitey Ford. They pitched against one another throughout the 1950s and into the 1960s. Both became Hall of Famers (National Baseball Hall of Fame Library, Cooperstown, N.Y.).

Huntersville itself had grown to more than 61,000 people by the 2020 United States census—not huge but not quite the cozy place of Wilhelm's youth. In the 21st century, the most prominent local sporting connection was the fact Joe Gibbs Racing is based there. He had supervised the success of five NASCAR championships produced by Bobby Labonte, Tony Stewart and Kyle Busch, but that was a considerably later era.

Also in later years, Huntersville was a cog in the Mecklenburg County machine, where more than 1.1 million people resided. That was essentially because of Charlotte. Even when Huntersville was more farmland it was within easy reach of city amenities.

The region became more sophisticated, and long after the Wilhelms got by with tenant farming, the largest employers in the county included Atrium Health, Bank of America, American Airlines, government agencies and the University of North Carolina at Charlotte.

Hoyt Wilhelm grew up when baseball was king of the American

1. A North Carolina Guy

sporting landscape, indeed the National Pastime. As times changed, the Carolina Panthers National Football League team and the Charlotte Hornets National Basketball Association team became widely popular professional sports representatives in the area, as well as NASCAR, with its Charlotte Motor Speedway. The speedway, located in Concord, advertises that it can host between 94,000 and 171,000 fans for an event depending on the set-up of seating, an unfathomable number of spectators during Wilhelm's pre–World War II years growing up in the region.

Hager said she did not know how Wilhelm's date of birth became confused.

"I just know there was some discrepancy at some time," she said. "I honestly don't know. But I remember at one time my parents tried to get a birth certificate for me."[3] Since they had difficulty doing so, she wondered if such issues were more common years ago. Still, she knows her real date of birth is October 6, 1938.

Young Hoyt took to baseball with much more passion than his brothers did, though Hager remembers the family being excited when the pitcher advanced to play professionally and his parents and siblings sometimes traveling to away games to see him pitch live. When he was in the majors, they watched television when Wilhelm's teams were playing and they knew he was going to throw.

That lay far in the future for Wilhelm growing up in the 1920s and 1930s. He may well have ended up like the many American boys who dream big but come to realize their enthusiasm exceeds their talents and they will never make good in the big leagues.

Wilhelm experienced his epiphany moment when he was in high school and good enough to compete for the Cornelius High ball club. However, it was not the same eureka realization the vast majority experienced. Rather than admit he was not good enough to go far in the game he loved, Wilhelm came to a crossroads when he recognized he had to do something to enhance his capability.

In casual references in interviews over the years to a life-changing moment, Wilhelm did not make it clear exactly how old he was when he was influenced in the direction of taking up the knuckleball. He was, however, very clear in pinpointing the impetus. Apparently, the Wilhelm family regularly read the *Charlotte News* newspaper.

Wilhelm repeatedly told sportswriters over the decades that his courtship of the knuckleball began when he was leafing through the newspaper and saw a photograph of Dutch Leonard, a prominent knuckleball thrower. While it is not 100 percent certain that the pivotal moment in Wilhelm's development stemmed from the *Charlotte News* of March 14, 1941, when he already would have been 19 years old, it is likely. On that day, the paper ran a trio of photographs highlighting the unusual combination in the pitching rotation for the Washington Senators. The team had Leonard, Ken Chase, and a rookie named Sid Hudson running out to the mound to start games—and all were knuckleball throwers. The caption under the photo called them "experts" and said they were currently the only three knuckleball throwers in the majors.[4]

As a high school player, when Wilhelm was not pitching, he played some outfield and third base, but he admitted even for that level of competition he was not a hard thrower. "I started messing with the knuckleball in high school," Wilhelm said.[5]

Inspired by Leonard, who had a track record better than his lesser-known Senators teammates, Wilhelm decided the knuckler was for him. It was mostly solo work, experimenting with grip, with technique, with throwing. Wilhelm gradually incorporated the knuckleball into his pitching routine, his right hand grasping the ball between the tips of his index and middle fingers and his thumb. He squeezed the ball, exerting pressure with his fingertips, when he let it fly to the plate.

Living on a farm, Wilhelm had plenty of room for practice. Although the knuckler was never going to travel very fast, there was always going to be some difficulty in mastering it. Actually, mastering the knuckler, even for Hoyt Wilhelm, is a misnomer, because the best veterans employing it had occasions when the knuckler seemed to go off and do what it wished, like an automobile with a busted steering wheel.

"As a kid in high school, I just didn't have a fast one," Wilhelm said, "and I picked up the knuckler. Nobody taught me. I just found out about throwing it."[6]

Wilhelm was soft-spoken and not terribly loquacious in interviews, and he rarely dove deep into his emotions when speaking to sportswriters about his early years. For decades, he talked about Dutch Leonard's influence, just about single-handedly keeping alive the memory of Leonard's career long after the man had retired.

Emil John "Dutch" Leonard was born March 25, 1909, in Auburn, Illinois. He threw right-handed like Wilhelm, was a spear-carrier for the knuckleball like Wilhelm, spent 20 years in the majors like Wilhelm, and later moved on to coaching like Wilhelm. So he was an appropriate role model and there were definitely parallels between the two men's

1. A North Carolina Guy

careers, even though they only barely overlapped in the majors during their playing days.

It should be noted that in the course of big-league baseball history there was another pitching Dutch Leonard. Hubert Benjamin "Dutch" Leonard, born in 1892, pre-dated both the other Dutch and Wilhelm. He was a southpaw. He passed away in 1952, just as the second Dutch Leonard's career was winding down and Hoyt Wilhelm's was revving up.

The original Dutch pitched in the majors between 1913 and 1925 and won 139 games. His most memorable and sterling accomplishment was recording a 0.96 earned run average in 1914 while pitching for the Boston Red Sox. That remains the all-time record for the lowest ERA posted during a single season in the modern era. This Leonard did not throw a knuckleball to batters.

The Dutch Leonard who caught Wilhelm's eye and changed his life broke into the majors in 1933 with the Brooklyn Dodgers and managed 20 seasons in the bigs, concluding his career in 1953 with the Chicago Cubs. He won 191 games in a solid career. This Leonard's nickname of Dutch was borrowed from the original.

He experienced several notable moments on the mound. One was being the complete-game winning pitcher over the New York Yankees on July 4, 1939, the day his Senators served as opponents on Lou Gehrig Day at Yankee Stadium. This was when Gehrig issued his famous, heartfelt address to fans that became known as the "Luckiest Man" speech as he was dying of amyotrophic lateral sclerosis.

On October 1, 1944, Leonard won the game that gave the St. Louis Browns the only pennant in their existence. Besides Wilhelm, another admirer of the second Dutch Leonard was famed crime novelist Elmore Leonard, who died in 2013 at age 87. Not only was he nicknamed Dutch in an homage to the thrower but the author also sported "Dutch" as a tattoo.

When Dutch Leonard the right-handed pitcher was a member of the Washington Senators, he was joined by three other knuckleball specialists. This was 1945, a few years after the photograph of the three Senators appeared in the Charlotte newspaper that must be the one that caught Wilhelm's eye. During that era clubs often relied on four-man starting rotations; they didn't have the enlarged versions of the 2020s. Leonard, Mickey Haefner, Johnny Niggeling and Roger Wolff were the Washington hurlers, the only time in history one team featured four knuckleball starters simultaneously.

Hoyt Wilhelm

Washington fared pretty well with this unusual combination of slow-ballers. Leonard was not even the best of the group, despite going 17–7 with a 2.13 earned run average. Wolff notched by far the best season of his career with a 20–10 record and a 2.12 ERA. Haefner went 16–14 with a 3.47 ERA. Niggeling did not do so well, ending up 7–12, though his earned run average wasn't bad at 3.16.

The starters were supplemented by Marino Pieretti, who went 14–13 with a 3.32 ERA. This was also his best year in a short career. Presumably, even though Pieretti was not a knuckleball thrower, the others still talked to him.

As was the case for many knuckleballing specialists, Leonard did not count on his knuckles to fling the ball. One headline writer in a Charlotte newspaper had fun dissecting this fact and a short story about Leonard in a 1938 read: "Dutch Uses Finger Tips. It May Be a Knuckler, But It Really Isn't."[7]

Somewhat ahead of his time in this matter, Leonard persevered at the big-league level with his knuckler to an advanced age—as did Wilhelm—out-lasting fastball pitchers of this period. Eventually, as he showed up for a new season each spring, sportswriters quizzed him about his staying power, how he did it, how long he would stick with it, and when he was going to retire. This same process was repeated with Wilhelm, and other longstanding knuckleball throwers with stamina, a generation or more later.

In the middle of the 1952 season, when Leonard was in the employ of the Chicago Cubs and turning 43 years old, a headline appeared in an Oklahoma newspaper from a syndicated wire service story: "Dutch Leonard Keeps Throwing His Knuckleball." The lead paragraph of the story read: "Dutch Leonard has been throwing baseballs for 20 years and the Chicago Cubs' knuckleball artist figured Wednesday he might keep going another 20."[8]

He was a reliever, called upon less frequently but always available. "I feel fine," he said. "I'd like more work. I need to keep my knuckleball sharp, but the warm weather helps me do that, too. I remember one stretch last season when I warmed up for 30 days in a row. That's too much, but with the pace the way it is now, I'd like to go another 20 years and I feel like I can."[9]

The reason why knuckleballers and Leonard often responded to questions about their futures in such a manner is that competing into their 40s was viewed with suspicion. Those specialists managed to do so in inordinate numbers because the knuckler put such slight

1. A North Carolina Guy

strain on their throwing arms and shoulders compared to fastballs and curveballs.

The same type of interviews followed Leonard in 1953, the season he began at 43 and ended at 44, still with the Cubs, who were throwing him a special day of honor that season. *The Saturday Evening Post*, one of America's most popular general interest magazines at the time, sought Leonard out to discuss his long run in the majors.

"At the age of 43, it's more of a surprise to me than to anyone else," Leonard said of how he kept hanging on.[10] He actually showed how he was hanging on, literally, by posing for a photograph displaying his knuckler grip on the ball. The index finger and middle finger stuck up in the air, his thumb cradled the ball from beneath, and his fourth finger nestled against a side.

He was the last man standing from active rosters of 1933 still playing in the majors in 1953. Leonard boasted of no outstanding athletic talent whatsoever. "No other ballplayer ever went as far—or as long—on limited ability," Leonard said.[11]

While no such thing was ever stated about the heralded pitchers who came into the game blazing fastballs past hitters or stunning them into disbelief with wide breaking curveballs, Leonard, who stood six feet tall and weighed 175 pounds in his playing days, was very aware of his limitations.

"I never was a world-beater," said Leonard, who suited up for the Dodgers, Senators, Phillies and Cubs over his 20 years of service. "Maybe that's why I've had the equivalent of three big-league careers. During my time, at least 1,000 pitchers have come and gone. Practically all of them could throw harder than I and the majority had better curveballs.

"To hold one of the 100 pitching jobs for grabs annually in the majors, I had to develop a trick delivery, a knuckleball that has been my meal ticket for the last 15 years."[12]

The knuckler, he added, allowed him to win 20 games one season (1939) and become an All-Star five times. He was the winning pitcher for the American League in the 1943 All-Star game in Philadelphia, so-called trick delivery or not.

What it did not do was enable Leonard to pitch another 20 years, until he was nearly 70 years old, or fulfill his goal of winning 200 games. He retired after the 1953 season. Leonard's coincidental appearance in Wilhelm's local newspaper showing off the knuckleball and his career as a whole could serve as templates for the young North Carolinian's baseball future.

Hoyt Wilhelm

Much like Dutch Leonard, Hoyt Wilhelm had no false modesty about the effectiveness of his fastball. Often, a high school pitcher with a zooming fastball can get by with no other tool than a change-up. Then, when he seeks to advance to college baseball or the professional minors, he is rudely awakened by facing better hitters who do not view his fastball as quite so fast at all. Their acumen at the plate allows them to pick and choose—and importantly—tell the difference between a fastball of 80 miles an hour and 90 miles an hour. Those may have been more or less the digits when Wilhelm was young. Nowadays, many players flirt with or top 100 mph.

In either case, Wilhelm did not fool himself. He wished to somehow make a living throwing a baseball after high school, but he understood he wasn't going to make the cut with a Grade B fastball. On his own initiative, he taught himself the knuckleball, putting long hours into perfecting something that could hardly be perfected, but which made him a much more effective commodity.

"I fell in love with the pitch, reading about it," Wilhelm said of what he owed to the publicity surrounding Leonard.[13]

Even when managers are the bosses of superb knuckleball specialists, they don't seem to trust the pitch. That makes sense, because it is something they don't really understand. If they don't comprehend how or why it works, then they more readily abandon a knuckleballer when something goes wrong or he goes into a slump.

In the athletic world, it is often said that no one can teach speed. That mostly applies to humans running on a field. It also applies to those blessed with bazookas for arms. It turns out that no one can really teach lack of speed either.

In the pitching world, or at least before every toss was analyzed and dissected by mathematicians, it was good enough if a hurler could get batters out any way possible. Rarely does a pitcher get challenged about what he is doing if he puts zeroes on the scoreboard. The exception seems to be for knuckleballers.

Those like Wilhelm who counted on the knuckleball might as well have been magicians, playing before wide audiences watching in wonder but never receiving an explanation for the trick. They were supposed to take the results on faith.

While he uttered the statement many years after adopting the knuckleball as the guiding light of his baseball career, surely general managers, managers and coaches flinched if they read Wilhelm's blunt assessment about the conundrum of the knuckler, further solidifying their view that it was some sort of voodoo or black art.

1. A North Carolina Guy

"I don't throw so much to spots as I pitch to an area," Wilhelm said. "I get it over the plate a high percentage of the time, but wind resistance seems to make it dart up or drop off or break one way or another all of a sudden. Usually, it dances. The big thing is it has to break every time since I'm not pitching to spots or overpowering anyone. If I lose the feel for it for awhile and it doesn't break, it doesn't do anything and it's murdered. Fortunately, this has been rare."[14]

Yet somehow over time from his first experimentation on, Wilhelm manufactured a certain level of mastery (though he and other knuckleball stars tend to shun that word about their prowess) over the knuckleball. Better than most, he might admit. Better than most all others, admirers might say.

2

From North Carolina to North Carolina

As a youth in North Carolina, Hoyt Wilhelm competed in sandlot baseball on playgrounds with friends in the area. His first real organized ball was playing for his high school team. Little League, founded in 1939, was in its early stages as Wilhelm was nearing the end of his time at Cornelius High School, not the ubiquitous opportunity it is for children now.

Nor were there youth leagues for teens as there are now and certainly there was no concept of summer travel teams representing communities. Wilhelm, who could be notoriously reticent when it came to dealing with personal questions despite participating in uncounted numbers of interviews with sportswriters after ascending to the big leagues, always said his only pre-professional baseball experience occurred as a high schooler.

In an oddly composed short item in the *Charlotte Observer,* apparently submitted by a parent or a coach discussing the action in the first person rather than in a journalistic style, Wilhelm received some local publicity. In part, the few-paragraphs-long report under the headline "First Ball Game" read, "Our baseball team has started off with a bang! And I do mean bang—with a 9–6 victory over the highly touted Long Creek nine! Thanks to the superb pitching and batting of Hoyt Wilhelm, who struck out 11, yes 11 men, and got four singles. We came back to take over a three-run lead and march on to our first victory of the year."[1] Indeed, this news item did employ exclamation points and used the word "we."

In April of 1941, the *Charlotte Observer* again took note of Wilhelm for throwing a no-hitter on behalf of Cornelius High. Wilhelm's team won the game easily and the short report went this way: "Hoyt Wilhelm hurled a no-hit, no-run game for the Cornelius High school yesterday over Long Creek on the latter's diamond, 14 to 0. Aside from

2. From North Carolina to North Carolina

the pitching of Wilhelm, the fielding of Long Creek's Kidd was a feature of the game. Knox with 3 for 4 and Mays, with 2 for 3, paced the winners."[2] Except for Wilhelm, not even the other stars of the contest rated their first names being mentioned.

As someone not destined to attend college in the years immediately following the Great Depression, Wilhelm seemed to have a sole career track in his head—becoming a professional baseball player as a pitcher. He may have dabbled in the outfield or wherever his coach placed him during his high school days, but pitching was the opportunity he pursued.

The trail he followed was a long one, offering limited promise in the beginning, and it took determination, patience and perseverance for Wilhelm to find the yellow-brick road and stay on the path. In the beginning, besides his innate ability, there really was just one genuine plus in his favor—minor league teams were situated all over the American landscape.

While the majors were more condensed, with a mere eight teams in each of the two big leagues, following the lead of Branch Rickey with the St. Louis Cardinals and Brooklyn Dodgers, squads in both the American League and the National League were expanding their farm systems and fighting back at Rickey's efforts to corner the market on young talent. Rickey invented the farm system and literally did try to sign any player of promise. If a player showed some skill and Rickey was conscious of it, he was pleased to offer a contract. His motives were twofold. If the player was good enough, great, he would eventually make his way to the big club and help win pennants. If the player was borderline, he was still under Rickey's control and that meant he kept the prospect out of the clutches of any other club.

Rickey was so aggressive in this manner that ultimately Commissioner Kennesaw Mountain Landis stepped in and released Rickey's and the St. Louis Cardinals' hold on a large group of players. Landis took the dramatic step in March of 1938. He made 74 Cardinal players free agents and fined the operators of six minor-league teams. St. Louis and Rickey were the target, because it was stated they controlled more than one team in the same league.

By 1940, there was a much wider dispersal of minor-league talent. Two years after Landis wielded his muscle, this is how the minor-league clubs were distributed: Boston Bees (Braves), five teams; Boston Red Sox, eight teams; Brooklyn Dodgers, 18 teams; Chicago Cubs, six teams; Chicago White Sox, five teams; Cincinnati Reds, seven teams; Cleveland

Hoyt Wilhelm

Indians, 10 teams; Detroit Tigers, six teams; New York Giants, seven teams; New York Yankees, 14 teams; Philadelphia Athletics, four teams; Philadelphia Phillies, eight teams; Pittsburgh Pirates, 10 teams; St. Louis Browns, 11 teams; St. Louis Cardinals, 31 teams; Washington Senators, nine teams. The 31 teams still affiliated with the Cardinals was a somewhat hilarious illustration of that club still operating under the Rickey premise, even if he couldn't sign everyone to contracts.

That minor-league club count did not include non-affiliated teams, but what the large number of teams out there overall meant for a hopeful such as Wilhelm was that if he displayed any skill whatsoever, there should have been a roster for him to land on and to show what he could do.

Then, as now, it was all about getting noticed, about having some scout see you throw and then writing a report for the front office telling the readers about you and projecting a future. There were no radar guns measuring the speed a high-school pitcher threw at the time and the machine would not have been telling in Wilhelm's case anyway. Word spread in print slower than it does now. There were no computers with websites posting highlight films or reports about young hurlers with potential. Much like gold hidden in the hills, a pitcher had to be discovered—either that or somehow sell himself to a knowledgeable coach who could spread the word to a scout he knew.

It was easier to be overlooked than discovered, easier to languish in a small town far from a major league hub than to be spotted and endorsed by a scout representing anybody in the big-time. There was also no way to predict just how a scout who happened upon a knuckleball artist might react to or judge a young thrower who wasn't throwing hard.

Wilhelm seemed to have the backing of his family to pursue his goal. This was not true of every young athlete who came from limited circumstances. Parents sometimes felt their boys were wasting their time and their efforts would be better spent working and earning money.

It was not as if Wilhelm's father was counting on him to take over the family business, such as it was, in their case, not seeing a future of grand opportunity in tenant farming. Several years after Wilhelm reached the big leagues, Cooper, one of his brothers, confirmed this outlook. "Hoyt never had trouble getting out of the chores if there was a game to be played," this younger sibling said. "Dad always believed that if Hoyt wanted to play ball, he should have the chance."[3]

2. From North Carolina to North Carolina

Wilhelm knew he did not want to be a farmer if he didn't have to become one, so he had to work to make a baseball connection. After high school Wilhelm did have the opportunity to attend Davidson College in Davidson, North Carolina. The school is located just down the road, seven miles, from Huntersville. But he rolled the dice on pro ball.

What Wilhelm could not have imagined coming out of high school is how long it would take him to make it to the top. Of all of the most prominent Major League Baseball players who reached the Hall of Fame, who had special careers, Wilhelm was just about the slowest-starting of them all.

Another notable exception to the majority of players who reached the top was another future Hall of Famer, Dazzy Vance, who paralleled Wilhelm's slow ascent. After a few brief trials, he did not make the majors full-time until he was 31.

Dazzy Vance was born March 4, 1891, as Charles Arthur Vance in Orient, Iowa, a tiny community less than 70 miles north of Des Moines, but when he was still a child he moved to Nebraska. It was there he began showing off a fastball in semi-pro competition that earned him a look-see with the Pittsburgh Pirates and the New York Yankees.

Vance was already 24 in 1915 when he pitched once for Pittsburgh, getting clobbered to the tune of a 10.13 earned run average and a 0–1 record. He went 0–3 for the Yankees in eight appearances and then disappeared completely from the majors until 1918. That year he made it into two more games for the Yankees but with an unsightly ERA of 15.43.

Arm woes kept Vance down on the farm—lots of farms—a virtually forgotten figure until 1922. During his years in the baseball wilderness, Vance seemingly played for as many minor-league clubs as the Cardinals connected with, pitching for squads in Superior, Wisconsin; Columbus, Ohio; Memphis, Tennessee; Sacramento, California; and New Orleans, among others. Rarely during his decade floating around America did Vance truly excel for entire seasons until he won 21 games for New Orleans of the Southern League in 1921.

In 1922, Vance was a rookie overnight sensation for Brooklyn, winning 18 games at age 31. Twice he led the National League in victories during the 1920s, captured three league earned run average titles, won 197 Major League games and a Most Valuable Player award, and became a Hall of Famer.

While Hoyt Wilhelm lived for baseball, it was not clear how much of a student of the game he was, if he was conscious of Vance's travails and challenges when the younger man was setting out to make his own way. Certainly, he had no way in 1942 to think his own convoluted route to the majors might parallel such an odyssey.

Appropriately enough, Wilhelm found a home for the 1942 season in the North Carolina State League. Before baseball rewrote its classifications so as not to demoralize minor leaguers by rating their level of play downward from Class A through Class D and no longer referring to anything with anything less than "As," this was Class D ball.

The entire league was situated within the boundaries of North Carolina, with teams located in Hickory, Concord, Lexington, Landis, Mooresville, Salisbury, Statesville and Thomasville. Salisbury had an affiliation with the New York Giants and Thomasville with the Cleveland Indians.

Putting it another way, one might say Wilhelm was surrounded by professional baseball opportunity within his home state. He ended up signing with the Mooresville Moors. Mooresville is just 17 miles north of Huntersville. He did not, however, get off to a very good start with Mooresville.

"When the manager saw my knuckler, he sent me home," Wilhelm said. "But I was back for another look in two weeks and when I used the knuckler to win a game, and then go on to nine straight, nobody objected again to the pitch."[4]

There was nothing glitzy about the operation at the lowest level of the minors, but it was a big step for Wilhelm, making the move from high school competition to professional ball. Wilhelm did not go into great detail about how he landed with Mooresville. He described the Moors as an independent team. They were part of an organized league, but it was true they had no big-league affiliation.

In his first stopover in pro ball, Wilhelm was fairly successful, doing well enough to believe he had chosen well. That season, Wilhelm pitched in 23 games for the Moors, eight of them starts. His record was an excellent 10–3, but his earned run average was a very average 4.25. The showing was compiled over 108 innings, during which he permitted 105 hits.

Wilhelm had enough faith in himself as he was growing into manhood and approaching the six-foot height and 190 pounds distributed on his frame that he would eventually reach to think he was in a good place and would just advance from his performance in 1942.

Of course, given that he was of sound health and had no impediments, he might have been delusional to think he would simply slip back

2. From North Carolina to North Carolina

into a second season of pitching for Mooresville given the backdrop of World War II galvanizing the country. In some ways he was fortunate to even gain that year of baseball experience.

Once the Japanese bombed Pearl Harbor on December 7, 1941, the United States was at war. Young men rushed to enlist. Other young men were drafted. War had already come to other areas of the globe in previous years and it was all the United States could do to stay out of the fighting until then. Germany invaded Poland on September 1, 1939, and was marching across Europe. Japan had already been spreading destruction in China since July 7, 1937.

The raining of bombs on Pearl Harbor in Hawaii fully embroiled the United States. President Franklin D. Roosevelt responded to a letter from baseball commissioner Kenesaw Mountain Landis asking for guidance, with FDR's famous green light letter giving Major League Baseball the go-ahead to continue playing its games. Simultaneously, the president made it clear that no ballplayers would be exempted from military service because they were playing a sport. Big-league ball continued throughout the war years, with some difficulties, especially manpower issues, though there was a general retreat from the scene by many minor league teams.

Some of the most famous Hall of Fame players in baseball history either signed up for various branches of the service or were drafted. Cleveland pitcher Bob Feller promptly signed up. Boston Red Sox outfielder Ted Williams became a decorated pilot. Joe DiMaggio of the Yankees served. Before his barrier-breaking career even got started, Jackie Robinson was in the military. The Detroit Tigers' Hank Greenberg missed years of playing time.

There were also future stars, Hall of Famers, who had not yet reached the majors and were not known quantities when they went off to war. Among those was Yankee catcher Yogi Berra and Warren Spahn, who became the winningest left-handed pitcher of all time for the Boston and Milwaukee Braves. Spahn did not really start his career until the hostilities ceased. He played in four games for Boston in 1942, got on the wrong side of manager Casey Stengel and was immediately sent back to the minors. Many years later, after Spahn was on his way to 363 victories and Stengel was concluding one of the most successful stints ever by a manager leading the dynastic New York Yankees, Stengel said his rash demotion of Spahn was the worst mistake he ever made.

World War II, which did not end until 1945, was the deadliest war in world history, with an estimated 70 million to 85 million military

Hoyt Wilhelm

personnel and civilians killed. For many who served, it was fate that decreed that they were able to return home and not die in a far-away corner of the world they knew nothing of and removed from their own personal universes and families. A wrong turn in a muddy field, one step taken either way, and those like Berra and Spahn, unlike Feller or Williams, with no real baseball record yet, might never have been heard from again or ever heard of at all.

Hoyt Wilhelm, a fellow Hall of Famer with those men, and a professional baseball beginner in 1942, might well have become one of the unfortunates who disappeared in anonymity. Instead, like Berra and Spahn, Wilhelm returned to his home and was able to resume his baseball career, over time making himself into a somebody in the sport.

Wilhelm was barely graduated from high school ball, just inching his way into the professional game. His lifetime resume was a single line in length in the record books. Mooresville would not be the end of the trail for Hoyt Wilhelm in baseball, but he would have to start all over again once peace arrived.

3

War

When he was a much older player and had been in the majors for many years, one of Hoyt Wilhelm's nicknames bestowed by a younger generation of ballplayers was "Old Sarge." For them, those who came along a bit later, World War II was more an historical event than one that had to be endured.

Wilhelm, though, was in it, part of the fight, an American who knew war up close and did his part. After throwing for Mooresville in 1942, Wilhelm wore a different type of uniform from 1943 until 1946. From age 20 to 24, Wilhelm was most of the time too otherwise occupied to throw knuckleballs.

The pitcher became a soldier when he entered military service on November 23, 1942, the fall after that debut baseball season with Mooresville. Wilhelm went into the Army at Camp Croft in South Carolina.

Initially Wilhelm was part of the 393rd Infantry Regiment and then the 395th, stationed at Camp Maxey in Texas in 1943 and 1944. Identified as a ballplayer, Wilhelm did compete for the local team in the service as a pitcher but also as a first baseman, reprising a role from his high school days. With him on the roster the 395th won the 99th Infantry Division championship in 1944. It was a chance to stay in the game for a little while, in a small way, while removed from civilian life.

Camp Maxey's baseball field was situated about nine miles north of Paris, Texas, not far from the Oklahoma state line. Apparently, it was not manicured to the specifications of a big-league field, becoming renowned for its dustiness. There was nothing fancy about the park, but the service players made do and it so happened that Wilhelm's team won a championship on September 2, 1944. In a semi-final game of the title round, Wilhelm produced a two-run homer that advanced his squad.

Following the OK given by President Franklin Delano Roosevelt, Commissioner Kenesaw Mountain Landis presided over the continuation of Major League Baseball while some of the game's loftiest stars played on the equivalent of sandlots like Wilhelm, were in foxholes, or made public relations appearances.

In 1942 and 1943, just as they had since the 1920s when Babe Ruth came on the scene, the New York Yankees still ruled the American League and won pennants both of those seasons when the nation was on full-time war footing. Similarly, in the National League, the St. Louis Cardinals won pennants both times. The Cardinals captured the World Series in '42 and the Yankees in '43. No team had a better stretch of play throughout the war years than the Cardinals, who won three Series titles and four pennants between 1942 and 1946.

Teams were desperate for manpower, and those exempt from military service, 4-F for a variety of physical reasons, who had reached the AAA fringes of the majors got chances to play when they otherwise might never have made a big-league roster.

Probably the most famous fresh face in the majors during the war was Pete Gray, who through extraordinary devotion to the game and determination played the 1945 season for the St. Louis Browns. Gray was a one-armed outfielder who batted .218 in 77 games at the age of 30. He had lost his right arm in an accident as a six-year-old child while hitching a ride on the running board of a truck. He fell off when the driver made a short stop and caught his arm in a wheel.

It was said Gray was not only an inspiration to fans at large but to disabled soldiers returning from overseas service. He never portrayed himself as a hero but understood he could be a role model.

"Boys, I can't fight," Gray said. "And so there is no courage about me. Courage belongs on the battlefield not on the baseball diamond. But if I could prove to any boy who has been physically handicapped that he, too, can compete with the best—well then, I've done my little bit."[1]

Gray competed for the Browns one year after the "other" St. Louis team won its only pennant during its half-century in the city before pulling up stakes for Baltimore in the early 1950s. The Browns lost the World Series to the Cardinals in six games in 1944.

Compared to many other Army men in the service, during that time at Camp Maxey Wilhelm was safe on American soil. His outfit and his circumstances changed in September of 1944. The 99th Infantry sailed to England at the beginning of the fall, arriving there on October 10. A few weeks later it moved on to France, arriving on November 3. Whether it was because of his performance on the baseball diamond (though battlefield promotions were not distributed for hitting or

3. War

pitching well), or his overall performance, by the time he truly went to war, Wilhelm was a sergeant.

Upon returning to normal daily life in the United States after the war, Wilhelm did not illuminate questioners with much information about his experiences, like many who had experienced combat and witnessed horrible things. At least once he completely sloughed off a question about playing ball while in uniform, never mind combat reflections.

Never a chatterbox, especially about personal matters, Wilhelm shunned discussion of life in the trenches, but it is certain the defining period he spent in an Army uniform took him to the Battle of the Bulge in Belgium, one of the pivotal battles of the war.

The Battle of the Bulge was a major conflict that was the final German offensive seeking to stave off defeat in Europe. Besides the memorable name applied, it was also called the Ardennes Offensive on the Western Front. The battle began on December 16, 1944, and lasted until January 25, 1945. It took place during the heart of winter with attendant freezing cold and snowy weather. Primarily taking place in the forests of Belgium, the battle also crossed into Luxembourg.

Winston Churchill, the esteemed British prime minister during World War II, and to whose aid Americans rallied after some of the early dark days of the conflict, said this about the Battle of the Bulge: "This is undoubtedly the greatest American battle of the war, and will, I believe, be regarded as an ever-famous American victory."[2]

According to the chronicle of the 99th Infantry Division, comprised of three regiments, that Army group was activated November 15, 1942, and engaged in three different combat campaigns. After its final preparations were completed in Belgium, the 99th began fighting on November 9. It was calculated that the division engaged in 151 days of combat under the guidance of three different commanding generals, Major General Thompson Lawrence, Major General Walter F. Lauer and Brigadier General Frederick H. Black, the latter presiding over the final stretch as the division was deactivated in August of 1945. The division report states the 99th suffered 6,553 casualties altogether during its existence.

The Battle of the Bulge began in mid–December of 1944 as a last-gasp operation of the Germans, who felt the war slipping away. It was a surprise attack that the Allied troops in the area representing the United States, Great Britain, Belgium, Canada and France were not prepared for as they were busy thinking ahead to taking Germany. Grim winter weather aided the Germans, preventing the Allies from obtaining up-to-date aerial intelligence. The Germans mustered as much manpower and remaining equipment as they could to forge the attack, most of it initially centered on American forces.

German military leaders pulled together 410,000 men and accumulated 1,400 tanks for the offensive, plus 1,000 airplanes. Even as the desperate move began to cut off the Allies and prevent them from proceeding to Berlin, leaders at home kept throwing reinforcements into the breech, adding another 40,000 troops and another 100 tanks. The Germans were playing poker with their resources, betting everything on one winning hand. In the end, the Allies were holding the cards for a royal straight flush that trumped the attempt.

The harsh weather helped neutralize the skies for a time, but by Christmas Eve, the weather had sufficiently cleared for the United States' superior air power to begin bombing the German combatants. American planes were also able to deliver necessary equipment, food, and other supplies to the front lines and that beefed up the Allied resistance and forward approach. General George S. Patton's Third Army rolled to the front and by December 26 halted the Germans at Bastogne, Belgium.

Bastogne had been removed from the front until the Germans made a charge to capture it. It was even considered a layover for those resting from combat. When the Germans made their unexpected lightning strike to try to turn the direction of the war, they came hard at Bastogne, which was defended by the 101st Airborne Division.

There were some 14,000 members of the division in the city, which was suddenly being surrounded by a force of Germans perhaps five times as large. The Americans well understood the abrupt turnaround in circumstances as they ran short on food and equipment while the Germans besieged them. A few days before Christmas, the German command sent forth a small group under a white flag of truce to speak to the commanding officer in Bastogne.

German officers were blindfolded and led to the American command post about a quarter of a mile from where they had arrived on the edge of town. Optimistic American fighters on the scene wanted to believe that this was an advance guard of Germans who wished to give up because they had had enough of war. They were wrong. These Germans came bearing a typewritten message requesting that the Americans surrender and to do so within two hours or face "total annihilation."[3]

Commanding general Anthony C. McAuliffe was actually just

3. War

waking up from a nap in his sleeping bag when one of his top colonels approached to inform him of the German offer. Lt. Colonel Ned Moore told McAuliffe that the Germans had hand-delivered a note asking for the Americans to capitulate. In one of the most famous and briefest of retorts to such a suggestion, McAuliffe, who was admittedly still half-asleep, said, "Nuts!"[4]

McAuliffe subsequently read the entire German message typed in English and German after briefly interpreting the paper he held in his hand as an offer of the Germans to surrender to him. He said, "They want to surrender?" Other officers said no, that's not what was being outlined. McAuliffe then laughed, let the paper fall to the floor, and said, "Us surrender, aw, nuts!"[5]

The still-blindfolded German message carriers awaited a formal response to the formal offer to deliver to their own superiors. McAuliffe pondered out loud what to say and his key supporters urged him to put down exactly what he initially said. So he wrote and sent back a reply that said simply, "To the German Commander, N U T S ! The American Commander," as in "Nuts to you" or "Are you crazy?" or "No way" or "Buzz off." While that meaning was loud and clear to his own officers, the Germans on site did not understand the slang and had to have it interpreted. A PFC medic named Ernest Premetz fulfilled that task, telling the Germans to go to hell.[6]

Rarely has so important a message at any time in history been so succinctly delivered. McAuliffe, whose name eventually became forgotten except by historians due to the sheer bravado of the comment, has at least been recalled as the man who used "Nuts" as a response in dangerous circumstances.

When the fighting finally ceased, ending the Battle of the Bulge, it was estimated somewhere between 63,000 and 98,000 German combatants were killed, wounded, or missing in action and of the estimated 89,000 American casualties about 19,000 were killed. At the peak of the battle, it was believed the Allies had a combined 705,000 men in the field.

Hoyt Wilhelm was one of the wounded, though after the battle itself, when his division moved on. He was injured in action on March 2 or March 3, 1945, depending on the source, as the men moved towards Cologne, Germany. The *Charlotte Observer* ran a small item about five weeks later, when word reached the paper, accompanied by a picture of a baseball-throwing Wilhelm. The single paragraph was topped by the word "Wounded." The caption described Wilhelm as a "former star pitcher for Mooresville of the N.C. State league." It said of Wilhelm's pitching achievements he "was ticketed to go higher when drafted."[7]

Wilhelm was leading a heavy machine gun section in Germany and he and three of the soldiers in his group were wounded by shrapnel when an enemy shell hit a tree near them. "The tree wasn't too far from me," Wilhelm said about 25 years later in a rare discourse on the subject. "When the shell hit it, fragments sprayed all over the place. I thought I was a goner."[8]

Wilhelm incurred wounds to his back and his right (pitching) hand and was awarded a Purple Heart. The damage to his throwing hand was slight and did not interfere with his baseball future. The shrapnel that penetrated his back stayed there the rest of his life.

As World War II ended, Wilhelm was able to return home to Huntersville, North Carolina. His youngest sister, Viki Hager, who was seven years old in 1945 at the conclusion of the war, said there was much joy when Hoyt came home. "I remember the day he came home from the war," Hager said in 2022.[9]

It was quite the occasion, especially since he had been wounded but now was healed. Still, Wilhelm was an adult brother, a decade and a half older than she was. She also remembers something else about that time period in her life—and Hoyt's. "He was gone a lot,"[10] Hager said.

Now that Wilhelm was back in North Carolina, like other American military service veterans, he was anxious to get on with the rest of his peacetime life. If he was going to continue his professional baseball career, it was mandatory he be gone a lot. There was no pro team in Huntersville.

4

Starting Over

After being discharged from the Army, being back in North Carolina, and still looking to jump-start a professional baseball career, Hoyt Wilhelm was virtually in the same place he was when he completed high school, only several years older.

At 24, Wilhelm had the same primary goal in 1946 as he had in 1942—to become a big-league pitcher—and he was essentially as far removed from that reality as he was when he departed for the trenches in Europe, if not further.

Wilhelm still had no advocate to help sell his career to a Major League club. He was probably viewed as rusty because of inactivity. Plus, the competition for a paid baseball job was likely even fiercer than it was when he departed for the service.

Major League teams were loaded with contenders for roster spots. There were the groups of players who kept the squads alive during the war who still wanted to play ball. There were the groups of familiar players who left for the war from the big-league rosters who wanted to resume their careers. There were the groups of minor-leaguers who were returning from military service, the players like Wilhelm, only better known to a major-league club, who wanted to break into the bigs.

Stars like Ted Williams, Bob Feller, Hank Greenberg and Joe DiMaggio were welcomed back to their teams with enthusiasm. More than 500 players served in the military during World War II. Just two died, Elmer Gedeon and Harry O'Neill. Neither had long big-league careers and neither were stars of the game.

Perhaps the most astounding comeback from World War II wounds was pitcher Lou Brissie. Brissie, who was born in Anderson, South Carolina, was scouted by Connie Mack with the Philadelphia Athletics in the early 1940s while attending Presbyterian College. He enlisted in the Army in December of 1942.

In late 1944, Brissie, who earned several medals for his military service, including a Bronze Star and a Purple Heart with Oak Leaf Cluster, was embroiled in fighting in Italy as a member of the 88th Infantry Division. During that campaign, an artillery shell landed nearby and his left leg suffered extensive damage, blown into 30 pieces, a devastating injury to an athlete, or to anyone.

Doctors sought to amputate the leg, believing they had to do so to save his life, yet Brissie argued them out of it. He underwent 23 surgeries over two years before he could resume playing baseball, eventually making his debut on September 28, 1947—Mack gave him a fresh chance—while wearing a heavy metal brace.

After putting his ordeal behind him, Brissie, who participated in a book about his life, made his first start for the A's at Yankee Stadium against the Yankees. "I was nervous," he said. "I had read where someone asked Warren Spahn when he came back after having fought in the Battle of the Bulge if he was nervous and he said, 'No! There was no one in the stands pointing a gun at me.'"[1]

Brissie was nervous anyway, due to all he had been through, and he lost the game to the pennant-winning Yankees. But he was in the majors and returned to compile a lifetime 44–48 record despite the obstacles he faced.

Wilhelm was still carrying around shrapnel in his back, but it did not hinder him as much. He had no Connie Mack in his corner, only a resumé with a short body of work listed on it from his showing in the North Carolina State League in 1942. He made a logical move, approaching his former team for a new start, and he signed anew with the Mooresville Moors for 1946.

The country as a whole was embracing a fresh start after years of the gloom of war ruling every day. Military personnel came home to their loved ones. A leisure time age was dawning across the United States. More and more families took to the roads in their new automobiles during a time of prosperity. The television set became an omnipresent item in living rooms, affecting free time plans for families.

A new All-America Football Conference came on the scene to challenge the National Football League. Similarly, high-level professional basketball was organized into leagues that became the National Basketball Association.

In baseball, Ted Williams won the American League Most Valuable Player award for the Boston Red Sox while batting .342 after missing play in 1943, 1944 and 1945. DiMaggio hit 25 home runs and a low-for-him .290, returning to the game after also missing the same

4. Starting Over

three seasons. Feller, who had swiftly joined the Navy, missed play on a slightly different schedule, out for 1942, 1943 and 1944 and making it back to go 5–3 in 1945. Then he won a league-leading 26 games in 1946.

The St. Louis Cardinals won the World Series in a suspenseful showdown with Williams' Red Sox in 1946, considered Major League Baseball's first normal season since 1941.

Baseball normalcy was especially welcome for Wilhelm, back with Mooresville for a second go. Although his memory could be sketchy on selected topics, Wilhelm did say he earned $85 a month for his pre-war Mooresville salary. It is not clear how much money he made later with Mooresville, though it is unlikely he received much of a raise. For that matter, by contemporary standards, as well as later, when he was a well-established major leaguer, Wilhelm was a low-paid employee. He did not gripe about that later in life, though.

"There were no bonuses in those days," he once said, reminiscing about his first paydays. "But you will never hear me complain I was born 20 years too soon. Baseball has been good to me."[2]

He probably had more confidence going into the 1946 season than as a younger player, though certainly there must have been some concern coming back to the game after the war's interruption. The good news for Wilhelm was that he was better than ever. During that return-to-the-game season in Class D he finished 21–8 with a 2.47 earned run average. He threw 233 innings and hurled 22 complete games.

In the modern era of the game, a big-league club would have been knocking on his door after 1946, seeking a signature on a contract for affiliation with a Major League team but also no doubt moving him up at least one level, to the equivalent of Class C, or even higher. Not so for Wilhelm then. Whether it was because his primary pitch was a knuckleball and few wished to invest much in that flighty weapon, or whether he was still throwing in obscurity, the right-hander's fine season produced no valued result.

The only thing that first-rate season earned Wilhelm was an opportunity to come back and do it all over again for Mooresville. Basically, he did so. In 1947, he was again a key element in the Moors' pitching rotation, finishing 20–7, this time with a 3.38 earned run average. He hurled 250 innings and recorded 25 complete games.

During his second stay with Mooresville, despite his superb all-around pitching, Wilhelm learned perception, more than results, could affect his long-term future. The rarity of the knuckleball—despite his steady success with it—provoked one baseball man to suggest he give it up and stick to a so-called normal repertoire like most other pitchers. That was after winning 41 games in two seasons and hurling 47 complete games and almost 500 innings. Talk about being disrespected.

"The manager at Mooresville was an old-timer named Ginger Watts," Wilhelm said, "and he had the same idea most everybody else had then—that the knuckleball was something you developed only after you lost your fastball. He told me I had to change or I'd never get anywhere in baseball."[3]

Watts' advice may have been well-meaning, or just blunt in his own mind, but it had the effect of briefly shaking Wilhelm's confidence. The knuckler seemed to have so many enemies. The young pitcher was apparently bucking common wisdom and prejudice. Wilhelm had proven he was a good solider by serving in the Army and following orders in combat. Initially, he took Watts' suggestions the same way, and for the only time in his career, he temporarily abandoned his reliance on the knuckleball to get batters out.

The only issue was that all of a sudden, he could no longer get batters out at the plate. The knuckler was essentially his super power and without it he was a mere mortal. "I tried switching to curves and fastballs like other pitchers," Wilhelm said, "and I got my brains knocked out. So, I went back to the knuckleball and Ginger never brought it up again."[4] Neither did anyone else in any kind of serious way over the course of Wilhelm's long career.

In 1947, when Wilhelm was winning 20 for the second time in a row—he was the only 20-game-winner in the league that summer—there was some formidable hitting in the North Carolina State League. Jim Miller, 29, batted .402 for the Landis team, though he never advanced beyond the minors.

Following the pre-war season at Mooresville at the end of his teen years and the two additional seasons at Mooresville after his return to the game after his World War II hiatus, Wilhelm had nothing left to prove in Class D. He needed a chance to move to a higher minor-league classification, which he finally got for the 1948 season.

The way Wilhelm remembers this part of his odyssey, Mooresville wished to capitalize on his success by selling him to the Boston Braves. However, he was quickly picked off by the New York Giants instead, who appeared to have a stronger interest in his future. "The Giants drafted me from the Braves that winter," Wilhelm said. "So, I never actually played in the Boston Braves' organization."[5] Someone

4. Starting Over

once asked Wilhelm if he commanded a portion of the sale price and he only laughed at the notion.

Still, at last a Major League club showed some interest in what Wilhelm might be able to accomplish on the mound and brought him into the organization. Wilhelm was first assigned to Jacksonville in the South Atlantic League, also known as the Sally League, then at the Class A level. His stay there was limited; he appeared in six games and pitched 11 innings. Then he was shifted to Knoxville of the Class B Tri-State League. He performed well there, going 13–9 with a 3.62 earned run average in 189 innings.

Periodically, the Charlotte newspaper would make mention of Wilhelm's exploits on the diamond, though they were generally just passing mentions. They did not represent in-depth catching up. In a report on one Knoxville game a writer noted Wilhelm's presence this way: "Smokie hurler Hoyt Wilhelm, the Huntersville boy, had a 4–1 margin going into the closing frame."[6]

It could fairly be said that the Knoxville Smokies needed Wilhelm more than the Jacksonville Tars (whose nickname soon changed to Braves, matching the parent club). Two of the three leading win totals were put on the board by Jacksonville hurlers that year, Bob Hooper with 20 and Art Fowler with 19. That was the finest season of Hooper's long minor-league career and he went 40–41 between 1950 and 1955 in the majors. He later managed in the minors and scouted for big-league clubs.

Fowler, who once won as many as 23 games in a season in the Carolina League, finished 54–51 in the majors between 1954 and 1964. He then had a lengthy big-league coaching career of more prominence, five different times acting as manager Billy Martin's pitching coach with various teams. Knoxville, meanwhile, ended up with a 71–76 record.

Wilhelm's showing for Knoxville, though, encouraged the front office to promote him back to Jacksonville for the 1949 season. He continued to do well—even better—in Florida. The thrower's record was 17–12 and his ERA dipped to 2.66. The competition got stiffer, but Wilhelm persisted. Wilhelm must have made an impression. Except for his passing-through stopover previously, this was his only full season pitching for Jacksonville, yet someone reviewing Jacksonville's entire baseball history, going back to 1904, included Wilhelm on the city's all-time team. Certainly, Wilhelm must have scored extra points in team lore for his big-league career, not solely for his good year in Jacksonville.

Southern newspapers, even those that were not located in the towns where Sally League clubs were situated, tended to run short round-ups of league play, though the details were limited. On a day the Macon Peaches allowed 15 walks in a game to the Greenville Spinners, Macon somehow won anyway, 8–7. A few paragraphs into that summation it was noted "Hoyt Wilhelm of Jacksonville's Tar gave up only four hits to Augusta as the Tars whipped the Tigers, 6 to 2, in the only other Sally League contest."[7] It was not the same notoriety as making the ESPN nightly *SportsCenter* highlights, but at least somebody was taking note of Wilhelm's name outside of his original North Carolina neighborhood.

Time was working against Wilhelm, if administrators were paying attention, but Giants officials liked what they saw in his results, whether or not they could explain the effectiveness of the knuckleball. It was easy to think they considered a promotion to AAA Minneapolis in the American Association for Wilhelm in 1950 to be a tipping point. That season he was in his late twenties by anyone's paperwork, slipping into old age for a potential rookie.

Minneapolis, however, was miles from the North Carolina State League, and not just geographically. The Millers were a well-respected institution at the highest level of the minors and someone passing the trials presented by the American Association—and faring well—might optimistically, and realistically, think he was a simple phone call away from the majors. But uncounted numbers of hopefuls had washed out in AAA, getting so close to reaching their goal, then being sent home without the glory of ever being able to say they took a swing or threw a pitch in the majors.

Hoyt Wilhelm was on the doorstep of making it, but the door between the AAA minors and the majors still had a lock on it, and it only could be opened from the other side.

5

Minneapolis

Make It or Break It

Being assigned to Minneapolis by the New York Giants for the 1950 season spelled a major opportunity for Hoyt Wilhelm. The minor leagues in many ways were a free-for-all, cut-throat in the sense the players were evaluated every time they took a deep breath but at the same time studied for their potential. Moving up the ladder became increasingly difficult as one grew older and above the lower classifications.

Somehow, older than most, having battled through the lower levels of the minors, Wilhelm had reached the top of the minor-league ladder. He had maintained faith in his knuckleball and his knuckler had led him through Mooresville, Knoxville and Jacksonville to the big city of Minneapolis. The Giants were giving him a real chance, it seemed. Now it was up to him.

The Minneapolis Millers were a prominent minor-league club with ties to various league affiliations dating to 1884. From the Northwestern League to the Western Association, from the Western League to the American League, back to the Western League and then between 1902 and 1960 as members of the American Association, the Millers were a staple franchise.

On many occasions, the Millers were a colossus in the American Association, winning nine pennants over the decades. The Millers provided not only an excellent brand of ball but featured some players on the field who went on to become greats of the game, including Ted Williams, Willie Mays and Carl Yastrzemski. When it comes to the all-time roster, that is hardly everyone worthy of being mentioned. Other stars included Monte Irvin, Orlando Cepeda, Roger Bresnahan (the catcher who invented shin guards), Zach Wheat and Rube Waddell and such notable managers as Bill McKechnie and Chuck Dressen.

In 1938, the year before Williams broke in as a rookie with the Red Sox, he put on a memorable show for Minneapolis, batting .366 with 43

Hoyt Wilhelm

home runs and 142 runs batted in. And among those stars and future Hall of Famers, Hoyt Wilhelm came along in the early 1950s, though during his two seasons it would have taken a pretty savvy seer to predict his Hall of Fame credentials.

The Millers, as stable as any minor-league outpost in the country, paved the way for the Minnesota Twins when the Washington Senators were looking for a new home and the American League was looking to expand in the early 1960s.

For those without long memories, the Twins are the original Washington Senators, founded in 1901, belonging to owner Clark Griffith and carried later by pitching great Walter Johnson. Those Senators fled from Washington, D.C., for the 1961 season to become the Twins as the American League put an expansion team in D.C., adding a replacement Washington Senators bunch, plus the then–Los Angeles Angels, competing these days just down the road in Anaheim.

It should be noted that Wilhelm's post–World War II minor-league career almost exactly coincided with the integration of baseball. Jackie Robinson signed with the Brooklyn Dodgers and spent the 1946 season with the Montreal Royals before breaking into the National League in 1947.

During 1950 and 1951, as Wilhelm fought to climb his way past Minneapolis to the New York Giants, he shared Miller rosters with former Negro Leagues great Ray Dandridge, Irvin, Mays, and Hank Thompson, Black players getting their first true chances to play in high-level White leagues. Although they played for a team located just about as far north as possible in the United States, instead of competing for teams in the Deep South, these were still turbulent times for a Black man anywhere in the country. Baseball was integrating, incrementally, at best, but the initial lonely times of Robinson and the Cleveland Indians' Larry Doby had passed as teams one by one opened their clubhouses to Black players during the 1950s.

Wilhelm, in his own odd way, was a smaller minority than the Black individuals because his bread and butter was his knuckleball. He was still trying to crack a big-league roster when he was shipped to Minneapolis.

Wilhelm made a good first impression in Minneapolis in front of the home fans—and sports reporters—when he began pitching at Nicollet Park. Nicollet Park was already a local institution, inaugurated with the Millers' first game played there in 1896, although the name was not affixed until 1897. It was a wooden structure periodically updated

5. *Minneapolis*

over the decades, and from an early capacity of around 4,000, it was expanded to hold 10,000 spectators at its peak. The park closed in 1955.

On the occasion of Wilhelm's second victory in Minneapolis in 1950, his knuckleball gained some attention. By early May, one local newspaper writer referred to Hoyt Wilhelm as "Kaiser" Wilhelm, harkening back to the last of the German emperors who led that nation through the end of World War I.[1] Wilhelm pitched a four-hitter in a 4–1 win over rival St. Paul, the other of the Twin Cities.

Wilhelm was still familiarizing himself with his surroundings and seemed totally unfazed by any of Nicollet's quirky dimensions when quizzed about his reaction to the outfield's size, especially the 280-foot wall in right. "I guess I don't know about that fence yet," Wilhelm said.[2]

Ironically enough, given what lay ahead in Wilhelm's career, he was asked the same question he faced over and over again—how did he come to reply on the knuckler? "Nobody taught it to me," Wilhelm said. "I started to use it in high school and worked on it by myself. It just came naturally, I guess."[3]

Just as humorous, in foreshadowing of the same kinds of reactions he would receive from catchers throughout his career, his catcher of the day, Bob Brady, explained that the floater was indeed difficult to hang onto, never mind to hit by opposing batters. "I ruined my thumb on one of 'em and another banged me on the ear," Brady said.[4] The story added that Brady was laughing when he said this. Not all catchers on Wilhelm's future teams responded so light-heartedly.

Wilhelm continued to make noise for the Millers as the season progressed. One local newspaper story about him discussed how a strong wind might mess up the effect of his knuckler, almost as if he had to be a weatherman to weather the circumstances on the field.

A sportswriter examined his entire minor-league career to date and realized that regardless of gusts blowing out toward left field or a windchill factor when he threw, Wilhelm compiled stellar results. It was noted that wherever Wilhelm pitched he not only won games but also he won games at a higher rate than his teams did in settling into their spots in the standings.

"Hoyt either has led a remarkably pure life through his 26 years, or he is a master at making adjustments because of wind or no," the story stated, "he has an overall pitching percentage of .675 for his professional career."[5] The piece appeared in the *Minneapolis Star Tribune* in June of that first season in Minnesota, and to date, the writer observed,

Hoyt Wilhelm

Wilhelm's career pro record stood at 87–42. This certainly implied that someone at the highest levels of the game should notice him.

Intriguingly, veteran scribes seemed to constantly be on alert to the possibility that Wilhelm could become concerned by the proximity of that right-field fence at Nicollet Park. At the end of the decade this became a common topic after the Dodgers abandoned Brooklyn for Los Angeles and had to play home games in the Los Angeles Memorial Coliseum, which was friendlier for football and had a looming left field just 250 feet over the pitcher's right-field shoulder.

"I didn't give that right-field fence a thought," Wilhelm said. "Why worry about it? If you make a mistake, someone will hit it out of a big park." The writer chimed in: "That's proved a sound and winning philosophy for Wilhelm. He's been hit hard and far at times, but usually has pitched his way out of trouble. That knuckler, plus that unshakeable poise, is a tough combination to beat."[6]

Come September, Wilhelm was still pitching well and the Millers, on their way to a 90-win season, were still playing well. In mid–September, during an American Association semi-final playoff series with the Columbus, Ohio, Red Birds, Wilhelm captured a 4–1 victory.

Minneapolis recorded the best regular-season mark in a league that included teams located in Indianapolis, St. Paul (down the block), Louisville, Milwaukee, Toledo and Kansas City. More than 70 years later, all of those cities are either still represented by AAA clubs or are Major League franchise-holders. The hitters were ahead of the pitchers that season, with Minneapolis second in the league in batting with a .273 average and Columbus leading in earned run average with a surprisingly high 4.14 mark.

"I felt just as good at the end as I did at the start," Wilhelm said of his win over the Red Birds. "I had a week's rest. That's the difference. Nobody is going to beat me when I'm rested and I like to beat these cocky guys better than anybody in the league."[7]

Wilhelm and his teammates may have reveled in that win, but they did not keep it up. Columbus, the Association's third-place regular season finisher with an 84–69 mark, won the series 4–2. Indianapolis ended up winning the crown with a four-game sweep of St. Paul.

Wilhelm impressed long-time Minneapolis Millers baseball observers from the beginning of his tenure in the Midwestern city. General Manager Rosy Ryan, born Wilfred Patrick Dolan Ryan on March 15, 1898, and whose big-league career spanned parts of 1919 to 1933 with 52 hurling victories and a World Series championship, managed

5. Minneapolis

the Millers from 1944 to 1946. He liked what he saw Hoyt bring to the mound with his knuckleball, and from personal knowledge, he thought Nicollet Park would be friendlier to him than it would be to the run-of-the-mill fastball hurler.

"A young, unseasoned fastball pitcher can be spoiled by that park," Ryan said. "Once in a while a young southpaw may do pretty well from the outset, but a right-hander has to have good breaking stuff. Wilhelm has that. When he comes to that pitch which the batter has to swing at, Wilhelm will give them the knuckler. He is not afraid to use that pitch on the 3–1 or the 3–2 count and it is a really good knuckler. It will get him out of a lot of jams."[8]

After that 1950 season in Minnesota, Wilhelm adjourned to Cuba and winter ball, teaming with, among others, Negro Leagues star Ray Dandridge on the Havana club. In his first game, very early on in that season, Wilhelm threw a four-hit shutout.

The question now facing Wilhelm following year after year in the minors, his military service, and his time in winter ball was whether he could make the New York Giants' roster coming out of spring training in 1951. It may have been the shaky 4.95 earned run average of 1950 that doomed Wilhelm to a second campaign in Minneapolis, but he did not make the cut with the Giants that year. Dandridge, Willie Mays and Hank Thompson were there with him.

A March review of Wilhelm's prospects by a local columnist predicted he would at some point be one of the Millers beckoned to the majors by the Giants. "Wilhelm also came a long way to pitch against AAA hitting," writer Dick Cullum said. "He got away to a fine start, then had his troubles. Here again, it was a matter of picking up experience, some of which, naturally, was unpleasant. But Wilhelm can pitch. He has an inherent cunning. He is one of those about whom baseball people say, 'He knows how to pitch.' He has a variety of pitches and a tricky way of using them. Having had a taste of AAA ball, it is his turn to show what experience has done for him."[9]

Mays was just shy of 20 years old when the season began and his residency in Minneapolis would not last very long. In all, he appeared in 35 games for the Millers and batted .477. The man some historians consider the greatest player of all-time was bursting with talent. Wilhelm never did provoke such excitement among scouts. He had to battle for every inch of progress he made in the minors. When Wilhelm came to camp for the Millers in 1951, he was referred to in print as "the calm knuckleballer."[10] That was a little bit lower on the enthusiasm meter than Mays rated.

Hoyt Wilhelm

The early talk with Wilhelm when he showed up for spring training in Sanford, Florida, was about his stay in Cuba and his play with Havana. He went 8–6. "We had a staff of five starters, all from Triple A," Wilhelm said. "Each of us starters only had to pitch about once in seven days." Wilhelm said he and each of the other American players were "treated like a hero," but not as much as Roberto Gonzalo Ortiz Núñez, a lifetime .255 hitter who in 1950 completed his six-year Major League career as an outfielder with the Philadelphia Athletics. "Boy, their hearts were broken if he struck out," Wilhelm said of local fans. "But they still cheered him. When he hit one, it was the occasion for firecrackers."[11]

As the AAA season was beginning, one Minneapolis sports columnist allowed the Millers' beat writer to express his opinion about what he saw from Wilhelm's right arm in Florida spring training. "Hoyt Wilhelm is going to be great," was the take.[12]

This may have been the moment Wilhelm had waited so long for. He was under some pressure to take advantage of his big chance to finally reach the big leagues.

Seasons began later in that era, and Wilhelm pitched the home opener on May 1, 1951, and won against Columbus. He got some help at the plate from Mays. The 19-year-old Mays stroked three hits at Nicollet Park before 6,477 fans that day. He also made what would become one of his signature plays—a glittering outfield catch up against a flag pole—as the Millers won 11–0 on a day cut short by rain. (Just two weeks later, Mays was called up by the Giants, though he was sent down briefly later in the season.) The game was halted after 6⅔ innings with Wilhelm allowing just five hits. It was noteworthy that Dandridge collected four hits that day, making for an all-around sterling performance in AAA by three future Hall of Famers.

Intriguingly, a AAA rookie, Ray Katt, served as Wilhelm's catcher much of the 1951 season, as if trying to show suitable stuff to be promoted to the majors wasn't a big enough challenge. Katt did make the American Association all-star team, but it was noted in a late-season newspaper article that he "battled Hoyt Wilhelm's knuckleball all summer."[13] The punch line was that Wilhelm and Katt would both play for Havana in the winter, meaning Katt would have no respite from the dancing pitch.

That was not necessarily good news for either man. Katt could probably be heard groaning beyond clubhouse walls when he was given the assignment. For Wilhelm, it meant he was still proving himself before earning a place on the Giants' roster for 1952. Indeed, Wilhelm

5. Minneapolis

finished the 1951 summer with an 11–14 record and a 3.94 earned run average. He may have been an essential man in the pitching rotation for the Millers, but the Giants likely still harbored questions about whether this veteran knuckleball thrower could be a difference-maker in the majors.

6

The Majors at Last

The New York Giants team that Hoyt Wilhelm sought to make in the spring of 1952 was coming off one of the most spectacular, unlikely, and still-remembered seasons in baseball history.

While Wilhelm was toiling in Minneapolis, the Giants put together one of the most astonishing pennant runs of all time, capped by the most stunning denouement ever in a playoff series.

The Giants of '51 came from 13½ games behind the Brooklyn Dodgers in August to tie the so-called "Bums" and force a best-of-three playoff series to determine the National League pennant victor.

These were the Giants of Sal "The Barber" Maglie, who finished 23–6, Larry Jansen, who went 23–11, and future Hall of Fame outfielders Monte Irvin and Willie Mays. As he turned 20, Mays vacated Minnesota and arrived in New York in time to play in 120 games, hitting 20 home runs and batting .274. Mays made his Major League debut on May 25 and won the NL Rookie of the Year Award. It was an OK beginning for the superstar who only improved from there, initially nurtured and encouraged by manager Leo Durocher.

Before summer's end the Giants seemed dead in the Hudson River, or water of some kind. But as the autumn leaves began to fall, they put together a remarkable run as the Dodgers faded. Despite being carried by Roy Campanella (who won the league's Most Valuable Player Award), Gil Hodges, Jackie Robinson, Pee Wee Reese, Don Newcombe and Preacher Roe, Brooklyn folded in the stretch.

The Giants, though, compiled a 50–12 run so the two squads finished the regular season even at 96–58, requiring the playoff that began at Ebbets Field on October 1. The teams split the first two games, then completed the suspense on October 3 at the Polo Grounds.

New York won the playoff and the pennant when Bobby Thomson slugged a home run off pitcher Ralph Branca with one of the most dramatic game-winning blasts in the sport's history. The home run came

6. The Majors at Last

to be known as the "Shot Heard 'Round the World." After all the weeks-long, heart-thumping suspense, the Giants still had to face the waiting-for-a-foe New York Yankees in the World Series. The Yankees being the Yankees at that time cooled off the Giants, winning the Series 4–2, their fifth straight championship.

As successful as the duo of Maglie and Jansen had been (even throwing in Jim Hearn and his 17–9 record), when Durocher surveyed his options in the spring of 1952, he seemed conscious that he and the Giants could benefit from improved depth on the mound.

After such a prolonged wait, it was finally

Some of the best seasons of Wilhelm's 21-year career were spent with the Chicago White Sox. He was a pitching factor for the team between 1963 and 1968 (National Baseball Hall of Fame Library, Cooperstown, N.Y.).

Hoyt Wilhelm's time. Nobody realized Wilhelm would celebrate his 30th birthday that summer. He was thought to be 28 in spring training and turning 29 at the end of July. Wilhelm reported to the Giants in Phoenix, Arizona.

"I had played in the minor leagues for what, seven or eight years," Wilhelm said, "and I was beginning to think that, you know, I might never get a chance to play in the big leagues. But when [it] came finally, I got a chance at it. I had felt for three or four years…. I know I could have pitched in the big leagues five years before I got there. I threw the same things when I got there that I did before I got there."[1]

The Giants may have fallen to the powerhouse Yankees, but they had achieved national admiration in coming from so far back in the standings to tie the Dodgers and then to capture the playoff in such dramatic fashion. Durocher had often been controversial because of his flamboyance, his directness, and more. But even though he did not win a World Series in 1951, he gained a great many admirers.

"Durocher was an inspired manager that year," Monte Irvin said. "He kept making the most astounding moves and seeing them pay off. Things like the right pinch hitter at the right time, the right pitching change at the right time, moving his fielders around. It seemed over the last few months of the season he just couldn't make a wrong move."[2]

As always happens between seasons, there was some shifting on the Giants roster for 1952. Mays only played in 34 games (and missed all of 1953 before returning to baseball in 1954) because he went into the U.S. Army. Then Irvin broke his ankle in an exhibition game and only played in 46 games for the Giants that year. Neither Maglie, Jansen, or Hearn recorded the same number of wins as the year before. It was not completely the same club, but the Giants still finished second with 92 victories in Wilhelm's rookie season—and he was one of the big reasons why.

Durocher was suspended by Major League Baseball as the Dodgers manager for an entire season. He courted a fast lifestyle, dating, and marrying, Hollywood actresses, and enjoying the nightclub routines. He spoke loudly, but in the end his baseball acumen was sufficient to gain him enshrinement in the National Baseball Hall of Fame. Some ballplayers hated playing for him and others swore by him.

Wilhelm had not torn up AAA during his second season in Minneapolis, but the Giants were open-minded enough to invite him to camp. It took some effort to convince Durocher that Wilhelm belonged. After some time in training camp, the boss talked about the hurler with Bill Rigney, a veteran infielder nearing retirement who was a future manager, expressing skepticism.

"I don't know," Durocher said to Rigney. "His ball doesn't do much. What do you think?" Rigney replied, "I'd like to see what he does in a game." Durocher said, "Warm him up and we'll see." Acting in the role of catcher, Rigney grabbed a mitt and had Wilhelm throw to him. The knucklers were impossible to handle and made a major impression on Rigney, who said if they were that hard to catch, hitters would not be able to connect with them.[3]

Wilhelm turned Rigney into a believer in such simple fashion and the Giants made the right call to keep him in 1952. He was one of those players who had been lurking in the shadows of the minor leagues for years and when at last given an opportunity became an overnight sensation.

6. The Majors at Last

It is probable that few New York sportswriters knew Hoyt Wilhelm's name in the spring of 1952 and just as likely that every single one of them knew something about him before Halloween.

Wilhelm made a name for himself that summer and did it not only by relying on the rare knuckleball but also as a relief pitcher. A relief pitcher, of all things, was the way he was analyzed. For decades, baseball had been uneasy about strategies counting on relief pitchers. The whole idea was to build a staff of stalwart pitchers who in turn, every few days, were thrust out on the mound to start a game and stay in it as long as possible. It was taken as a virtual insult, a sign of a lack of faith, to be designated as a hurler who was not valuable enough to start games, and for decades no one counted on by the club was solely a relief pitcher.

Certainly, there were occasions when a starting pitcher got hurt, ejected by an umpire, or was on his way to allowing 15 runs in a game when a relief pitcher was summoned by a manager. But the manager did not want to make a habit out of that and a pitcher did not wish to become known as that type of specialist.

An illustration of how seemingly unimportant a reliever was to a team is that it was not until 1959 that the "save" statistic to calculate a reliever's effectiveness was invented by baseball writer and historian Jerome Holtzman and it was not until 1969 that it was officially recognized. Holtzman was reporting for the *Chicago Sun-Times* and wanted a handy statistic to measure relief pitcher production. The definition of a save has been altered over the years, along with the manner in which relief pitchers have been used. But it has evolved and grown in importance.

Between 1876, when the National League was established, and the end of World War II, a relief pitcher was mostly regarded as a failed starting pitcher. There was no formula for a manager to follow going to the bullpen. There are anomalies that stick in the mind as brilliant relief performances from baseball's early days, but no famous steady relievers of the distant past.

The most astonishing relief showing of all time, combining luck, talent and circumstance, belongs to Boston Red Sox righty Ernie Shore who went up against the Washington Senators on June 23, 1917. The Boston starter that day was Babe Ruth. However, Ruth walked the first batter, Ray Morgan, and when he vigorously disputed the call with home-plate umpire Brick Owens, the arbiter threw Ruth out of the game. This became an even bigger rhubarb when Ruth punched Owens and Boston catcher Pinch Thomas was also heaved.

Hoyt Wilhelm

Shore was called on in relief, a new catcher was brought in, and when Shore threw to his first hitter, Morgan tried to steal second. He was thrown out, erased. Shore then set down the other 26 batters he faced for a perfect performance. It was not considered a perfect game because Ruth started, allowed the base runner, and then was replaced, though it was still 27 men up, 27 men down. The record books now call the game a combined no-hitter.

A prominent relief performance that lives on in baseball lore took place during the seventh game of the 1926 World Series between the New York Yankees and the St. Louis Cardinals. The Yankees loaded the bases in the bottom of the seventh inning, trailing 3–2. Due at the plate was dangerous Tony Lazzeri. Coming out of the bullpen just a day after throwing a complete game was Grover Cleveland Alexander, a future Hall of Famer with 373 career victories. Alexander pitched out of the jam by striking out Lazzeri, another future Hall of Famer, and then finishing off New York's late-innings threat.

For all of the hoopla following Shore's accomplishment and Alexander's achievement, the fundamental role of the reliever was not viewed as heroic. It was not until after World War II that the job of a relief pitcher began to take on a description the modern fan would recognize. Over the first half of his eight-season career, Joe Page regularly started games for the Yankees, but for three years in a row, 1947, 1948, and 1949, his new manager, Casey Stengel, who was a master of employing players as specialists, made him an important reliever. Page led the American League in games finished all three of those seasons.

The Yankees won the world championship all three years, and the spotlight on Page helped highlight the critical nature of the relief pitcher's role shortly before Wilhelm moved into the majors. The significance of the role has only increased in the years since, though the manner in which managers use relievers has changed considerably. It was in 1960 that *The Sporting News*, called the Bible of Baseball at the time, established a Fireman of the Year Award going to the finest reliever in each league.

In the 2020s, bullpens are so cluttered pitchers can hardly find a seat in the early innings of games. By the second decade of the century, relievers were often relied on for a single inning, perhaps only one-third of an inning or even for one pitch. When Page was pitching and when Wilhelm was starting out, relievers were not seen as one-and-done throwers to opposing line-ups. They stuck around for two, three or more innings at a time.

6. The Majors at Last

After Wilhelm sold himself to Rigney (and Durocher by proxy), and stayed with the Giants in 1952, he excelled. To that point in his professional career, Wilhelm was a starting pitcher. Yet he never started a single game during his first season. He was used often and had the confidence of the dugout management team, but he was indeed a fireman, deployed to douse blazes that started on others' watches.

Wilhelm authored some memorable statistics as a rookie, finishing 15–3 for an .833 winning percentage, the best in the National League that season. He also led the league in earned run average at 2.43 and in pitching appearances with 71. Retroactively, when a formula was applied, Wilhelm was credited with 11 saves. He hurled 159⅓ innings, an unfathomable number by modern standards. Those eye-catching numbers made Wilhelm the runner-up for NL Rookie of the Year to Brooklyn's Joe Black. Black was also a right-handed relief pitcher. He finished 15–4 with a 2.15 earned run average, though he did not have the minimum number of innings required to best Wilhelm. Black led the league with 41 games finished to Wilhelm's 32.

Black's age, 28, was similar to Wilhelm's, but his seasoning occurred in the Negro National League rather than in the White minors. Black handily won the rookie voting with 19 first-place votes to Wilhelm's three. The only other NL rookies gaining support that year were Dick Groat and Eddie Mathews. Over the long run—a very long run—Wilhelm outdid Black in every category.

If there was uncertainty in spring training in the beginning, in the end, Wilhelm was grateful to Durocher. It was Durocher who kept him on the team and it was Durocher who relied on him throughout that season, giving him many opportunities to show what he had. Durocher knew no more about the knuckleball's behavior than most baseball men, but as long as Wilhelm got people out the boss really didn't seem to care how he accomplished it and kept him walking out to the mound dousing those blazes begun by other pitchers.

The Giants' regular season began on April 16, nearly three weeks later than the regular season begins in the 2020s, partially because teams of that era played 154 games, not 162. The team's home base was the historic Polo Grounds and somewhat of a glow still surrounded the club because of its fantastic late-season run and stunning home-run victory over the Dodgers. In an era when drawing a million fans through the turnstiles was notable, the team on its way to a runner-up campaign drew 984,940 spectators.

New York opened play with a Wednesday night game, starting at

Hoyt Wilhelm

8:30, against the Philadelphia Phillies before 17,742 fans. Sal Maglie faced Hall of Famer Robin Roberts and got the 5–3 win with a complete game. Game number two, the next day at 1:30 p.m., attracting just 13,697, was a 2–0 loss in 11 innings with Larry Jansen going nine of them. The reliever Durocher pointed to was George Spencer. He threw two innings, gave up two runs, and took the loss.

Having spent his two aces from 1951, Durocher logically went with his third-leading winner of that season in starting Jim Hearn in the third game. This was the first rematch of the season versus the Dodgers, the first meeting between the great rivals since the playoff epic. The Giants moved across the boroughs from the Polo Grounds to Ebbets Field and the still-smarting local supporters turned out in force, some 31,032 strong.

As so many of the Giants-Dodgers showdowns did, this contest provided value for the dollar, lasting three hours and 50 minutes and going 12 innings before Brooklyn prevailed. Hearn was hit hard early for four runs and lasted just 1⅓ innings. This time when Durocher waved to the bullpen he signaled for Wilhelm.

In what must have felt like a space odyssey through the galaxy taken by an astronaut, a decade after first throwing for Mooresville in North Carolina, Hoyt Wilhelm landed at his destination and his name first appeared in a Major League box score. It wasn't much of an entry, but it was there for all time.

Wilhelm pitched just one-third of an inning in the second inning and he didn't stick around very long because he allowed a hit and two walks. He was also charged with a wild pitch. The first man Wilhelm faced was future Hall of Fame shortstop Pee Wee Reese, who flied out to center field. However, the shot scored future Hall of Famer Gil Hodges, with the run charged to Hearn. Billy Cox doubled off Wilhelm next and future Hall of Famer Jackie Robinson walked. Next up? Another future Hall of Famer, Roy Campanella. The wild pitch occurred during that at-bat. Dodgers pitcher Carl Erskine scored. When Wilhelm then walked Campanella, he was lifted. Other than the fact that it was a rookie debut, there was little to preserve in the memory bank.

Wilhelm next pitched in a lost-cause game on April 19, the third pitcher for the Giants in an 11–6 defeat to Brooklyn. Wilhelm threw the last inning for New York, allowing no hits but giving up one walk. The Giants produced a series of complete games after that, but on April 23, versus the Boston Braves, Wilhelm collected his first Major League victory with a lengthy relief outing.

6. The Majors at Last

Just 4,611 fans paid their way into the Polo Grounds for a 1:30 game against the Braves ultimately won by the Giants, 9–5. Roger Bowman started for New York but gave up three runs in 2⅓ innings before the bench beckoned for Wilhelm. This was a much better outing for Wilhelm than his first one. He covered 5⅓ innings, allowed six hits and two runs, struck out three and walked two.

Even if the first decision, his first win in the bigs, was a milestone, something else happened in that game involving Wilhelm that is better remembered by most baseball historians. In the fourth inning, with the bases empty and one out, facing Dick Hoover, Wilhelm cracked a home run to right field. A six-foot, 170-pound left-hander, Hoover was a 26-year-old rookie who made his big-league debut just a week earlier. As it turned out, this second appearance at the top of the sport was his final one. Hoover's entire career line consisted of those two games spread over 4⅔ innings.

Whereas like most professional pitchers, Wilhelm was a good hitter in high school, when he came up against better pitching, even in the low minors, his arm was what carried him. Nobody cared what kind of batting average he maintained. That was a good thing, because Wilhelm was worse than most. In his long Major League career, his lifetime average was .088, which could charitably be termed horrible. In 493 plate appearances, 432 of them official at-bats, Wilhelm managed just 38 hits. Among those hits was just a single home run. One. This one smacked off of Hoover was the only four-bagger Wilhelm recorded.

Wilhelm's at-bats were spread over 1,070 games, but as mostly a reliever, he rarely played a full nine innings, regularly came to bat once or not at all in his relief outings, and was a poor hitter. Still, it might be expected that in 20 years of play he might have accidentally hit another homer. He did not.

Wilhelm hit the solo shot in his first big-league at-bat and never matched that swing. Hitting a home run in a player's first-ever at-bat is rare but not unique. As of September 2022, 133 players had managed that feat. Among the others are New York Yankee Aaron Judge and Hall of Famer Earl Averill. The first time(s) this happened was April 16, 1887. George Tebeau of the Cincinnati Red Stockings and Mike Griffin of the Baltimore Orioles hit homers in their first Major League at-bats on the same day.

Other notable players to hit homers right off the bat included Whitey Lockman, Wilhelm's teammate with the Giants, who did so in 1945, Will Clark, Bill White, and Adam Wainwright. None of the big-gun sluggers in the Hall of Fame, or likely to soon be in the Hall of Fame, accomplished this. Like Wilhelm, many of those first-at-bat home-run hitters, hit just one home run during their careers, but unlike Wilhelm, they did not stay in the majors for two decades. Mostly they were short-termers.

One official who works at the National Baseball Hall of Fame in Cooperstown, New York, has used the Wilhelm homer as a favorite trivia question when making fan-related appearances at the annual All-Star game: "Who is the only Hall of Famer to hit a home run in his first at-bat and never hit another one?"

It might fairly be said that Hoyt Wilhelm hitting a home run was a fluke. In that same game, Wilhelm drove in a second run with a groundout and did not gather another RBI for more than a year. The closest Wilhelm ever came to hitting a second home run in the majors was a triple he belted in 1953.

As time passed and Wilhelm competed in more and more games without hitting another home run, his one blast became historic lore. Sometimes he joked about it, and sometimes he gave a straightforward retelling of it when a sportswriter from another generation asked him about it.

"Durocher put me in the game against the Braves," Wilhelm said. "Score was tied, I think. Hit a homer my first time at-bat. Right field. That was 258 feet in the Polo Grounds. We won the game. I kinda went on from there. I remember that year like it was yesterday. I hit a home run in my first game. First swing, actually. I was ahead of Babe Ruth's pace there for a while."[4]

After this brief show of power against the Braves coinciding with Wilhelm's first major-league win, one might say he dipped into an extended slump. The flip side, however, was that he began winning games with his arm and his knuckler.

7

A Hot Commodity

All of a sudden, after years of neglect, Hoyt Wilhelm was one of the hottest pitchers in the National League, a rookie find by the New York Giants who had been begging to be found for years.

After cataloguing his first win, Wilhelm was on his way to a 15-victory season in 1952, viewed as an out-of-nowhere guy because of his non-traditional rise to the majors and probably, too, because of his reliance on a non-traditional pitch. By then, Wilhelm understood that his knuckler was always going to place him in a minority category. Wilhelm knew it labeled him an oddity.

Given that not even the most accomplished of knuckleball practitioners could explain what made it work, couldn't predict where it would go or how it would spin, those who counted on the pitch were always going to be surrounded by doubters. Wilhelm had come to comprehend that, but he didn't care very much as long as the pitch kept working for him and enabled him to get enemy hitters out.

Managers were just getting the hang of this relief pitcher thing. They were tip-toeing into cold waters to see if the risk was worth it. They never really thought for a moment of using a reliever for a single batter—that came later. What was really involved in evaluating how often manager Leo Durocher should use Wilhelm was how often he came out of the pen in the clutch to get batters out and strand batters on base.

If Wilhelm, who was adapting to the reliever's job himself, had been belted all around the field when called upon, he might have found himself back in Minneapolis in a New York minute. Instead, when Durocher beckoned, Wilhelm baffled. He did not toss 90 mph stuff, but his 65-mph stuff had the foes flailing all over the place. He harnessed super control rather than overpowering speed.

Wilhelm moved to 2–0 on May 2 when the Giants beat the Pittsburgh Pirates at Forbes Field, with one inning of solid work, including

Hoyt Wilhelm

a walk and a strikeout. Just two days later, Wilhelm's yeoman's work against the Chicago Cubs bridged a shaky start by usually reliable Larry Jansen and George Spencer finishing out a 5–3 game. Wilhelm threw 5⅓ innings this time, allowing four hits, striking out five and permitting zero runs. At 3–0, Wilhelm saw his earned run average dip to 1.38. Bill Rigney was looking like a pretty smart guy for his recommendation to Durocher.

That long relief stint seemed to provide more confidence and more cache. On May 24, when Wilhelm's record improved to 4–0, he pitched seven innings of relief of Max Lanier. Nothing lasts forever, though, and Wilhelm lost the first game of his Major League career to the Philadelphia Phillies at Shibe Park on May 29. It was an odd game, Jansen again leaving after throwing 1⅓ innings and Wilhelm being followed in the 6–5 defeat by two other relievers.

As someone who did not have a particular spot in the rotation, Wilhelm never knew when he would pitch next. It was always at the expense of another teammate who was having an off day, got injured, or needed to be replaced as part of an overall strategy. As relief pitchers well know, of course, they are usually more at risk and have more pressure on them not to make a mistake when they are summoned into a game and the opposition has runners on base and is threatening to score. The smallest of mistakes can be the costliest, meaning a lost game.

Sal Maglie produced seven strong innings versus the Cincinnati Reds on June 10, but the teams went into extra innings in a long one, Wilhelm losing his second straight decision after 4⅓ innings of one-run ball. Cincinnati won, 6–5, in 14 innings at Crosley Field. The once-undefeated Wilhelm was 4–2.

Yet he pretty much ran the table after that. Except for an August 24 loss to Cincinnati, for the rest of the summer any time Wilhelm's name appeared next to a decision it featured a "W." He won 11 more games and every few days he also picked up a save. The unheralded Wilhelm was rolling through the National League.

June 24, Wilhelm beats Cincinnati. July 29, Wilhelm beats Philadelphia. July 1, Wilhelm beats the Boston Braves. July 30, Wilhelm beats the Chicago Cubs. August 2, Wilhelm beats the Pittsburgh Pirates. August 13, Wilhelm beats the Brooklyn Dodgers. August 19, Wilhelm beats the Cubs. August 26, Wilhelm beats the Pirates. September 10, Wilhelm beats the Pirates again. September 24, Wilhelm beats the Braves. And September 25, Wilhelm beats the Braves once more.

The August 2 triumph pushed Wilhelm's record to 9–2. On a

7. A Hot Commodity

day Larry Jansen started and allowed three runs on four hits in ⅓ of an inning, Wilhelm came to the rescue, going 5⅔ with four strikeouts while surrendering just one hit before rain shut down the game early. "Wilhelm bamboozled the Bucs the rest of the way," went part of the *New York Daily News*' account of the 4–3 contest.[1]

Then, as baseball statistic addicts updated information retroactively, Wilhelm's saves were added up too. He had saves that summer on July 3, July 12, July 13, July 15, July 19, August 7, August 21, September 11, September 12, September 13 and September 26.

It got to the point that summer where Dodgers manager Chuck Dressen did everything but bluntly express fear of what Wilhelm could do with the mystery pitch. He did not wish to send Carl Erskine, one of his top guys, head to head with Wilhelm. "I won't pitch him against Wilhelm," Dressen said. "Let's face it, we just don't hit his knuckler, so why should I waste Erskine against him if Leo [Durocher] starts him?"[2]

When he appeared in his 58th game on the mound that season, Wilhelm set a record for most pitching appearances by a rookie. It was not a terribly old record; teammate George Spencer had set the old one of 57 the year before. This was also an indicator Durocher was open to relief pitcher contributions before he ever saw Wilhelm.

In the home stretch, just as the season was ending, Wilhelm broke the Giants' record for appearances by any pitcher in a single season with a one-inning showing versus the Phillies on September 27, a game won by Philadelphia 7–3. That was Wilhelm's 71st showing of the season. The old team mark was 70 by Ace Adams in 1943. Wilhelm, who made $7,500 in salary that season, gave the Giants their money's worth.

No question Wilhelm stayed busy and he came through almost all of the time after a few shaky appearances early. That was 159-plus innings of relief in 1952. Most of Wilhelm's outings exceeded two innings and he tossed six innings in relief one time and seven innings another time. While he was never asked to start a game, Wilhelm, in a sense could have been a starter.

It had never been Wilhelm's aspiration to be a relief pitcher. Virtually no one moving up the professional chain felt that way in his era. Still, Wilhelm, like everyone else working his way through Class A and B and everywhere else, desired to have the golden chance to pitch in the majors, so he was not about to refuse if the method that was going to get him onto a big-league roster was filling this job.

Wilhelm much later in his career wondered if he had been a failed relief pitcher, or one who performed just so-so, what would have become

Hoyt Wilhelm

of his career in the long run. He wouldn't have given up pursuing his dream, but what might have happened was just one blur of an idea.

"I had never pitched relief before," Wilhelm said, "but I was a relief pitcher from then on for most of my career. If I had been just fair in relief, maybe I'd have been a starting pitcher and everything would have been different all those years. I might have just lasted a couple of years and then again maybe I'd still be pitching up here as a starter. This is something no one can possibly know."[3]

After his long apprenticeship, Wilhelm was a success, his 15–3 record catching baseball off-guard. The number of his showings, 71 games, leading the league. His winning percentage besting that of any of the more famous guys. And winning the ERA title to boot. If few members of the Giants' organization and practically no one else in the National League knew his name before spring training, everyone did by the end of the season.

Wilhelm became the first rookie to lead the NL in winning percentage and earned run average.

Neither for the first time (including his minor-league stays) nor the last time (all the way through retirement), Wilhelm was asked fundamental questions about the knuckleball. How did he hold it? How did he throw it? How did he pick it up? So few knuckleball experts flitted across the baseball firmament, each generation needed a refresher course on the darned thing, which looked so easy to hit, to learn how it actually worked.

It only drove questioners, sportswriters and the like, who probed like detectives or scientists trying to pinpoint the origin of the universe, battier when they could not get a straight answer out of Wilhelm or another top-notch knuckleball thrower. It was all counterintuitive. It seemed self-evident why a hitter could not connect with a Walter Johnson, Bob Feller or Nolan Ryan fastball. You couldn't hit what you couldn't see. But a knuckler? It floated to the plate so slowly you could see it all too well. Why couldn't the batter—among the best hitters in the world—adjust his sights to smack it into the next county?

Then you had Wilhelm and the Phil Niekros of the world, Niekro being another knuckleball Hall of Famer, simply replying that they didn't know why it worked either and frowning at anyone who suggested they were masters of the knuckler.

Wilhelm was 100 percent committed to the knuckleball. When he was asked who taught him to throw it, he told the story about seeing Dutch Leonard in the newspaper when he was a kid. He was self-taught,

7. A Hot Commodity

he said, causing the skeptic to turn his head sideways and look askance at him the way dogs sometimes do when trying to figure out an owner's command.

"Nobody," Wilhelm insisted. "Really, I picked it up and worked at it myself. I threw it off the front two fingers, yeah." Then he was quizzed on if he knew what the knuckler would do when he released it. "No, not exactly. I don't think anybody does if those are real, true knuckleballs, you know. You can't throw two that will do the same thing. Then you might, because it's the idea of a knuckleball to get the spin off the ball."[4]

It is possible that Wilhelm lost an interviewer after he began delving into the science of what affected the knuckler, sometimes sounding more like a sailor about to go off by himself on a circumnavigation of the globe.

"The wind resistance on the seams is what makes it break and there's no way those seams are going to be in the exact same position, plus the wind difference," Wilhelm said. "There's nobody that can throw a knuckleball and say it can do this or it's going to do that. I'd say the majority of them [knucklers], at least mine did, the majority broke down away from the right-hand hitter, but that's not to say it did all of the time."[5] Got that?

Wilhelm said he was not surprised that he could deliver for the Giants as a first-year player and being someone who relied on a knuckleball meant he didn't really change anything, just kept doing what he was doing.

"I don't think anybody thought too much about it," he said of his rookie success. "I was having good years in the minor leagues and to me it was a big thing to get to the big leagues, of course. But the pitching difference in my style, I mean I didn't really find it that much harder because I pitched exactly the same as I did in AAA ball. It was just fortunate I had the knuckle ball and got big-league hitters out."[6]

In his own way, Wilhelm became a secret weapon for Durocher and the Giants but always with the understanding that no one is perfect and no baseball pitcher can expect to be perfect game after game, otherwise there would be more than 23 perfect games in history. Wilhelm never pretended to be perfect, but he could be untouchable in certain instances when the knuckleball obeyed the commands of his fingers.

Trying to pull personal details out of Wilhelm could be like trying to extract nuclear secrets from a spy, but Wilhelm revealed some of his character when discussing knuckleball origins. He repeated the Dutch Leonard story many a-time without pinpointing the year, but he did emphasize that his high school coach, Ben Brown, encouraged him to keep throwing it.

Lord knows what would have happened to young Wilhelm if he had been cast aside because his favorite pitch was anathema to many. He was indeed a poor boy from the farm, and baseball sustained him and propelled him.

"From as far back as I can remember, I loved baseball," Wilhelm said. "I grew up on a farm. When we didn't have baseballs, we'd use corn cobs, hickory nuts, walnuts, even rocks. We'd just make a bat out of a hickory stick or dogwood. Dogwood made a good one. You'd just go out in the woods, cut yourself a small one, let it dry a little, and you're ready to go. I never played any organized game until I got to high school. But my, I loved baseball."[7]

There is a purity of sentiment in that quote from Wilhelm that would seem to recall a bygone era. He almost sounds like the Robert Redford character in the movie *The Natural*, which did not come out until 1984. Indeed, that character came from a farming background. Coincidentally, Bernard Malamud's novel of the same name was released in 1952. Although about baseball, it did not relate to Wilhelm in any specific manner.

What did was the United States becoming involved in another major foreign conflict. Famously, Ted Williams, who fought in World War II, was conscripted to fly and fight again in the Korean War. If that had happened to Wilhelm, it surely would have wrecked his career for good right when he was getting his big chance. Williams, one of the greatest players of all time, did miss playing time, serving as a Marine Corps pilot again starting in 1952. Williams played in just six games for the Boston Red Sox that year, went overseas, and returned in time to play in 37 games in 1953.

Williams played for Boston between 1939 and 1960, except for time out for wars. He first became aware of Wilhelm from afar, but he would not have faced Wilhelm as a batter regularly until later in the 1950s when the hurler came over to the American League.

"The Splendid Splinter," as Williams was sometimes called, admired Wilhelm's success and his ability to make the knuckleball dance for him. Once, Williams named the five best pitchers he ever faced, for different reasons, and one of them was Wilhelm.

"Wilhelm had a sure-strike knuckler," Williams said, "then a real good knuckler, then with two strikes a real bastard of a knuckler, dancing in your face, the closest thing to an unhittable ball I ever saw."

7. A Hot Commodity

Wilhelm said he never wavered from his commitment to the knuckler as his meal ticket and threw it in games between 75 percent and 95 percent of the time. Williams recalled once that Wilhelm sought to cross him up and failed. "I remember one time waiting for that knuckler," Williams said, "and darned if Wilhelm didn't throw a fastball. I said, 'Well, gee, here's a nice fastball.' Line drive for a base hit. I had that much time. He never threw me another."[8] Williams was making the point that Wilhelm learned and adjusted and didn't repeat mistakes.

Alas, Wilhelm did not exactly repeat his sterling season of 1952 when he came back from winter break for a second season with the Giants, though he did receive a decent raise from the club, boosting his pay to $13,000 annually. In those days, ballplayers as a group were not necessarily better off than common American laborers. Only the biggest of stars made what was considered to be big money at the time. Hall of Fame slugger Hank Greenberg made his reputation with the Detroit Tigers but was playing for the Pittsburgh Pirates when he became baseball's first $100,000 player in 1951. The majority of players, especially a rookie coming to the big leagues with little fanfare, were paid like Wilhelm in those days. Raises were incremental. The nearly 50 percent increase for Wilhelm between 1952 and 1953 was considered quite generous.

Wilhelm was hard on himself and the team in discussing the 1953 campaign. Neither equaled the 1952 level of play. The Giants did not come close to their recent 90-plus-win seasons, finishing far down in the National League pack at 70–84.

In some ways that record was inexplicable. The Giants hit terrifically with Don Mueller at .333, Monte Irvin at .329, Hank Thompson at .302, Alvin Dark at .300, Davey Williams at .297 and Whitey Lockman at .295. It was the pitching that dropped off across the board.

The big two, Larry Jansen and Sal Maglie, were not their normal selves, Jansen going 11–16 and the Barber finishing at 8–9. Jim Hearn was just 9–12, so none of the top three starters did well. The best pitcher among the regular starting quartet was Ruben Gomez. Gomez, then 25, went 13–11 with a 3.40 earned run average. The Puerto Rico native seemed to have a promising future, but concluded his career with a 76–86 mark and an ERA over 4.00.

Maglie, who won 119 games in his career with an excellent lifetime 3.15 earned run average, was not in top form. The chapter in his biography that refers to 1953 is called "Sal's Season in Hell."[9] Suffering from a back problem from a strained muscle and then other physical ailments,

Hoyt Wilhelm

Maglie was heavily criticized in the sports pages as possibly being over the hill.

Compared to his first season, Wilhelm's year was a mixed bag. He came nowhere close to matching his 1952 won-loss record, ending up 7–8, but his earned run average was a still-solid, if not as-excellent 3.04 and he posted 15 saves. One of Wilhelm's most satisfying outings that year was shutting down Brooklyn for four innings in an early-season win with no hits and no runs. Also, in early May, a 5⅓-inning showing gave him a win over the Pirates. These were long relief stints. Wilhelm picked up his third victory of the season with five innings of relief against Cincinnati in an 11-inning game.

Wilhelm faltered late in the season, not winning a game after early August and seeing his ERA rise by nearly a run. However, it should be noted that Wilhelm (perhaps as a result of his first season) was chosen for the National League All-Star team.

The 1953 All-Star game was played at Crosley Field in Cincinnati on July 14. The hometown Reds changed their name to the Redlegs that year because of the Communist "red scare" hysteria being drummed up by U.S. Senator Joseph McCarthy of Wisconsin.

Billy Pierce started for the American League and Robin Roberts for the National League after Ted Williams threw out the ceremonial first pitch, honored because of his military service. The Yankees' Casey Stengel managed the AL and the Dodgers' Chuck Dressen managed the NL. Pierce, of the White Sox, and Roberts, of the Phillies, matched tosses, each going three innings and allowing just one hit. The National League gradually piled up runs from the middle of the game on, winning 5–1.

Unlike the 2020s contests when managers go out of their way to pitch starters for fewer innings and to get everyone on each roster into the game, not everyone played in this one. Hoyt Wilhelm was an honored spectator, a member of the National League team that included Stan Musial of the St. Louis Cardinals, Roy Campanella of the Dodgers, Eddie Mathews of the Braves, Warren Spahn of the Braves, and Jackie Robinson, another of the many Dodgers Dressen dressed up the team with.

Wilhelm was one of eight pitchers selected for the NL, but only four of them, Roberts, Spahn, Curt Simmons and Murray Dickson, got into the box score. Spahn was the winning pitcher. The Yankees' Allie Reynolds took the loss.

The recognition was notable for Wilhelm, especially because he was a relief specialist, and those in authority in Major League Baseball

7. A Hot Commodity

still were coping with the idea that a non-starting pitcher could be that valuable.

The Giants sinking in the standings and his own record concluding at an inferior mark than his 1952 season combined to leave Wilhelm feeling a bit melancholy despite the All-Star selection. "We had a bad year in '53 and I had a bad year," Wilhelm said. "We had a bad year all the way around."[10]

Although he did not seem to gain too much extra satisfaction from the event and it made little dent in his overall batting average, Wilhelm cracked the only triple of his career in 1953. Already, sportswriters seemed to understand that any offensive output from Wilhelm's bat was going to be a rarity.

The date was June 4 and the opponent was the Cincinnati Redlegs. Maglie gave the Giants six solid innings before Wilhelm was summoned in relief. The score was 3–3, but New York took command late, exploding for seven runs in the eighth inning on the way to the 11–3 final. Wilhelm's triple came in the bottom of the seventh inning, when the Giants inched ahead before the later-in-game eruption.

While it was his pitching that kept the Reds quiet, Wilhelm's smash was highly regarded in the *New York Times*' reporting. "Hoyt Wilhelm, whose specialty is tossing a knuckleball that baffles batters, catchers and umpires, stepped out of character at the Polo Grounds yesterday and forthwith produced a startling feat," the story said with a touch of whimsy. "Advancing to the plate as a batter in the seventh inning of the Giant-Redleg battle with the score tied at 3-all, which is where it stood when he entered as a mound replacement for Sal Maglie in the same round, the Carolinian relief specialist exploded a terrific triple into right center."[11]

8

The World Series

The 1954 season saw some of the most extraordinary events in baseball history, and Hoyt Wilhelm's New York Giants were at the heart of them. When the season concluded, Wilhelm was the owner of a World Series ring.

In his third season, Wilhelm was a solid member of the team. The Giants had taken a step back in 1953, at least partially because Willie Mays was in the military rather than in center field, and were from the start gunning for the pennant and shunting the Brooklyn Dodgers aside.

At least the Giants were thinking that way, if not playing that way, in the spring. New York was 8–6 in April and 15–13 in May but blew away everyone in the National League with a 24–4 June. The Giants ended up with a 97–57 record overall. In many ways, even though he never went near the rubber on the mound to start a game, Wilhelm was even better than he had been as a rookie two years earlier. In relief in 1954, Wilhelm went 12–4 with a 2.10 earned run average in 57 appearances spread over 111⅓ innings. Wilhelm was making $15,000 a year.

Manager Leo Durocher was so happy with the way things were going at the height of the summer that he began handing out $100 bonus checks to players when they hit home runs. It was an idea out of the blue, but the practice didn't last long, because league president Warren Giles spiked the plan. Giles told Durocher he would fine him personally $500 each time he paid the reward.

That season the Giants had great depth on the roster and Durocher became enamored with the notion of platooning a couple of players at one position here and there. Such strategy had worked splendidly for Casey Stengel across town with the New York Yankees.

Durocher, who could be loud and gruff and was closely identified with phrases that indicated the only thing he cared about was winning, offered a bit of sarcastic humor about his own status after the Giants went all the way to the crown. "In 1954," he said, "we not only won

8. The World Series

another pennant, we swept the World Series in four straight. And once again I was a genius, and just in the nick of time too, because for two years I'd been just another bum."[1]

Durocher, it might be said, was mixing his metaphors. He knew well that the Dodgers, who resided in Brooklyn, were sometimes affectionately called "the Bums."

By 1954, after three years in the majors, having reached the pinnacle of his profession, Wilhelm was even somewhat of a celebrity in his own household. In North Carolina, at least, his parents and brothers and sisters kept track of the movement of his knuckleball as best they could in a much less technology-oriented era. Sometimes they could catch Giants games on television or radio, although since Wilhelm was a relief pitcher, there was no way to know when he might appear in a game. Other times some members of the large family would make trips to attend some of his big-league games.

Even though she was 20 years younger than her big brother, Viki Hager, the youngest of Hoyt's sisters, remembered the long-ago excitement of watching him play in the big leagues in person.

"I remember when he hit his home run in 1952 and I remember my dad hearing some games on the radio," Hager said in 2022. "Once he got called up, he didn't live at home too much. Later, oh Lord, I always watched. You didn't miss a game."

When she was around 15, after school let out for the summer, Viki was part of a trip to New York to visit Hoyt and watched the Giants every day during a homestand. "That was a lot of fun," she said. "I went to all the games, though we never knew when he was going to pitch." The family took pride in Wilhelm's accomplishments and young as she was, she always had thoughts like "Hey, that's my big brother." "I was certainly proud."[2]

When the 1954 season began it was not immediately obvious that Wilhelm was on his way to a league-leading .750 winning percentage. He was among those affected somewhat by the Giants' mediocre April start. There was really nothing major wrong with his delivery since his earned run average was 1.64, but by May 1 Wilhelm was just 0–1 with a single save. He didn't get his first victory of the season until May 14 when the Giants topped the Chicago Cubs, 9–6. In between, despite not being saddled with a defeat, Wilhelm's ERA jumped to 3.38. The guy who led the NL in winning percentage and only suffered four losses all year did not move to 3–2 until June 8. Two immaculate outings gave him a proper push in the win-loss column and in diminishing that ERA.

Hoyt Wilhelm

Wilhelm was a major contributor to the Giants dominating June, the month they went to 20 games above .500. Wilhelm won four times and picked up four saves as the sun shone brightly on him as well as the team.

First came that win over the Milwaukee Braves, who had relocated to the Midwest from their old home in Boston. On June 19, Wilhelm bested the St. Louis Cardinals. On June 22, he edged the Braves again. On June 29, he prevailed over the Chicago Cubs. That made four victories and no losses during the month—and Wilhelm did not allow a run in any of those outings.

The saves of the month were catalogued on June 4 against the Cincinnati Redlegs (no runs allowed), June 12 against the Cubs (no runs allowed), over the Cubs again June 13 (this time permitting two earned runs in 3⅓ innings) and June 30 versus the Dodgers (one run allowed). It was a month for not only little sister Viki to be proud of but for all the Wilhems to be pleased with.

Hoyt Wilhelm had much to be proud of by this point. Not only had he reached his long-held goal of making it to the big leagues but he was also making it in the big leagues. He had done it his own way, the hard way, and that included sticking with and relying on his knuckleball.

Wilhelm became a success by throwing a pitch that few understood and many were skeptical of, no matter how often he came out of the bullpen to help his team win. Wilhelm was an affable man, and for the most part teammates were his friends, got along well with him, and even if they couldn't really identify with his trick pitch, they supported him. They saw the results and recognized that game after game—over lots of games—he was helping the team.

While there is little hard evidence that the men who played the position of catcher on the Giants disliked Wilhelm, beginning with his first seasons in New York and throughout the years, Wilhelm regularly came across players who hated catching his knuckleball. They feared it would make them look bad—and it did—because its twists and turns were so unpredictable. At times they were as helpless to corral the ball as a wild swinging batter was to hit it. There was nothing routine about catching a regular knuckleball artist.

Pitchers and catchers have long been referred to as batterymates. They are a duo, forming a partnership, and always have been. The catcher signals to the pitcher what he wants the hurler to throw, a fastball, a curveball, or something else, and then he hunkers down even tighter behind the plate. Pitchers and catchers can be like dance

8. The World Series

partners, in rhythm with one another's moves and steps. When it comes to the crazy knuckler, though, the catcher is often in the dark, caught off-guard by the pitcher's move.

When a pitcher throws a pitch far off target, way out of the strike zone, he is penalized on scorecards for throwing a wild pitch. When a catcher drops or misses a good pitch, he is charged with a passed ball. Some catchers are better fielders than others, but all make flukey mistakes. However, trying to catch a knuckleball thrower involves a greater degree of difficulty. More bad things happen when a knuckler is unleashed toward the plate than when a fastball is thrown.

In AAA Minneapolis, Wilhelm was teammates with catcher Ray Katt. Like the pitcher, Katt was on his way up through the Giants' chain, hoping to make the big-league roster and proclaim he had made it to the majors. Katt grumbled about the challenges of catching Wilhelm when they were both on the Millers' roster in Minnesota. But he couldn't escape the knuckleball. When Wilhelm broke in as a rookie with the Giants in 1952, so did Katt.

Katt, who was born in 1927, was not a particularly young rookie either. His first major-league appearance took place in September of 1952 with the Giants, a handful of months after Wilhelm. He was already 25 years old. The Giants' regular catcher in the early 1950s was Wes Westrum, approaching and passing age 30. He was a light hitter with a bit of power but with a poor average. He hit .220 in Wilhelm's rookie year and an embarrassing .187 in 1954.

By that season, the younger Katt was getting almost as much playing time, appearing in 86 games to Westrum's 98. Katt hit .255 during that pennant-winning year. The only problem he periodically faced was catching Wilhelm, his nemesis from the minors whose knuckleballs' flutters drove him mad.

For the Giants' September 10, 1954, game against the Reds, Katt was behind the plate and Wilhelm was on the mound. The Giants, cruising toward the pennant, were having an off day against Cincinnati. The Reds were ahead 6–1 by the time Wilhelm entered the game and won it 8–1. Before the last out, Katt had committed four passed balls. All four occurred in the eighth inning, the lone inning Wilhelm pitched. It was a disaster for Katt and the Giants, even though the game was essentially meaningless.

Wilhelm came on in relief of Bob Lennon to start the eighth and the top of the inning unfolded in a messy manner. Wally Post grounded out and then second baseman Johnny Temple singled to center. Andy

Hoyt Wilhelm

Seminick made a fly-ball out. Thus far nothing unusual had transpired. Reds pitcher Art Fowler stepped into the batter's box and the first passed ball happened, sending Temple to second safely. Wilhelm walked Fowler, and when Bobby Adams was up, the second passed ball occurred. Adams walked to load the bases.

The next two pitches, both to shortstop Roy McMillan, were both passed balls, creating chaos on the basepaths and leading to a Cincinnati run. Temple scored on the first mishap.

The inning ended with Katt charged with four passed balls, a record for a single inning that still stands. Twice in subsequent decades the mark was tied but never broken. Texas Rangers catcher Geno Petralli endured the same type of frustration in 1987 and Boston Red Sox receiver Ryan Lavarnway lived the nightmare in 2013. As it so happened, Petralli was catching knuckleballer Charlie Hough and Lavarnway was catching knuckleballer Steven Wright. The fact that the three catchers had the worst-ever games by a receiver when they were trying to catch knuckleball experts is a surprise to no one. It is not clear if Wilhelm sent Katt Christmas cards for the rest of his life to soothe his bruised ego, though he probably should have.

This was not an otherwise memorable game and the regular season wound to its end. The Reds left the Polo Grounds 20 games behind the Giants after their surprising strong perfomrance and there were few paying witnesses—3,107—who had seen Katt's shame. One of those in attendance, though presumably he had gotten in free, was syndicated writer Red Smith, possibly the greatest newspaper sports columnist of all.

In a game of no note in the standings, Smith found himself drawn to the drama surrounding Katt and his shaky fielding. "As it turned out," Smith wrote, "there were two battles—between the Reds and the Giants on one hand—and between Ray Katt, the catcher, and Hoyt Wilhelm's knuckleball, on the other. The home forces lost both, and all the league leaders got out of the afternoon was a major-league record." Taking note of the vagaries of knuckleball behavior, Smith said, "It was one of those days when the mightiest managerial brain spins and whirls and gives off sparks and might as well have been checked at the gate."[3]

The way Smith described the scene it was as if Katt was at war with some superior supernatural force and was also lucky that he wasn't charged with a fifth passed ball as action played out.

"In a series of no more than a dozen pitches, five eluded Katt's plunging grasp," Smith wrote, "though one of those wasn't scored as a

8. The World Series

passed ball because it didn't get far away and no runner advanced. To Katt's credit, though, he went right on calling the knuckler and weaving, bobbing, lunging in a willing struggle to handle it."[4]

The writer overlooks one thing. When Wilhelm was pitching, he was always throwing the knuckler. Katt really couldn't ask the hurler to throw something different. Durocher could have declared mercy and yanked Katt altogether from the game, but winning the game did not seem within reach.

The post-mortem in the Giants' locker room was subdued. Katt sat quietly in front of his locker trying to process what happened. Teammates walked past and tried to cheer him up after learning he set such a negative record.

"All those tricky winds today made that ball act up extra special," said Johnny "Windy" McCall. "It's bad enough without winds." Given his nickname, McCall should have known. Westrum, the other catcher, who was probably glad to sit this one out, said, "Anybody can get fooled on his knuckler. It's impossible to guess. You can get black and blue from getting hit with it, but you can't bet you'll catch it."[5]

Katt had every opportunity to bemoan his fate to sportswriters, or to duck blame, but he refused to do either. He manned up to the mistakes while acknowledging the knuckleball is indeed the knuckleball and sometimes things happen.

"Those were scored right," Katt said, not casting aspersions on the official scorer's call or suggesting Wilhelm should have been assigned wild pitches in any instance. "Those were passed balls. I got my glove on every one of them. Trouble was I had no idea where one was going until it hit me on the heel of the glove. This way, that way, up, down, it jumps and it dips and if you move one way and it twists that other way—you ought to see that thing."[6]

Ironically, Katt said he received some sympathy from home-plate umpire Jocko Conlan, who sounded as if he was thinking a bit like Red Smith, once the situation became repetitive and testy.

"When two of them went by," Katt told the sportswriters, "'Conlan said, 'Call for the fastball.' But I didn't. I was going to ride that darned thing."[7]

Of course, the batters were still being driven crazy by Wilhelm's best knucklers too. They couldn't track the pitch well and they didn't know where it was going to go. Jim Greengrass, then a young outfielder who had plenty of time to witness Wilhelm's flings during his own early 1950s stays with Cincinnati and then the Philadelphia Phillies, was given advice on hitting Wilhelm's specialty by Cincinnati manager Rogers Hornsby.

"He said, 'This knuckleball, just play pepper with it,'" Greengrass said. "You hit it by him, you've got a base hit. He's only sixty feet, six inches from you. Just try to hit a line drive. A nice, easy, short swing right back at him.' So, I get up there. Wilhelm throws that dancer at me. I swung straight down at that damned ball. If I hadn't hit the ground with my bat, I'd have hit my leg and broke it. Wes Westrum was catching [for the Giants]. He just rolled over laughing. The umpire was laughing. Forty thousand people were laughing."[8] Ray Katt wasn't the only guy who had difficulty coping with Hoyt Wilhelm's knuckler. He probably wasn't laughing.

Despite the occasional glitch like Katt's four passed balls in an inning, 1954 was good to the Giants. Willie Mays was now a full-blown star, batting .345 with 41 home runs and 110 runs batted in. Don Mueller hit .342 and Hank Thompson slugged 26 homers. At a time when not every team in baseball had integrated, Thompson was a Negro League veteran of the Kansas City Monarchs who supplemented Mays and Irvin, giving the Giants three potent bats from Black players.

Larry Jansen was gone, but the new ace of the staff was bonus baby Johnny Antonelli, who finished 21–7 with a 2.30 earned run average. Sal Maglie was hanging in at 14–6, and Ruben Gomez, a native of Puerto Rico, had a 17–9 record. Although the Giants were not the pioneers in integrating Major League Baseball, they quickly followed the first teams that did so, and reaped benefits from signing players who only a few years earlier would have been banned from the game.

The Giants won the National League pennant by five games over the Dodgers, with Brooklyn finishing 92–62. The Milwaukee Braves were three games back of the Dodgers. This was the era of New York City baseball, when the Giants, Dodgers and especially the American League New York Yankees were powerhouses of the game. It seemed there was always a New York team playing for the championship. The phrase "subway series" was coined to describe how easy it was for fan bases of the New York teams to access the opposing teams' stadiums, almost as commuters heading to a job in another borough or in another area of the city.

The Brooklyn Dodgers won NL pennants in 1947, 1949, 1952, 1953, 1955 and 1956 with the "Boys of Summer" bunch led by Jackie Robinson, Roy Campanella, Duke Snider and other stars. The New York Giants won pennants in 1951 and 1954. The Yankees, under Casey Stengel, won

8. The World Series

10 pennants in 12 seasons between 1949 and 1960, plus pennants in 1947 under Bucky Harris, and in 1961, 1962, 1963 and 1964 under Ralph Houk and Yogi Berra.

In the midst of all of that wild success, and with the Yankees winners of five straight World Series between 1949 and 1953, the biggest surprise in the sport in 1954 was that the Yanks did not win the American League pennant.

This time the Cleveland Indians, under manager Al Lopez, a future Hall of Famer, romped through the regular schedule, compiling a record of 111–43. That marked a record for wins by an AL franchise. It was not as if the Yankees even slumped, winning 103 games, but that was only good enough to finish eight games back in the standings.

The Indians were unstoppable and put together one of the greatest regular seasons in baseball history. Second baseman Bobby Avila led the league in average at .341. Hall of Famer Al Rosen hit .300 with 24 home runs and 102 runs batted in. Larry Doby, the first Black player in the American League and also later a Hall of Famer, clubbed 32 home runs and drove in 126 runs, best on the team.

However, it was the starting pitching, more than anything else, that opponents feared when facing the Indians. The team was loaded with aces. Early Wynn, headed to the Hall of Fame with 300 victories, went 23–11. Bob Lemon, another hurler working his way to the Hall, went 23–7. Mike Garcia was 19–8. Bob Feller, at 35 and nearing the end of his World War II–interrupted career, was 13–3. Hal Newhouser, only a few years before the top hurler in the league, mostly came out of the bullpen and went 7–2. Completely unheralded compared to the rest of these pitchers was Art Houtteman and he was 15–7. The team earned average was 2.78. It seemed impossible for the Giants to fare well against such depth in a pitching staff.

When the World Series opened on September 29, the game was played at the Polo Grounds in front of 52,751 optimistic fans who worried that their hometown team would not be able to keep up with the spectacular Indians. The ceremonial pitch of the first game was thrown out by a young man named Jim Barbieri. Barbieri would later become a Major League outfielder and compete in a World Series (as well as play one season of professional ball in Japan in 1970). In 1954, though, he represented his team from Schenectady, New York, that had won the Little League World Series. Despite their seeming glut of arms, the Indians should have signed Barbieri right then and there.

With all three of the New York big-league clubs playing well each year and two of them liable to face off in the World Series year after year, come October the city enjoyed a baseball holiday of sorts. Forget about autumn's falling leaves or the early weeks of the National Football League season, they were playing for the world championship in their backyard.

For once, there were not two New York teams in the World Series in the fall of 1954. What baseball fans got instead was one of the greatest upsets in championship-round history. There was barely a soul in the country who felt the Indians were vulnerable after their thorough domination of the summer. Their 111 wins stood as an American League record until 2001.

The Giants felt they should show up anyway. Many felt Cleveland would sweep. Many were shocked by what transpired. And the drama began with the first game, one of the more memorable World Series games of all thanks to Willie Mays. Throughout the Series, he was aided and abetted by the hustling, somewhat bit player Dusty Rhodes. James Lamar Rhodes wasn't even a starter, but he had proven his ability in clutch situations to Durocher over the course of the season. When the manager needed instant offense off the bench, he turned to Rhodes.

Rhodes' seven-year Major League career covered just a chunk of the 1950s and at no time was he better than in 1954. He was better still in that season's World Series. The spotlight found him as if fated that fall and he responded well to the bright lights. Durocher said not every player has the wherewithal to come in cold to hit after sitting on the bench for a game's first several innings—acting as the offensive counterpart to the relief pitcher and the Hoyt Wilhelms of the world.

"At the start of the season, I tried in every way I knew to trade Dusty Rhodes," Durocher said later. "Half of the time he was drunk and everybody in the league had heard about his drinking problems. But nobody would claim him. Thank the Lord nobody did."[9]

Rhodes was retired by age 32 in 1959, but he hit a career high .341 in 1954. He even received Most Valuable Player votes despite playing in just 82 games. His lifetime average was only .253.

"Every time we needed a pinch hit to win an important game, there was Dusty Rhodes to deliver it for us," Durocher said. "Confident? The average fan may think a manager has to fight his men off when he's looking for a pinch hitter. Don't kid yourself. You look down on the bench and more often than not every eye is averted. But not Dusty Rhodes. Dusty would always be up on his feet, at the far end of the dugout, swinging a bat." Imitating Rhodes' Alabama drawl, Durocher said, "'Ah'm your man. What are you waiting for, Skipper?'"[10]

8. The World Series

Righty Bob Lemon started Game 1 of the Series for the Indians and right-hander Sal Maglie started for the Giants. The Indians shook things up immediately by scoring two runs in the top of the first. Maglie hit Al Smith with a pitch and Bobby Avila singled to right. Vic Wertz smashed a triple to score the runs, but Maglie wiggled out of any additional trouble. The Giants tied the game in the bottom of the third. Singles by Whitey Lockman, Al Dark, Hank Thompson and a walk to Mays contributed.

The score was still 2–2 when the Indians came to bat in the top of the eighth inning. After Maglie walked Larry Doby and gave up a single to Al Rosen on an infield hit to short, Durocher replaced Maglie on the mound with Don Liddle.

Next up was Wertz, who collected four hits this day, though he is best remembered for this at-bat when he made an out. Wertz tagged an offering from Liddle to deep center. The speedy Mays dashed deep, losing his cap in the process, caught up to the shot and fielded the ball over his shoulder much like a football player catching a long pass. Mays did not pause but whirled around and hurled the ball back to the infield as fans screamed support and players were astonished. The ball's swift return prevented Indians base-runners from advancing into better scoring position and they did not tally a run that inning. Nearly 70 years have passed since Mays made the tremendous catch and some baseball figures believe it was the greatest catch of all time.

At the least, Mays' catch halted a Cleveland rally. Durocher must have figured a ball hit that hard meant Liddle did not have his best stuff and he immediately replaced him on the mound with Marv Grissom. Wilhelm received neither the first call nor second call from the bullpen, and indeed, he sat this one out.

The game remained deadlocked through regulation innings. Lemon held steady for the Indians, headed for a complete-game loss when he allowed three runs in the bottom of the 10th inning.

Mays reached base on a walk and stole second. Lemon intentionally walked Thompson. Then, with one out, Rhodes pinch-hit for Monte Irvin and lofted a three-run homer to deep right field to win the game, 5–2.

There was plenty to discuss after the game that provided New York with a 1–0 lead in the Series, but much focus was centered on Mays and Wertz. Over a 17-year career, Wertz batted .277 with 1,178 RBIs and 266 home runs. That day he stroked a triple, a double and two singles, a home run short of the cycle.

Hoyt Wilhelm

"I never hit a ball harder in my life," Wertz said of the fly ball that Mays gathered in. "I know this sounds funny, but I actually thought that thing was going to carry into the bleachers. When I smacked the ball, it felt so good and I was so sure of how hard I tagged it, that all the details were erased from my mind. I can't even tell you what I hit."[11]

Forevermore, while others raved about the brilliance of his fielding play, which came to be nicknamed "The Catch," Mays insisted the grab wasn't as challenging as it looked and that he had a bead on the ball all the way. "Everyone said, 'well, it was a hard catch,'" Mays said. "I said nah, it was an easy catch."[12] Perhaps if you have super powers.

The second game of the Series took place the next day, September 30, also at the Polo Grounds. It was a pitcher's duel and southpaw Johnny Antonelli went the distance for the Giants in a 3–1 win, besting Early Wynn.

The Indians again began the scoring in the top of the first inning when Cleveland outfielder Al Smith greeted Antonelli and the still-settling-in crowd with a solo home run. That was it on offense for the Indians. New York took the lead with two runs in the bottom of the fifth.

Mays scored after opening the inning with a walk. Hank Thompson singled, sending him to third, and Dusty Rhodes pinch-hit for Irvin. His single to center scored Mays and later in the inning the Giants squeezed out another run on an Antonelli groundout. So Rhodes was already the hero again when he came to the plate in the bottom of the seventh and crashed a solo home run off Wynn for the final margin. The man was on fire.

Syndicated columnist Jimmy Cannon aimed his notetaking and prose at Rhodes' miraculous play. The lead of Cannon's column the day after the second victory went like this: "You're Dusty Rhodes who holds the hot hand. You feel all the jackpots in all the slot machines in the world belong to you. Nothing's impossible when a guy realizes he has the touch. The price doesn't matter either."[13]

There was someone who recognized Rhodes had been sprinkled with fairy dust. Oh, there was more, much more, another New York sportswriter Jimmy Powers taking the same kind of fun ride with his words as Rhodes was with his bat.

"Luck makes a dumb man smart," he wrote. "It makes a short man taller. It gets you where you're going after all the trains have left. You have it inside, but you're afraid to talk about it. People would swear you're crazy if you told them."[14]

After two games in New York, the underdog Giants led the Series

8. The World Series

2–0, and the teams were on their way to Cleveland where the Indians hoped to conjure some hometown magic. Both the players and their fans were a bit stunned to find themselves trailing in this manner.

Cleveland came out 71,555 fans strong for Game 3 at Cleveland Stadium, hoping to help rescue their Indians with enthusiasm. Mike Garcia, the 19-game winner, was chosen by Al Lopez to start. Durocher picked 17-game winner Ruben Gomez.

This time there was less suspense. The result was not as close. New York scored one run in the first, three in the third, one in the fifth and one in the sixth. Cleveland almost didn't score, putting up just a single run in the seventh and another in the eighth. New York's biggest rally was sparked by no major blow. Alvin Dark, Don Mueller and that guy Dusty Rhodes each contributed singles, Rhodes knocking in two more runs in the clutch. Rhodes was pinch-hitting again. Hank Thompson collected an intentional walk and Davey Williams reached on an error.

Gomez tamed the Indians for 7⅓ innings before being lifted after surrendering two runs. This time Durocher beckoned for Wilhelm in relief. This could have been a tipping point. The Indians were threatening after a double by pinch-hitter Bill Glynn and Al Smith reached base on an error that scored Glynn. Gomez came out after he walked AL batting champ Bobby Avila.

Wilhelm's World Series debut, easily watchable around the country, including in rural North Carolina, pitted him first against Larry Doby. Doby got hold of a pitch but grounded it to first base, where he was out as runners advanced to second and third.

Then Mr. Danger, Vic Wertz, stepped in. Durocher had conducted a pitcher's meeting to remind his mounds-men how potent Wertz could be. But Wilhelm struck him out to end the inning. Wilhelm did not give up a hit, a run or a walk and he was later awarded a save.

It seemed almost unimaginable after the season the Indians had that they would be on the brink of elimination in the World Series after just three games. Professional sports teams in post-season playoffs almost never come back to win seven-game series after they fall behind 3–0. The Giants were in complete control.

The fourth and, yes, the last game of the 1954 World Series took place on October 3 in Cleveland, 78,102 hopeful and howling fans looking for any type of comeback hint, one "W," even. They didn't even get that.

Bob Lemon got the ball for the Indians and was one of five Cleveland hurlers, though the one who took the loss in the 7–4 defeat. Don

Hoyt Wilhelm

Liddle started for New York and went 6⅔. He gave up three unearned runs and one earned run, yielding to Wilhelm for his second Series appearance.

Wilhelm arrived on the mound with two outs in the seventh and quickly induced pinch-hitter Dave Pope to ground out, concluding the inning. Wilhelm started the eighth with a strikeout of Avila, but the Cleveland infielder was safe at first after the K. Doby lined out, but after Wilhelm allowed a single to Al Rosen, Durocher played a hunch. He removed Wilhelm from the game and brought in his ace starter Antonelli. Antonelli finished just two games during the regular season, but he finished this one, wrapping up the World Series with 1⅔ innings of work.

The Giants polished off the Indians in four straight games, their first World Series title since 1933. The scribes were not all pleasant in reviewing the Indians' demise. "All the king's horses and all the king's men couldn't put Humpty-Dumpty together again," a sports writer said, quoting the children's nursery rhyme. "The humiliation of Cleveland's winningest team in American League history, a ball club that will be remembered through the years as much for its World Series embarrassment as its rich regular-season record, was completed today in the shortest time possible."[15]

Although the Series lasted just four games, ballparks in each host city allowed good attendance totals and created a player payment pot of $1.5 million. The winning player share of Series money was $11,147.90 apiece. Some 30 Giants, Wilhelm included, received that payout. The losers' share to Cleveland players was $6,712.50.

Wilhelm pitched in two of the four Series games and they turned out to be the only two World Series appearances of his 21-year career. His World Series totals were 2⅓ innings, with no runs permitted and one hit allowed plus one save and a 0–0 record. But he definitely contributed, coming in from the bullpen in times of need.

9

Entrenched with New York

By the 1955 season, Hoyt Wilhelm was a solid member of the New York Giants, owner of a World Series championship souvenir, and an All-Star selectee, and based on his performances, he did not have to worry about hustling for a spot on the regular-season roster coming out of spring training camp.

By then, Wilhelm was making $20,000 in salary and doing his best to conservatively handle his money. Wilhelm was married to wife Peggy and they were starting a family that would include three children: Patti, James and Pam.

Unlike many of the single players, Hoyt did not live in New York City. Those unattached young men looking for love were charmed by its many off-the-field entertainment opportunities. When the Giants were in-season, and after school ended for the year, Wilhelm lived with his family on the outskirts of the city. Wilhelm was from small-town North Carolina and he did not really spend much energy trying to adapt to the nation's biggest city, except as a ballplayer in the majors.

"I never really lived in the city," Wilhelm said. "I didn't find it to be any big problem. I never went up there. I lived upstate, 10 or 15 miles north of New York City. Of course, you know, it was a big city to me, but still I was just playing baseball. We'd go into the park and play in the afternoon and play at night and then go back up to Dobbs Ferry (located in Westchester County). It was more or less a quiet country setting."[1]

While Wilhelm heard many family men in baseball speak about the difficulties about moving constantly and switching kids from school to school, he never considered that to be a particular challenge, even though the Wilhelms followed a migration pattern.

"I've heard players say that," Wilhelm said of the family shifting. "My kids, they all went to three different schools every year just about as long as I was playing. They'd go to their school at home and in spring training I'd put them in school for a month and then back in the city I was playing for. I think it would be better—that's one thing that I might change if I had in mind to do it over again—I would probably live in the town that I played in, just stay there year-round. I think that's one thing that I would probably change. Then again, I don't know because I always looked forward to going home at the end of the season. So, it's really hard to say."[2]

Moving around and switching schools did not seem detrimental to his kids, Wilhelm said. "The most important thing to raising kids is that they are with their parents wherever they are with that moving and stuff," Wilhelm said. "I don't buy that [moving harm] as long as they're with their parents and are being taken care of."[3]

Wilhelm apparently took care of his money, too. Teammate Johnny Antonelli remembers Wilhelm sidling up to him at the beginning of some seasons and informing him that he took some of his Giants pay-outs during the off-season and bought land at home in North Carolina, adding to his acreage each year. For someone whose father was an tenant farmer, being the owner of farmland meant something.

Wilhelm not being from a wealthy background stayed with him, Antonelli said sometime later. He had the simple goal of financial stability for his own family. "All he ever worried about was paying off his mortgage before his baseball career was over," Antonelli said. "Those days, you figured your career would last about six years because that was the average career—six years. Ballplayers weren't making a lot of money in those days and that was an important thing, to use those years you had to pay for as much as you could."[4] Antonelli said each year Wilhelm would report that he added perhaps 50 acres here or there to his property holdings in North Carolina.

Antonelli was a six-time All-Star who won 126 big-league games in 12 years but retired at 31 because he was weary of the travel. He referred to Wilhelm as a quiet type of guy with quite a bit of country in him. The married Antonellis and married Wilhelms sometimes spent social time together in spring training when both pitchers were with the Giants.

Antonelli, who attempted to throw a knuckleball periodically, just for fun, said Wilhelm always stuck with his pitch and with a reliever's mentality seemed to be ready to go on any day of the schedule. "He wanted the ball and somehow you knew he always wanted it," Antonelli said.[5]

Those who experienced the euphoria as players for the Giants in the 1954 World Series were able to bask in the achievement for some time to come. Capturing the win was no routine but an extra-special one given

9. Entrenched with New York

that the Indians won those American League–record 111 games and that the National League had been held in check by AL clubs (mostly the Yankees) since 1946 when the St. Louis Cardinals won it all.

Baseball observers such as longtime writer Frederick G. Lieb in *The Sporting News* meshed the Giants' accomplishment as one of baseball's greatest upsets with the Indians' loss as one of the sport's biggest collapses. Not only did the underdog Giants win but they also swept the Series.

Lieb compared the result to the 1906 World Series when the Chicago Cubs represented the National League after winning 116 regular-season games (still the league mark), only to fall to the Chicago White Sox, 93-game winners on the season, in six games.

When his Indians trailed in the series 3–0, Cleveland manager Al Lopez said, "They can't be that good and we can't be that bad."[6] Of course, both parts of his comment proved true, at least over four games.

This Series triumph seemed likely to spread a glow forever, but that's not how sports work. Almost immediately after one season ends, a new one begins, at least in terms of contract negotiations or, in a more modern era, free agency begins. Teams are promptly under pressure to build for next year, especially if they did not win it all the previous year, or are under pressure to maintain, if they did win it all. While the Giants' tremendous sweep of the Indians was preserved for good in history books, those who participated had to go on living, go on playing, and preparing for and competing next year.

The 1955 season wasn't nearly as good for Hoyt Wilhelm's New York Giants as 1954 had been. It was the year of the Brooklyn Dodgers, a year of redemption for a franchise that had come so close so many times without recording a title. Brooklyn was the dominant team in the National League in 1955 and no one else was really close in the standings, certainly not the Giants, who finished 80–74, roughly 18 games behind the Dodgers' 98–55 mark. The Giants came home third, trailing the Milwaukee Braves, who finished 13½ games behind the Dodgers in the standings.

Nineteen fifty-five was a year of great joy in Brooklyn. The Dodgers fielded one of the best and most popular teams of all time. The regulars in the field included Roy Campanella, Gil Hodges, Pee Wee Reese, Jackie Robinson and Duke Snider, all Hall of Famers, as well as All-Star Carl Furillo, plus pitchers Don Newcombe, Carl Erskine, Johnny Podres. Billy Loes, Clem Labine and a 19-year-old bonus baby named Sandy Koufax who rarely took the mound and went 2–2.

Hoyt Wilhelm

Appropriately enough, things went back to usual in the American League that season with the Yankees rebounding from their missed pennant of 1954 to face the Dodgers in their vindication year. Brooklyn's joy was complete when it topped New York in the Series four games to two.

It was Brooklyn's year all the way. The season is still celebrated in Dodgers history because Brooklyn was soon to be abandoned by the big leagues. The Dodgers-Giants rivalry had generated much excitement and drama, but soon that New York chapter of baseball history would be over.

Wilhelm's work load declined slightly in 1955 compared to his first three seasons and his earned run average spiked. He participated in 59 games out of the bullpen, two more than in 1954, but his innings pitched dropped to 103. His won-loss decisions were just a fraction of what they had been in previous years, though there was nothing wrong with a 4–1 record.

The earned run average, however, was concerning, jumping to 3.93. For once, hitters connected with a bit more regularity. That could simply have been the law of averages, because the frequency of the runs did not cost Wilhelm often in the win column. Somehow, in all of those relief innings and in those appearances, Wilhelm was not credited with a single save that year.

Wilhelm didn't earn his first victory until May 20; he had been hit hard in a couple of showings. That day he went 3⅔ innings, throwing virtually perfectly without allowing a hit or a run in a 6–3 victory over the Pittsburgh Pirates.

Two days later, May 22, Wilhelm was called on again versus the Pirates and recorded his second win in a 5–3 Giants victory, permitting two hits but no runs in two innings of work.

Wilhelm took his lone loss of 1955 on May 26 when he gave up one run to the Phillies in 1⅔ innings of pitching.

Wilhelm went seemingly ages, until September 4, before gaining his third victory in a 7–4 victory over the Philadelphia Phillies. By then Wilhelm had lost his only game of the year, and even after this scoreless outing, his ERA stood at 4.18. The knuckler wasn't as crisp that summer.

The hurler's final decision of the season came on September 20, once more versus the Pirates, this time in a 14–8 Giants win. In a ballgame with considerable action, Wilhelm threw 5⅓ innings and gave up three hits and one run for the win. In contrast to the enthusiasm demonstrated by Giants fans a year earlier, this game had an announced attendance of 1,165 fans at the Polo Grounds.

9. Entrenched with New York

Wilhelm's knuckleball presented difficulty to catchers. He was pleased when he came across a teammate who was good at catching the knuckler. With the Giants, Katt wrestled with hanging onto the knuckler, but older veteran Wes Westrum was better at it. Overall, he was renowned as a sterling defensive catcher and his glove kept him in the majors for 11 years since his lifetime batting average was just .217.

"I was a low-ball catcher and you know, in baseball, you've got to keep the ball down," Westrum said years after he retired. "They [the best pitchers he caught] weren't afraid to throw the ball in the dirt, make the batters go fishing."[7]

Westrum was not intimidated by Wilhelm's dipsy-doodle throws, though he did recognize the knuckler was apt to behave as if it had a mind of its own and not always pay attention to where Wilhelm wanted it to land.

"I didn't have many problems [with Wilhelm]," Westrum said. "The only thing is I was warming him up one day in Milwaukee—he came in in relief—and he got the end of my finger. There was another time I was hitting pretty good. Blood was pouring out and [manager Leo] Durocher said, 'Let's put a piece of tape on it and just keep going.' So, we did. Then I couldn't grip the bat."[8]

That showed how Wilhelm could be a menace to catchers, even those on his side, with the wild and wooly knuckler. Yet Westrum respected how well Wilhelm normally utilized it as a weapon.

"If he got the ball around the plate, nobody could hit it," Westrum said. "He had one of those knuckleballs that went all directions. Most of the knuckleball pitchers today [late 1980s, early 1990s] have a pitch that breaks downwards. His broke in all directions. The hitter didn't know where it was going. I didn't, and neither did he."[9] Westrum laughed when he said that, but it was true and is pretty much the same perspective other baseball people have employed in joking about knuckleball pitchers for decades.

Knuckleball pitchers remained an anomaly. There was no flood of Hoyt imitators coming of age in the minors. Shortly before Wilhelm broke into the majors, Gene Bearden had made a huge impact for the Indians but only briefly. Bearden was a rookie for Cleveland in 1947, a star in 1948 when he helped the Indians win their most recent World Series championship, and out of the big leagues by 1953 when he finished up with the White Sox.

Bob Purkey broke in with the Pirates in 1954 and struggled for a few years before finding himself on the mound and becoming a five-time

Hoyt Wilhelm

All-Star. His first years were poor and Purkey suffered an injured shoulder. He then became one of those knuckleballers who turned to the pitch to save his career. Branch Rickey, then running the Pirates, was his instructor.

While the knuckler may have rescued him, Purkey had a much broader pitch repertoire than Wilhelm and many other prominent knuckleballers, also throwing a fastball, slider, change and sinker. He did not identify closely with other knuckleball specialists but is often lumped together with them on the short list of those who used the pitch.

"I don't depend mainly on any one pitch," Purkey said. "My knuckler isn't as good as Hoyt Wilhelm's, my fastball not so overpowering as Ryne Duren's, my curve not so sharp as Vernon Law's. But put them all together and they give me a pretty fair repertoire. If I'm right I can set up any batter with almost any type of pitch."[10]

Purkey peaked in 1962 with a 23–5 record for Cincinnati and won 129 games in the majors in a 13-year career, mostly as a starter.

In 1956, another knuckleballer appeared in the bigs. Wally Burnette broke in with the Kansas City Athletics. Burnette had a short career, going 14–21. Originally signed by the New York Yankees, he was traded to K.C. for future Hall-of-Fame manager Tommy Lasorda. Burnette was brought up to the majors when the Athletics had a pitcher shortage due to injuries but was gone by the end of the 1958 season.

Except for the occasional new knuckler on the scene like Burnette, and Purkey, who relied part-time on the the pitch, Wilhelm was pretty much the only well-known and lasting pitcher in Major League Baseball counting on the knuckleball in the mid–1950s.

It would not be much longer, though, before the New York Giants stopped counting on him. Wilhelm had his worst season in the majors to date in 1956, when the team thought he was 33 (though he was really 34) and began to lose confidence in him.

Wilhelm still appeared in 64 games out of the bullpen that year, but his record was 4–9 and his earned run average, at 3.83, was only marginally better than it had been in 1955. By then, Leo Durocher was out as manager and the Giants were reshaping the team, going 67–87 under Bill Rigney. Except for Johnny Antonelli excelling with a 20–13 record, only two other Giants, Steve Ridzik at 6–2 and Ramon Monzant at 1-0, had winning marks on the mound.

The team was ripe for an overhaul, but the franchise itself was on the verge of being transported to San Francisco. Not many people knew

9. Entrenched with New York

about this developing situation. Owner Horace Stoneham took his club to the West Coast after the 1957 season.

By then, that earth-shattering move did not make any difference to Hoyt Wilhelm's career. He had already been exiled from the team earlier that year. Wilhelm's career in New York concluded months before the revered New York Giants became the San Francisco Giants. Whether New York management believed Wilhelm was through as a reliable pitcher or just shaking up a losing team, the Giants chapter, on whichever coast, ended for Wilhelm.

Not that he was close to being done as a pitcher at all. In the ensuing years, as he aged from these early 30s on, he was often underestimated. Teams failed to realize the value of his arm and repeatedly failed to take into account that the good old knuckleball did not produce wear and tear on his right arm the way a fastball might have.

That was one great beauty of the knuckler. It did not exert such powerful torque on the arm and the shoulder, so the men who employed it could seemingly pitch forever as long as nothing else interfered.

10

On to Other Teams

Hoyt Wilhelm's tenure with the New York Giants ended abruptly on February 26, 1957, when he was traded to the St. Louis Cardinals. Both the Giants and Wilhelm had been victims of tumbling fortunes the previous season and the perennial pennant contenders felt it was time for a shake-up.

Twice, Wilhelm had led the National League in appearances for the Giants and won at least 12 games in relief and once he had led the league in earned run average. But he endured an off season in 1956 that coincided with an off season for New York. Team management likely looked at his age—thought to be 34—and considered him over the hill.

Even for some games prior to World War II military service and from 1947 into 1956, Whitey Lockman had been a valued hitter for the Giants. Then the team sent him and others to the Cardinals in a multi-player blockbuster trade that involved nine players. Key Giants headed west were Lockman, Alvin Dark, Ray Katt and Don Liddle. The Giants acquired Red Schoendienst, Jackie Brandt, and Dick Littlefield, among others.

However, upon further thought, the Giants decided they wanted Lockman back, so as spring training of 1957 was revving up, they traded Wilhelm for Lockman. Giants president Horace Stoneham felt pressure to make some moves to juice up the Giants' lineup again after finishing 20 games below .500 in 1956. One newspaper described Wilhelm as a swap of the Giants' "ace reliever" for "an old friend."[1]

The Giants found themselves desperate for a quality first baseman. After the 1956 season, in a move that shocked the sport, Brooklyn traded Jackie Robinson to the despised Giants, but Robinson chose to retire rather than report. The Giants then counted on young Bill White, an up-and-coming star who later served as president of the National League, but White was drafted into the Army. New York had a big hole to fill.

10. On to Other Teams

Stoneham announced the deal to sportswriters himself and made it sound as if the trade came about as an impulsive decision, but he also made it sound as if the Giants were in the market to make changes after their poor 1956 season.

"This one came up pretty suddenly," Stoneham said, "and I hope it is not the last we can swing before the season starts."[2]

The farewell story in the New York *Daily News* referred to Wilhelm as "the best knuckleballer in the NL, if not in all of baseball."[3] The timing of the deal caught Wilhelm by surprise as he had just arrived in Phoenix, Arizona. Following the end of the 1956 season, he had wondered about his future with the club, but with spring training on the immediate horizon, he thought he was going to remain a Giant.

"I fully expected to be traded over the winter," Wilhelm said, "but after I made it here, I fully expected I was going to stick."[4]

In a different era, before free agency and more movement between teams, players often reacted strongly when they were traded for the first time in their careers after spending years in the same organization. Wilhelm felt some of that emotion.

"At first it shook me a little bit," Wilhelm said, "then I figured as long as I was in the big leagues it didn't really matter, what the heck."[5]

Players had just reported to spring training to kick off the 1957 season, so Wilhelm was in Phoenix and Lockman was in St. Petersburg, Florida, with the Cardinals. Once the trade was announced, a funny situation unfolded as the two men were traveling in opposite directions. Wilhelm got behind the wheel of his car and headed East. Lockman got behind the wheel of his car and headed West.

Without such online aids as MapQuest or other electronic route finders, the players figured out the best way between their camps on their own. The Wilhelms and Lockmans were driving in Dallas, Texas, when Peggy Wilhelm looked up and saw the Lockmans, Whitey and Shirley, at an intersection and told Hoyt.

"We passed each other in Dallas, and saw each other," Lockman said, "and stopped and had a little chat and went on our ways. Can you believe that?"[6] What were the odds?

At least one of Wilhelm's new teammates, the esteemed Stan Musial, seemed glad to have the new face with his secret weapon joining the team. "The thing about a good knuckler is that it's tough to hit whether you're hitting .300 or .200," Musial said. "It jumps around like mercury in a bottle."[7]

After Wilhelm's years-long apprenticeship in the minors with a mix of teams as he battled his way to the top level of the sport, he had experienced stability, playing for just one big-league team between 1952 and 1957. What he could not know was that this trade represented the beginning of a more itinerant lifestyle. His career had a long way to go and he had many miles to travel.

The change of scenery, to St. Louis to play for the Cardinals, did not benefit Wilhelm's career, despite Musial's glowing endorsement. Wilhelm got into 40 games for St. Louis, but the knuckleball seemed to baffle him as much as batters that summer. His record was 1–4 with a 4.25 earned run average, mostly in short relief. Wilhelm hurled just 55 innings in all of his showings combined, whereas previously he had been relied on for multiple-inning outings out of the bullpen.

The Cardinals, managed by Fred Hutchinson, went 87–67 and finished second to the Milwaukee Braves in the NL pennant race. St. Louis used a trio of knowledgeable catchers that summer with work split between Hal Smith, Hobie Landrith and Walker Cooper. But things did not seem to jell with Wilhelm's throwing and their fielding. By his own admission, Wilhelm wasn't much help to the Cardinals.

"I could never get going there," Wilhelm recalled years later. "If I had, if I had a good year, the Cardinals would have won the pennant because they were in the race right to the end. If I could have done anything, I think it would have helped them win the pennant that year. The Cardinals had a good team, a good hitting team then. I got along real good with Fred. I just worked for him that one year, but I remember him as a good manager and a fair man."[8]

Hutchinson was a solid big-league pitcher with the Detroit Tigers, winning 96 games over 10 years. He managed the Cincinnati Reds to a pennant while dying of lung cancer in 1964. The Fred Hutchinson Cancer Research Center in Seattle, his hometown, was later named for him.

Before the end of the season, general manager Frank Lane cut Wilhelm from the roster. He said at the time it was not so much doubting Wilhelm's capabilities as reacting to catchers having so much difficulty handling the knuckler.

In St. Louis, Wilhelm played with Musial, who hit .351 that season and was someone the pitcher admired, and Alvin Dark for a second time after they were teammates on the Giants. Some of the pitchers stuck in memory. Though not all of them were great that year, at one time or another they had their moments, players such as Larry Jackson, Wilmer "Vinegar Bend" Mizell, and brothers Lindy and Von McDaniel.

"He was a good pitcher for a few years," Wilhelm said of Mizell,

10. On to Other Teams

who had one of the most distinctive nicknames in baseball history; it was drawn from the town in Alabama where he began playing ball. He later became a congressman representing a district in North Carolina.

Jackson went 15–9 with a 3.47 ERA and Lindy McDaniel posted the same record as a 21-year-old with a 3.49 earned run average. Von McDaniel was just 18 and went 7–5. Lindy had a long, 21-year career. Von didn't; he was out of the majors a year later.

Wilhelm was also trying to stay in the majors once the Cardinals jettisoned him and he was not without a team for long. Before the season ended, Wilhelm was signed by the Cleveland Indians. There was just enough time left in the campaign for Wilhelm to get fitted for a new uniform and be rushed into some games. Wilhelm made two relief appearances totaling 3⅔ innings, earned a victory, and notched a 2.45 earned run average. It was a good first impression and had carryover value, too, since Wilhelm was still a member of the Indians come the spring of 1958.

This was Wilhelm's first full-time employment in the American League, but the change did not faze him. "I didn't see that much difference in the two leagues," he said.[9]

At the time there was some debate about balls and strikes being called differently in the American League and National League, but Wilhelm said his knuckleball style made him impervious to such distinctions.

"I tried to pitch up in the strike zone, you know," he said. "I always pitched up in the strike zone because if I started a knuckleball low, it's a ball. My pitch usually broke down. The only time I would do that [throw at the knees] was if I had two strikes and no balls. I might try, you know, to throw a couple down there to see if I could get the guy to go for a bad pitch because I knew it was going to be out of the strike zone by the time he swung at it."[10]

Wilhelm arrived in Cleveland from St. Louis as the season was concluding, taken by the Indians off waivers on September 21. He made two appearances and went 1–0 and had a save.

Eddie Robinson was simultaneously concluding his 13 seasons as a player in the majors with four games for the Orioles, knowing the next year he would be coaching for his friend Paul Richards. Robinson, who passed away in the autumn of 2021 at age 100, spent 65 years in baseball in all capacities, including as a general manager. As a player he was selected for four All-Star teams and compiled a lifetime average of .268.

Robinson told a humorous tale in his autobiography about his final

Hoyt Wilhelm

time at the plate: "My last at-bat as a Major League player was against Cleveland's Hoyt Wilhelm and his knuckleball. It was an inauspicious way to end a career, hitting at Hoyt's knuckleball. In fact, Paul Richards knew it was going to be my last at-bat and was laughing in the dugout as I went up to try to hit that knuckleball. Hoyt struck me out and that was the end of my playing career."[11]

While that was a suitable tribute to Wilhelm and a fine story, there is something amiss in the details. Once with Cleveland, Wilhelm pitched in just two games and neither one of them was against the Orioles. A summary of Robinson's career states his final big-league appearance was September 15 of that year. The Orioles did meet Cleveland that day, which would have been the occasion for the duo to face off. The clubs played a doubleheader and neither man's name appears in the box score.

That followed a 16-inning first game at Memorial Stadium. Robinson came on as a pinch-hitter for pitcher George Zuverink in the bottom of the 13th inning in what became a 5–4 Baltimore victory. Only the hurler on the mound for Cleveland was Cal McLish, not Hoyt Wilhelm, who did not pitch that day. Versus McLish, Robinson hit a fly ball to center field for an out. That was Robinson's only plate appearance of the game. It is not clear if Robinson misremembered his last at-bat or if he confused it with another time Wilhelm struck him out.

During this time period (one of Wilhelm's shortest team affiliations was with the Indians), he was singled out for attention as part of a baseball television show called *The Inside Pitch*. This episode, hosted by a young Bob Wulf during the early days of his decades-long sportscasting career, can still be found on YouTube. The 1950s flavor comes through in the black-and-white video as the show's sponsor, Palmolive Rapid Shave, is mentioned. It might be thought a better match would have been with pitcher Sal "The Barber" Maglie who, like the product, was known for his close shaves of batters. But this show represented the baseball fan's never-ending fascination with the knuckleball.

As the show begins, Wulf goes right to the heart of the matter, asking Wilhelm if the knuckleball is truly accurately named because of the use of the knuckles on the throwing hand.

"Well, it's actually a floater is what it is, Bob, and the whole idea of throwing a knuckleball is to throw the ball where it won't spin," Wilhelm said, "and the wind tries taking the ball and making it do those tricks. I guess you just call it a floater. I throw it right off the end of the fingertips and push the ball out."[12]

10. On to Other Teams

As Wilhelm explained he only used two of his fingertips on the ball to guide his pitches, Wulf mentioned that different players use different grips.

"That's true," Wilhelm said. "There's different guys put three fingers on it. I've even seen guys throw it with four fingers, but I got started throwing it like this and that's the way it stuck to me and that's the way I throw it."[13]

Perhaps as a leading question in getting Wilhelm to establish the oddity of the knuckleball as compared to other pitches in throwers' repertoires, Wulf asked Wilhelm how often he used the knuckler. It was pretty much common knowledge that Wilhelm used it all the time.

"Well, if I'm getting it over the plate, that's the pitch I want," Wilhelm said, though he noted it did not always work. "Oh yeah. There's days when it doesn't do much and days when it does too much. It's just getting to control it and that's the main disadvantage of it, getting it over the plate."[14]

In the spirit of the name of the show, Wulf mentioned a knuckleball anecdote of the past, prompting him to ask Wilhelm if he had to keep his fingernails properly trimmed to help control the knuckler. Smoothly diving into the topic as if he was a manicurist in a beauty salon, Wilhelm admitted grooming was part of the game.

"Definitely, Bob," he said. "That's one of the big things about throwing a knuckleball is keeping your fingernails the right length and filed straight across the end. That's the way I do it."[15]

For their next move, Wulf and Wilhelm brought in reinforcements for a demonstration, Indians catcher J.W. Porter. Porter, also called Jay, played in the majors between 1952 and 1959. His only year with the Indians overlapped with Wilhelm in 1958 when he appeared in 40 games. Lifetime, over six seasons, he was a .228 hitter.

Porter narrated film catching the Hoyt Wilhelm knuckleball while trying to explain to viewers what they were seeing.

"That ball broke down and away from a right-handed hitter, which Hoyt would normally do however that ball went up there," Porter said. "That ball went down a little and away. That pitch there, it wasn't bad. It didn't move too much. That's called a pig-tail. Now that ball broke in a little. That was a good one. That ball broke down I would say anywhere from six to eight inches."[16]

Porter did not truly articulate the problems catchers had keeping up with knuckleballs; he only hinted at them.

"Bob, you never know what a ball is going to do until the very last instant and then all you can do is just grab at it and hope that you get enough glove on it to keep it close by," Porter said.[17]

Wulf delved into the crux of the matter, which managers always worried about with Wilhelm coming into games in crucial circumstances as a relief pitcher with opponents on base. He asked Porter if he was going to call for the knuckleball knowing it could be a challenge to catch, but the knuckleball and Wilhelm were a package. You didn't get one without the other.

"You have to call it because it happens to be Hoyt's best pitch and a good strikeout pitch, which you want with men on base," Porter said. "But you just have to fight it."[18]

During the 1958 season, Porter was the third most-used Indians catcher behind Russ Nixon and Dick Brown, neither of whom would rate catching the knuckler as more fun than taking a cruise on the ocean. The Indians were very much a team in flux that year. They began the season with Bobby Bragan as manager and concluded it with Joe Gordon as manager and with a record of 77–76.

Frank Lane, the Cardinals' general manager for 1957, became the Indians' GM for 1958. He was known as "Trader Lane" and he lived up to his reputation by shifting personnel constantly. Some 43 players came to the plate for Cleveland and 20, including a couple of fielders in emergency relief, threw a pitch. Wilhelm had a schizophrenic year. His overall record was a lousy 2–7, but his earned run average was a quite solid 2.49 in 30 games spread over 90⅓ innings. Wilhelm was on the outs with Lane again, two years running, so he ended up pitching for Baltimore.

These were strange times in Wilhelm's career. Teams seemed willing to take a chance on him, but not stick with him through the good and the bad and waiting for things to even out. Sure enough, he did not last through the whole next season in Cleveland. The Indians put Wilhelm on waivers and he was picked up by the Baltimore Orioles on August 23, 1958.

Wilhelm's stat line that year approximated the work he did for Cleveland. His won-loss mark was just 1–3 in nine games. Yet his earned run average was a superlative 1.99 for the 40⅔ innings he pitched.

Between 1952 and 1958, every single one of Wilhelm's pitching assignments had included the walk in from the bullpen after a game started. In '58, the Indians experimented a little bit, giving Wilhelm six starts. Then the Orioles did the same, starting him four times. That turned out to be creative thinking and a sneak preview.

10. On to Other Teams

Those stopovers in St. Louis and Cleveland could have announced that Wilhelm was at the end of his baseball career and that being listed at 35 years old meant he was a too-old pitcher. Instead, Wilhelm was about to demonstrate that as had always been the case, the law of averages and most rules of pitching did not apply in the same manner to pitchers who featured the knuckleball, and especially not to him.

If someone had told baseball front office executives and managers—or even Wilhelm—that he was still in the springtime of his big-league pitcher career, probably few people would have believed the comment. Wilhelm would become the embodiment of the saying that knuckleball specialists don't suffer arm injuries the way fastball and curveball artists do. Their arms never wear out.

In most if not all professional sports, , 35 is considered somewhat aged (and that's not taking into account that Wilhelm was really 36). Soon enough baseball people would begin applying a new nickname to Hoyt Wilhelm—"Old Folks." Yet he was not about to move into a baseball senior citizens' home or have a rocking chair placed in front of his locker in the clubhouse.

As the 1958 season ended, and the 1959 season began, Wilhelm was beginning an entirely different, exciting and renewed chapter of his baseball life with the Baltimore Orioles under leadership that did not care how old he was or how he managed to retire batters for opposing American League teams.

And who knew, or could guess, that Hoyt Wilhelm, "ace reliever" as that New York newspaper stated on his departure from the Big Apple, would be presented with a vast new set of opportunities as a starting pitcher in Baltimore.

11

Lightning Strikes

In late August of 1958, the Baltimore Orioles made a cash deal with the Cleveland Indians to acquire Hoyt Wilhelm for the $20,000 waiver price. At the same time, the Orioles cleared roster space by selling first baseman Jim Marshall to the Chicago Cubs.

What caught Baltimore manager Paul Richards' eye was Wilhelm's then-2.40 earned run average, which he felt showed Wilhelm was better than his 2–7 record with Cleveland.

The Orioles of 1958 finished with a 74–79 record, plus one tie, in sixth place in the American League. Richards was trying to build something out of the team that had shed its St. Louis Browns heritage a few seasons earlier. He was known for taking chances and unorthodox steps at times.

Wilhelm made nine appearances over the last month of the season despite a tender elbow and lowered his ERA to 1.99, but one start in particular made an impression that lasted a lifetime. Dabbling as a starter for Richards in four games, on September 20, 1958, Wilhelm wrote a little bit of history.

It was an afternoon game against the dominant New York Yankees, once more on their way to another pennant, played at Baltimore's Memorial Stadium. Some 10,941 fans paid their way into the ballpark and 100,000 wished they had. That was despite lousy weather. It rained at times during the game and there was mention of turning the lights on in the stadium as if it was a night game. Wilhelm had only recently begun filling in as a starter after coming over to the American League instead of being relied on only as a relief specialist.

Coincidentally, this start came on his and Peggy's wedding anniversary. Wilhelm cursed himself that he had forgotten to buy something for his wife before heading to the ballpark.

Once the game started, he didn't waste time thinking about it and concentrated on making perfect pitches. He had to since the Yankees

11. Lightning Strikes

Wilhelm (right) and Jack Fisher discuss the knuckleball. They were teammates both with the Baltimore Orioles (1959–1962) and Chicago White Sox (late 1960s). As the pitch's consummate practitioner, Wilhelm was often approached for advice by other hurlers who thought about giving the knuckler a try (National Baseball Hall of Fame Library, Cooperstown, N.Y.).

were 22 games ahead of the Orioles in the standings and were the powerhouse team of the league, one which jumped on any hurler's mistake.

The Yankees' starting lineup and batting order read this way: Hank Bauer, right field; Jerry Lumpe, shortstop; Mickey Mantle, center field; Bill Skowron, third base; Norm Siebern, left field; Elston Howard, catcher; Marv Throneberry, first base; Bobby Richardson, second base; and Don Larsen, pitcher. The right-hander had hurled the only perfect game in World Series history in 1956. Some changes were made later,

Hoyt Wilhelm

including future Hall of Famer Yogi Berra entering as a pinch-hitter and staying in at first.

Baltimore's starters were Dick Williams at third base; Bob Boyd, first base; Gene Woodling, right field; Bob Nieman, left field; Gus Triandos, catcher; Willie Tasby, center field; Billy Gardner, second base; Foster Castleman, shortstop; and Wilhelm on the mound. The Orioles also made some substitutions, including inserting a young Brooks Robinson, just settling into his Hall of Fame career, at third later in the game.

What an astounding game it turned out to be. The aging Wilhelm, with a new team, no-hit and shut out the imposing New York Yankees, 1–0, in one hour and 48 minutes.

No-hitters happen with no warning, a confluence of a pitcher's magnificent day when everything is clicking and hitters' off days, with a bit of luck mixed in that direct where line drives go to die and hard-hit flies fall into gloves instead of bounce off or over walls.

Through the 2022 big-league season, there have been 318 recognized no-hitters. The first one dates to July 15, 1876, authored by George Washington Bradley of the St. Louis Brown Stockings, a win over the Hartford Dark Blues during the National League's first year of existence.

The most recent recognized no-hitter was a combined job by the Houston Astros on November 2, 2022, on their way to the World Series championship with Cristian Javier, Bryan Abreu, Ryan Pressly and Rafael Montero sharing credit for the 5–0 playoff victory over the Philadelphia Phillies. Javier pitched six innings and the other three hurlers one inning apiece.

In an era where managers dig into the bullpen much more readily, the combined no-hitter is becoming more commonplace than the praised, singular achievement by one man. While any pitcher can have an exceptional day and produce a no-hitter, the handful of pitchers whose resume includes multiple no-hitters is a short list.

Nolan Ryan leads the no-hitter list with seven of them. Sandy Koufax hurled four of them. Cy Young and Bob Feller, Hall of Famers like Ryan and Koufax, active pitcher Justin Verlander, destined for the Hall of Fame, and Larry Corcoran are the only ones to fire a trio of no-hitters. (Corcoran threw his three in the 1880s under different rules.)

Other Hall of Famers who tossed no-hitters, not including stars who made their biggest impact in the Negro Leagues, where statistics were sketchy, are Pud Galvin, John Clarkson, Charles Radbourn, Amos Rusie, Christy Mathewson, Addie Joss, Chief Bender, Ed Walsh, Rube Marquard, Walter Johnson, Jesse Haines, Dazzy Vance, Ted Lyons, Carl

11. Lightning Strikes

Hubbell, Bob Lemon, Jim Bunning, Warren Spahn, Juan Marichal, Jim "Catfish" Hunter, Gaylord Perry, Jim Palmer, Bob Gibson, Phil Niekro, Dennis Eckersley, Bert Blyleven, Tom Seaver, Jack Morris, Randy Johnson and Roy Halladay. Add Hoyt Wilhelm, the only one on this list besides Niekro who was a knuckleball specialist.

Among Hall of Fame greats who never threw a no-hitter are Grover Cleveland Alexander (373 wins) and Greg Maddux (355). Only half of the 300-game winners in history also threw a no-hitter. In different ways, both are elite, exclusive clubs, one involving greatness spread over many years, the other involving greatness spread over one day or nine innings.

Hoyt Wilhelm's one day of greatness was September 20, 1958, versus the Yankees.

Since the Orioles were the home team, the Yankees led off the game. Bauer, who would become embroiled in some late-game controversy, popped out to shortstop. He was followed to the plate by Lumpe, who struck out. Mickey Mantle came next and hit a fly ball out to center. Nice start for Wilhelm.

Larsen, who was already two years past the apex of his career achievement with that unmatched World Series performance as his Yankees beat the Brooklyn Dodgers, saw his no-hitter end in the bottom of the first. The Orioles wouldn't threaten much this day, gathering five hits, but after Dick Williams, later a Hall of Fame manager, lifted an out in the air to short, the second Baltimore batter of the day reached base. Bob Boyd tipped a bunt down the third-base line for a single. Two quick outs followed.

The Yankees in the second inning did nothing with Wilhelm's knuckleball in this turn at the plate, either, Skowron, Siebern and Howard being swiftly retired.

Baltimore was three-up, three-down in the second inning against Larsen. Wilhelm's first time veering from perfection was issuing a walk to Bobby Richardson in the Yankee third, but he was caught stealing with the pitcher, Larsen, at the plate, who quietly ended the inning.

The next Baltimore baserunner, in the bottom of the third, was Wilhelm himself—not because the weak-hitting hurler stroked a solid base-hit, but because he reached on an error on a grounder to second base that was compounded by a throwing error by Richardson which advanced him to second. He didn't go any further, the Orioles unable to move him along or score him.

The usually powerful hitting Yankees were not doing any home-run bashing this day. Their play was the equivalent of small-ball, even if that was not ordinarily their style. Bauer led off the fourth by striking out. Lumpe worked Wilhelm for a walk—and worse—moved on to second base, into scoring position on a passed ball committed by Baltimore catcher Gus Triandos.

Of all the catchers that Wilhelm tortured over the course of his long career with his knuckleball, Triandos was seemingly bothered more than any other by the difficulties of handling the ups and downs of the knucklers. Later, after coping with Wilhelm's throws for a few years, and in retirement, Triandos would speak of how much he despised the task of handling the knuckler.

Triandos, who was a strong guy at 6-foot-3 and 205 pounds, was born in San Francisco in 1930 and he made his first appearance in the majors with the New York Yankees in 1953 when he was 22. In a 13-year Major League career he developed into a four-time All-Star for the Orioles.

He was a reliable hitter at times despite a .244 lifetime batting average but was viewed as probably the slowest runner in the sport when he was catching. Aside from his difficulty with and aversion to the knuckler, he was regarded as an OK fielder. The passed balls began mounting in 1959 and got into his head, however, so it was ironic that he committed one in the no-hitter even though Triandos allowed 12 all season in 1958.

There is no doubt the knuckler preyed upon his mind as his innings with Wilhelm accumulated.

"The batter didn't know where the danged thing was going, the umpire didn't know where it was going—even Wilhelm didn't know where it was going," Triandos said, "so how was I to know? I used to enjoy catching. It used to be fun for me. But not when I had to catch that thing. I hate to admit it, but it got the best of me. It really did."[1]

On the occasion of this passed ball, very early in Triandos' relationship with Wilhelm, no damage was done. Lumpe was safe at second, but New York sluggers Mickey Mantle and Bill Skowron could not get him to home plate.

The Orioles continued to flail at Larsen's offerings without success as they took their turns at bat in the bottom of the fourth, with Woodling, Nieman and Triandos all going down in order. The score was still 0–0.

That brought the game to the top of the fifth inning. Wilhelm fanned the first two Yankees, Siebern and Howard, and induced

11. Lightning Strikes

Throneberry into a fly-ball out to left field. Five innings in, halfway through the game, the Yankees were hitless and Wilhelm wasn't even breathing hard.

Not that Larsen was giving his mates anything to worry about either with his deliveries. In the bottom of the fifth he disposed of the Orioles, with quickness and efficiency, striking out Tasby and holding Gardner to a fly-ball out to left before walking Castleman. Wilhelm made the last out for the Orioles himself on a ground ball to first, an unassisted putout.

In the majors, where the best pitchers in the world work, the sixth inning is way too early to begin thinking about a no-hitter. Many times hurlers have carried no-hit prospects into the ninth inning only to lose them at the end, so such an opportunity is not worth talking about until later in the contest.

The Yankees half of the sixth passed quickly, just like the preceding innings. Richardson lofted a fly deep to left, but it was collected. Larsen, not a renowned hitting pitcher either, grounded a Wilhelm offering back to the mound and was thrown out at first. Then Bauer was caught looking on a strikeout. The Yankees' at-bats flew by.

If the Orioles came to the plate in the home half of the sixth inning determined to make something happen, they failed. The best they could come up with was a walk to Woodling, the one-time Yankee, and three outs, by Williams on a line drive, Boyd on a fly out, and Nieman on another fly, wrapped themselves around the one base runner, who never budged.

When Baltimore took the field for the top of the seventh, manager Paul Richards did some tinkering. He installed Jim Busby in center, while moving Tasby to right and removing Woodling. Didn't matter much to Wilhelm. Lumpe flew out to center, Mantle struck out, and Bill Skowron grounded the ball back to the knuckleballer, who threw him out at first.

New York manager Casey Stengel made his own major change to the Yankees' lineup for the bottom of the seventh. He lifted Larsen after six innings of superb pitching. Larsen allowed just one hit, two walks, and, of course, no runs. His replacement was Bobby Shantz.

Shantz, a southpaw who was one of the smallest players in the game at 5-foot-6 and 139 pounds, broke into the majors at 23 in 1949 with the Philadelphia Athletics and had a 16-season big-league career, the highlight of which came in 1952 when he finished 24–7, was an All-Star and won the American League Most Valuable Player Award. He joined the

Hoyt Wilhelm

Yankees in 1957, his last All-Star season in a 119-win career that also included winning eight Gold Gloves.

By 1959, he was almost fully transitioned from starter to relief man, so it was common enough for him to take the mound in a situation like this. Shantz walked into a no-hit-one-hit drama playing out in the bottom of the seventh and promptly allowed a lead-off home run to Triandos. The solo shot traveled 425 feet out of the park in center field. It was Triandos' 30th homer of the season. At the time the blow equaled Yogi Berra's record for most home runs in a year by an American League catcher.

The homer for the Orioles provided a run but didn't amount to much of a break-out. Shantz proceeded to strike out Tasby and get Gardner on a foul pop to the catcher. Castleman did stroke a single to left but was the third out at second on a play that turned messy, with the relay from the left fielder to the shortstop to the second baseman. Still, there was a run on the board and it was 1–0 Baltimore for Wilhelm.

Before the Yankees began the eighth inning at the plate, Richards shuffled more players around the field. Brooks Robinson, who had the day off, came in at third base. Dick Williams shifted to left and Bob Nieman went to the bench. Willy Miranda came in for Castleman at short.

Only then could Wilhelm throw. Siebern made an easy ground-ball out, second to first. Elston Howard took a good whack at the ball but lined out to left field. This is when Berra entered the game, pinch-hitting for Throneberry. The Stengel strategy did not pay off. Berra could only muster a ground out to second. Berra stayed in the game at first base.

Baltimore wanted to add to Wilhelm's lead, the 1–0 status only a slender margin to keep victory afloat. Wilhelm was the lead-off man in the bottom of the eighth but did not help himself, grounding out second to first. Williams offered significant optimism with a double to left field. Shantz then struck out Boyd. Busby mustered a single, but it was of the infield variety, just back to the pitcher, and while he was safe, Williams couldn't even get to third. Brooks Robinson came up for the first time and generated some excitement with a deep fly to left field, but all it turned out to be was a long out.

Ninth inning. Now the fans could buzz with a realistic hope of seeing a rare no-hitter. The players knew the situation, but conforming to the rules of superstition, they were not about to begin gabbing about it with Wilhelm. Certainly, there had to be talk among thems, however, even if only in whispers, about preserving the no-hitter.

Richardson led off the top of the ninth and connected on a fly

11. Lightning Strikes

ball to center. One out. Shantz was due up, but there was no chance he was going to bat. Future Hall of Famer Enos Slaughter was tabbed to pinch-hit for the pitcher. Slaughter got good wood on the ball and hit a liner to right field for the second out.

This brought Hank Bauer, the right fielder, to the plate. Bauer had contributed nothing off the bat this day, going 0–3 before stepping in. His day included striking out twice. On this at-bat, Bauer surprised most people in the ballpark when he attempted to bunt. He got a piece of the pitch, but the ball rolled foul. Later, some resented Bauer's maneuver, questioning whether it was sporting to try and bunt for a hit to break up a no-hitter. Bauer was unrepentant. "If he's going to get a no-hitter, let him earn it," Bauer said. "I was trying to get a hit. That's baseball. I'm sorry it rolled foul."[2]

Wilhelm, who said he began to feel jitters when he reached the seventh inning aware he had not allowed a hit, said he was trying to guard against that bunting possibility and threw only knuckleballs in the ninth when Bauer gave it his game shot.

"Geez, geez," Wilhelm said. "It started to get to me in the seventh. But I tried to keep it out of my mind. I threw all knucklers in the ninth inning because I was afraid of a bunt. I'd have hated to lose a no-hitter by falling down trying to field a ball."[3]

When Bauer was declared out and the game was official, Orioles broadcaster Ernie Harwell finally exhaled. Not wanting to jinx Wilhelm, he had refused to mention the no-hitter possibility. Now he could. "A no-hitter for Wilhelm!" Harwell announced. "He's got a no-hitter. Hoyt Wilhelm pitches the first no-hitter in modern Orioles history and he's mobbed by his teammates."[4]

Those who were present said that in the clubhouse after the game, Wilhelm acted like a man who barely believed what he had just done. In terms of Orioles history, his feat combined the distant past with the present. The Orioles of the 1890s were a terrific ballclub with a roster bursting with storied figures such as John McGraw, Wilbert Robinson, Ned Hanlon and "Wee" Willie Keeler. Jim Hughes, a hurler on that team, tossed a no-hitter on April 22, 1898. Of course, the Orioles had a lengthy time out without being a big-league club before their resurrection post–St. Louis Browns in time for the 1954 season.

It was at this point in the midst of the post-game festivities that it became public knowledge Wilhelm had failed to come up with an anniversary card or present for his wife Peggy.

Actually, Wilhelm realized he had made the mistake and he

telephoned home to Huntersville, North Carolina, long distance from the ballpark before the game. "Peggy," he said, "I neglected to send you a card." Of course, in those days he could not hurriedly make up for the error by jumping on a computer and zipping her an email. "What do you want for our anniversary?" Wilhelm said his wife replied, "Honey, send me something real good. Let's win one."[5]

Mrs. Wilhelm was home with the couple's three children, Patti, then five, Pam, three, and Jim, one. As it so happened, the Saturday game was available on the *Game of the Week*, so it was possible for Peggy to actually watch her husband's sterling triumph. He didn't know for sure yet but said it was likely the TV was on, even if she was taking care of the kids, and she may well have seen all of the action.

"Unless she fainted, that is," Wilhelm joked.[6]

It made sense for Peggy to be rooting for a win, because Wilhelm hadn't registered one yet for Baltimore during his short stay in Maryland.

One thing Wilhelm did, common among pitchers who record such games, was extend credit to his catcher, Triandos. Not only did the catcher smite the game-winning home run, Wilhelm said, "I thought Gus caught a great game for me. He's big and he's sure-handed and he's easy to pitch to."[7] Wilhelm sought out Triandos directly to compliment his home run. "Here's the guy I want," Wilhelm said. "Hey, Greek [referring to Triandos' heritage], that was a real wallop."[8]

Sportswriters kept probing under the assumption that at times Wilhelm used other key pitches to get Yankees out, but Triandos denied that the hurler ever lacked faith in the knuckler. "Just nothin' but knucklers," Triandos said, stressing his man tossed that pitch more than 90 percent of the time. "Boy, it was hoppin'."[9]

Triandos' average of the number of knuckleballs thrown was just about right on. Wilhelm threw only 99 pitches to complete the game; 87 were knuckleballs.

Mickey Mantle, who was victimized throughout the game by Wilhelm, joked, "I thought his fastball was lousy and so was his curve." Mantle knew full well he may not have even glimpsed either of those pitches. Mantle's teammate and fellow future Hall of Famer Yogi Berra addressed the knuckler effect. "It's a guessing game when you're hitting against him. You know it's coming, but you don't know where. I don't think he does, either."[10] That latter comment became a common refrain among Wilhelm watchers.

Assuredly, if Wilhelm was going to notch one win to make his

11. Lightning Strikes

presence felt with his new Orioles team, this was the way to do it. Richards had already tried Wilhelm starting and he lost a tough game against the Red Sox, 3–2. He was good enough to earn another look and the Yankees no-hitter was Wilhelm's third start for Baltimore.

He recorded that W with Baltimore after three losses after coming over from the Indians, but no one who saw the win was ever going to forget it. The performance may also have figured into the Orioles' off-season thinking of just maybe working Wilhelm into the starting rotation more in 1959.

It sounds quaint, but as a result of the no-hitter, the *Game of the Week* television team gave Wilhelm a $150 watch as the player of the game. Who else could it have been?

Also as an indication of how much that performance meant to Wilhelm beyond his "geez, geez" comments, a half-century later a ball used in that game was still a prized possession in the family. After the game, Wilhelm put aside a game ball and signed it.

In 2008, on the 50th anniversary of the no-hitter, Wilhelm's grandson Andy Collins, son of Hoyt's daughter Patti, had the family keepsake preserved in a special place. He said his grandfather was "a humble guy who never talked much about his career." But Peggy Wilhelm said that was one pitching effort that stood out in the Hall of Famer's memory—perhaps because it was a one-time achievement and it also happened on their anniversary. "That game, on that day, meant a lot to Hoyt," Peggy Wilhelm said.[11]

12

Rebirth with Orioles

During his decades in baseball, Paul Richards was known as a bit of a maverick but also as an innovator. He later said that when the Orioles obtained Wilhelm, he already had it in his mind that he might be useful as a starter instead of solely coming into games from the bullpen.

"I'd always wondered why he'd been used in relief," Richards said, "coming in with men on base where one passed ball could hurt him." He was giving voice to a major concern of managers in both leagues who had had Wilhelm on their roster. "I thought perhaps, if Hoyt started, the runners wouldn't get on base to begin with."[1]

Richards had been speaking philosophically, not as literally as implying Wilhelm would pitch a no-hitter every time out.

Young Brooks Robinson, who broke into the majors with the Orioles when he was just 18 in 1955, was still learning at the plate but was already so good in the field that Richards' pitchers lobbied for him to gain more playing time.

Robinson may have preserved Wilhelm's no-hitter on Bauer's attempted bunt by choosing not to make a play and just letting the ball roll to its destination on its own.

"Suddenly, that big, blocky man dipped his bat forward, squared away, and put a perfect surprise bunt down the third-base line," Robinson said. "Whoever would have thought that this hard-nosed ex–Marine gunner would employ that strategy to kill off Wilhelm's no-hit, no-run effort?" Robinson recalled charging in on the ball, glancing at Bauer running down the baseline and realizing if he picked up the ball Bauer would be safe and have a hit. "As I watched, the ball began to bend to my right toward the foul line. I decided to let it roll, hoping it would go foul. My prayer was answered."[2]

There was something special about being on the field for Wilhelm's no-hitter, Robinson said. The feeling stuck with him for years. He said playing a limited role in that game was the highlight of his 1958 season

12. Rebirth with Orioles

and the game gave a spark to the franchise and the city. Perhaps because the performance was so unexpected. Maybe because Wilhelm was the old man of the staff. But Robinson said the no-hitter "had special meaning for all of us on the club."³

There was a persistent feeling, among players and sportswriters both, that it was a kind of turning point for Baltimore sports. A few months later the Colts won their highly publicized sudden death National Football League title over the New York Giants, and Robinson, who became the city's biggest baseball icon, always felt the Wilhelm no-hitter in some way jump-started appreciation for the Orioles.

If nothing else, it was an energizing prelude to what might be expected from Wilhelm when the next season began about six months later.

Although he had years to go in his 21-year big-league career, sportswriters were already referring to Hoyt Wilhelm as an old man when he turned 40 in the early 1960s. He was with the White Sox between 1963 and 1968 (National Baseball Hall of Fame Library, Cooperstown, N.Y.).

The 1959 season, his first full one with the Baltimore Orioles, revived Hoyt Wilhelm's career. At 36 going on 37, he became nearly a full-time starter, though he still helped a bit coming out of the bullpen. Wilhelm won 15 games, threw 226 innings, including 13 complete games, and led the American League in earned run average with a 2.19 mark, a bookend achievement matching his National League accomplishment of 1952.

For four seasons, beginning in 1959, Major League Baseball decided to conduct two All-Star games per summer. That year, Wilhelm was chosen to represent the AL in both of them. It was the first time he was named an all-star selection by anyone since 1953.

Certainly, Wilhelm found

playing in Baltimore an elixir after being surrendered by the Giants and given up on by the Cardinals and Indians. Three teams had underestimated him and his knuckler and the Orioles capitalized.

Wilhelm had briefly introduced himself to the American League late in the 1958 season with his grand 1.99 ERA and the eye-catching no-hitter. After the earlier years of his career spent in the National League, he was playing to a fresh audience, a crop of other-league hitters who may never have faced or tried to cope with his knuckler before, and that may have enhanced his fresh effectiveness.

One thing his work in 1959 did was develop new fans. Ted Williams, who spent a lifetime studying pitchers, their habits, their strengths and weaknesses, favorably compared Wilhelm to any other knuckleballer he played against over his 21-year career.

"Out in front of all of them," Williams said. "He was the best I ever tried to hit. Don't let anybody ever tell you they saw a better knuckleball than Wilhelm's. The thing that distinguishes him from the others is that he'll throw a greater percentage of tough knuckleballs."[4]

That was an unsolicited endorsement that could have psychologically worked against other hitters. After all, if the godfather of hitting, Ted Williams, said so, it must be so.

One of the things that always drove batters batty about the knuckleball was that as it approached the plate after leaving the hurler's hand, it seemed so easy to hit, so available to swat. That's because it traveled so slowly. It was as if it was going well under the speed limit on the interstate.

Eddie Fisher, another much-appreciated knuckleball thrower who followed Wilhelm with the Chicago White Sox a few years later, agreed with Williams.

"He had the best knuckleball of all," Fisher said. "It moved all over. Wilhelm probably didn't break 50 mph some of the time. It looked like it wouldn't get to the plate."[5]

It is often said that when a fastball pitcher dominates, he blows hitters away, as if his speed blinds them and stifles their bats. The best comparison is that a knuckleballer makes hitters look silly, unable to slap good wood on a ball crawling to the plate the way Fisher described. Speed could not be conquered, but at least it was understandable. Slow motion was inexplicable.

Nonetheless, when the new campaign began, a rejuvenated Wilhelm, as slowly as ever, confused American League hitters through the early going as if the season was just a continuation of the no-hit game

12. Rebirth with Orioles

against the Yankees. He pretty much made Paul Richards look like a genius too, for using him in a starting role as a regular member of the rotation.

Wilhelm began the 1959 season by winning his first nine decisions. He lost for the first time on June 15. He was the talk of the town in Baltimore, and, to a degree, the sport. There were three reasons for that: (1) simply that he was unbeaten for a large chunk of the season; (2) he was old by professional athletic standards; and (3) he threw the knuckleball as his primary weapon. It always came back to the knuckleball, the weird pitch no one could comprehend and few could employ successfully. Wilhelm may not have been unique, but he was definitely not ordinary.

His first victory of the season was notched on April 21, a 5–2 win over the Boston Red Sox. Wilhelm threw a complete game, permitting eight hits and two runs, one of them earned. He struck out eight men but did allow five walks. Three different Sox players figured the knuckler out sufficiently to collect two hits apiece. Ted Williams did not play in the game.

Wilhelm got his second win on April 26, beating the Yankees, 3–2, with another complete game. He allowed just one earned run on five hits and fanned eight.

On to May 2 when the Orioles bested the Kansas City Athletics, 3–1, on still another Hoyt Wilhelm complete-game job. He gave up five hits and one run and struck out seven.

A week later, Wilhelm beat the Red Sox for a second time, but he wasn't as overpowering (if that is the word) as he had been in recent starts. He was touched for 10 hits in a 4–3 Baltimore win on two earned runs and pitched eight innings, yielding to relief for the ninth. But he was still 4–0.

A week after that, on May 16, Wilhelm handled the Detroit Tigers. While giving up nine hits, he gave up just one run in a 6–1 triumph. At 5–0, Wilhelm got his earned run average down to 1.49. This was dead-ball era stuff.

Soon enough, on May 22, Wilhelm turned in a masterpiece that topped his recent wins and nearly equaled his no-hitter against the Yankees the previous September. This contest was against those same Yankees and concluded with a 5–0 Baltimore win. This time Wilhelm gave up just one hit (though he did issue six walks). Jerry Lumpe managed the lone hit off Wilhelm this time. Lumpe played third base instead of shortstop as he did on September 20, 1958. Lumpe's single off Wilhelm did not occur until the top of the eighth inning.

Hoyt Wilhelm

As he had in the previous showdown, catcher Gus Triandos smacked a home run in this game, a two-run job in a four-run Oriole first that provided Wilhelm with a comfortable lead. It would have been quite the accomplishment to no-hit the powerful Yankees twice, but coming close again also made an impression. Bob Turley took the loss.

Then Wilhelm shut down the Yankees again, for a third time, on a four-hitter, before the end of the month on May 28. Another shutout of the Bronx Bombers who appeared to be wielding toothpicks, not bats, when facing Wilhelm. Same score too: 5–0. At that stage of the season Wilhelm was 7–0 with a 1.12 earned run average. The Hoyt Wilhelm knuckleball was the most feared pitch in the sport.

"I am glad there is only one of him in the league," Yogi Berra said after this defeat, no doubt speaking for the rest of his Yankee teammates too.[6]

There was something special going on in Baltimore with a team that was moved from another city but might as well have been an expansion club given the depths of quality on the roster that the St. Louis Browns brought with them. The club had not posted a winning season since 1945 when the Browns went 81–70, the season after they won their only pennant while stationed in St. Louis.

The Browns moved to Baltimore because baseball fans in that city wanted the big-league version of the sport back in town and because the Browns fought a losing battle for fans against the Cardinals in St. Louis. The Orioles drew more than one million fans in 1954, their first year back in business with their old name, but there was a drop-off over the next couple of years, likely attributable to fielding a losing team.

The spark, the enthusiasm for Major League play, had not quite worn off, but it may have been teetering as Richards and the Orioles sought to build a young and exciting club. It was a bit unexpected that an old-timer like Hoyt Wilhelm was infusing the club with fresh energy, but after that second 5–0 win over the Yankees, the Orioles were 24–18. Oh, and the Yankees, the perennial champs, were 15–23.

Baltimore at this time was ga-ga over the Colts, which in 1958 won the most dramatic National Football League title game of all and in 1959 was on the verge of repeating. The populace was also ga-ga over crabcakes, but the signature food did not have ebb and flow support. It was a staple.

Wilhelm was a big man on campus in Baltimore, so to speak, as his hot start on the mound garnered major attention in the city of Baltimore proper (population about 939,000) and the surrounding area.

12. Rebirth with Orioles

A column in the May 15, 1959, *Baltimore Sun* called "American Viewpoint" by Norman L. Wetzler singled him out for praise. It read, "Our weekly award of a famous BUD BERMA PRO-JAC goes with our very best wishes to HOYT WILHELM, whose knuckler has won him loads of fans in Baltimore and a host of disgruntled hitters around the rest of the League. Thus far, WILHELM has pitched great ball for the BIRDS and together with TRIANDOS, whom we honored in similar fashion last week, could go down in the books as one of baseball's great battery combinations. Keep it up, Hoyt ... we're 'witcha all-a-way!'"[7] PRO-JAC made jackets and shirts.

By 1959, Wilhelm was making $17,000 a year with the Orioles but probably still would have appreciated things like jackets and shirts from a sponsor.

Off the local professional baseball diamonds in 1959, one of the biggest controversies of the summer reported by the *Baltimore Sun* involved Miss Maryland in July abdicating her title for the Miss Universe pageant and passing her crown to a runner-up.

Marie Litz, the winner of the title initially, gave up the role after just five days after her crowning, transferring the honor to Diane White. The outgoing pageant winner said, "Since the excitement has died down, I don't desire a very glamorous career." The writer of the newspaper article compared it to the great Great Britain scandal precipitated by a king in 1936, "an abdication statement that may rank with Edward VIII."[8] Edward gave up the throne to marry divorced American commoner Wallis Simpson.

As an illustration of how Wilhelm had burst into the consciousness and taken over the minds of Baltimore citizenry, the article's author made another common-sense comparison he was certain his readers would understand: "The crown of Miss Maryland (potential Miss Universe variety), flutters around the way Hoyt Wilhelm's knuckleball used to."[9]

Used to? Well, by the time the beauty queen story broke, Wilhelm had actually lost a game.

Wilhelm moved his record to 8–0 on June 2 when the Orioles topped the Chicago White Sox, 3–2. It was yet another complete game notched in serene fashion, just one earned run over nine innings and seven hits, his ERA lowered to a microscopic 1.11. To defeat Hoyt Wilhelm at this point, opposing pitchers had to be nearly perfect themselves.

The law of averages plays out in sports and especially over the long baseball season, at this time still 154 games. There are too many variables. Players talk about being in the zone at the plate and whatever repetitive action makes their game function. No one knows when a hot streak will start or end. The superstitious tip-toe around any kind of threat, the stoic take what comes.

On June 7, Wilhelm took the mound again to face the Kansas City Athletics—and pitched another shutout. He blanked the A's on seven hits in under two hours and remarkably cut his earned run average down even more, to an even 1.00.

The all-time best recognized season-long earned run average was compiled, ironically, by Dutch Leonard, not the Dutch Leonard whom Wilhelm modeled his knuckleball after, but the Dutch Leonard who pitched for the Boston Red Sox and Detroit Tigers between 1913 and 1925. This non-knuckleballing Dutch Leonard led the American League in ERA in 1914 with a stupendous 0.96 mark.

After the Kansas City game, Wilhelm was sporting a 9–0 record and an earned run average that flirted with immortality. But it was only June, and as many thrills as he had provided, time was about to run out on the perfection meter.

On June 15, Wilhelm started again in a night game versus the Detroit Tigers at Memorial Stadium. On this day his knuckler deserted him. Wilhelm was hit hard and his winning streak went down the drain as the Tigers captured the game, 6–4. Wilhelm lasted 6⅔ innings before relief was summoned. He gave up eight hits and five earned runs. The winner, Ray Narleski, actually allowed 11 hits but prevailed.

A key blow was struck by Detroit outfielder Harvey Kuenn on a two-run homer and the slumping Orioles, who lost their third game in a row and were slipping toward a .500 record, stranded 11 runners. The headline in the June 16 *Baltimore Sun* read, "Hoyt's 1959 Win Streak Stops at 9."[10] The loss was bound to come at some point and it was a great ride while it lasted. Most prognosticators would have figured Wilhelm would pick up and start fresh with a new win streak, but some magic appeared to be lost.

At the time, the Orioles, who had started quickly, were at 30–29, trying to tread water near the front of the league. They were still the city's summer attraction for sporting pleasure and team management was still working hard to make friends and ingratiate itself with the fans. In early July, shortly before the nation's July 4 birthday, members of the team took a field trip to the Baltimore League for Crippled Children and Adults' Sheltered Workshop.

12. Rebirth with Orioles

Winning streak, losing streak, all those fans cared about was being in the presence of big leaguers. Catcher Gus Triandos, infielder Willy Miranda and outfielder Albie Pearson made the appearance on behalf of the team.

One Orioles fan asked Triandos what he tells his pitcher when he walks out to the mound. "Stop fooling around," was Triandos' reply.[11] Deep down inside Triandos probably wished he could tell Wilhelm during mound visits, "Stop throwing that darned knuckleball." But he didn't say that to Wilhelm and he didn't say that out loud at this event.

The players fielded a request to demonstrate Wilhelm's knuckleball. Presumably they wouldn't have been able to make the ball float with the same effectiveness if top-grade hitters were around to test them.

Triandos, Miranda and Pearson were informed those in the workshop listened to Orioles games on the radio as they made wastebaskets, lamps and bookends and sorted machine parts. One of the guides informed Triandos she charted all of his home runs and he autographed her personal scorebook.

It was a feel-good visit in what had thus far been a feel-good season, especially for Wilhelm, but the second half of the campaign wasn't a joyride. The day after Wilhelm lost his first game of the season, a teaser to the game recap offered an offbeat lead-in to the report. Headlined "The Orioles," it read, "Caesar had his Brutus; Charles the First, his Cromwell, and Hoyt Wilhelm—"

> Since we hear no cries of "treason," let us come right out with it: Hoyt had his Detroit Tigers. (Lie still, Patrick Henry!)
>
> Of course, Hoyt's no Caesar, but he did hang up a nice string of victories until Kuenn, [Al] Kaline and company battered him off the mound and sent the Orioles to defeat, 6–4, last night.
>
> The Bird batsmen kept hammering away in a 12-hit effort to keep Wilhelm's record clean, but the Tigers, scenting first-place meat, smeared their claws all over it.
>
> And so Hoyt's nice big bubble has burst. However, we suspect, he'll just chew his gum a little harder and start inflating another one.[12]

Most assuredly, a wacky way to get readers to study the game results.

Alas, after his wonderful streak, Wilhelm was not as good the rest of his season. He began losing as often as winning, giving up runs more frequently, though overall he still maintained a best-in-league earned run average. The Orioles faltered as a group, finishing 74–80–1, with almost the same record they had in 1958, and once again they finished sixth in the American League standings.

Hoyt Wilhelm

"What hurts us most is the lack of another dependable long-ball hitter," Richards said.[13] Triandos hit 25 homers and Bob Nieman 21.

Wilhelm's firecracker of a start garnered him enough attention to be named to the AL All-Star team. The main reason two such games were scheduled in the same year at all was to beef up the players' pension fund.

The first All-Star game was played on July 7 at Forbes Field in Pittsburgh and was won by the National League, 5–4. Vice President Richard Nixon threw out the ceremonial first pitch.

Early Wynn started for the AL and manager Casey Stengel used four other pitchers, but Wilhelm did not get into the game. Whitey Ford of the Yankees took the loss and Johnny Antonelli of the Giants got the win.

The second All-Star game of the summer was played on August 3 at Los Angeles Memorial Coliseum. The American League won this one, 5–3. Wilhelm's 20-year-old Orioles teammate Jerry Walker got the start, but Wilhelm entered the game in relief. He hurled the sixth inning and gave up one hit and no runs. He set down Willie Mays and Ernie Banks, ultimately two fellow Hall of Famers, gave up a single to another future Hall of Famer, Frank Robinson, and then retired Wally Moon.

Baltimore was a place a young man could go to party, though not necessarily a married man like Wilhelm, but certainly the single guys on the team. Before there was ever a renovated Inner Harbor for tourism, Baltimore was known for The Block, its sex district. Dating back to the late 19th century, the 400 block of East Baltimore Street featured brothels, strip-tease clubs, sex shops, and burlesque shows. It was one of the most famous such areas in a major city in the United States.

As time passed, the area became more renowned as a crime district. The newcomer Orioles were not above trying to play a little bit on the image, if only subtly. Of course, the team could argue it was only tap-dancing around the image by playing on the Broadway stage show *Damn Yankees*, which opened in 1955.

Late in the 1958 season, an eye-catching advertisement appeared in the evening edition of the *Baltimore Sun* about an opportunity the next day. "Tomorrow Nite, 9:30–10 p.m. Only! Meet the Baltimore Orioles. Starts with All Day Prevue Tomorrow, See 2 Top Shows All Day, 'Streetcar Named Desire' and 'Damn Yankees'" (the newly released film version) with show times listed. "Gals, Gags, Laffs, Music. In Person. In Our Lobby." Contained in the ad were hand-drawn stars around head shots of various Orioles players, "Gus" (as in Triandos), "Hoyt" (as in

12. Rebirth with Orioles

Wilhelm), "Willie" (probably as in Tasby) and "Bob" (probably as in Nieman). Featured larger than anything else was a picture of a somewhat scantily clad woman, hands on hips with the words "What Lola Wants, Lola Gets!" Those were words from "Damn Yankees" expressed by actress Gwen Verdon. Verdon handled the vixen role on stage and on screen wearing this costume and the pose was well known from posters and the like promoting the show.

If a good time was not had by all, it was not particularly publicized.

After the blistering start, Wilhelm completed his year with a 15–11 record. It was a good record but could have been better. Despite that, when he stopped winning and the Orioles started winning, his earned run average remained at a tremendously low level, the best in the league at 2.19 when the final tally was made.

Beginning with his no-hitter the previous September, continuing with his scorching 9–0 start, and concluding with his earned run average, Hoyt Wilhelm had single-handedly made the knuckleball trendy—at least as a topic of baseball conversation, if not through a bevy of imitators.

13

Trying to Make Sense of It

What gives the knuckleball its mystique is how it defies explanation. For more than 100 years even the best of those who can make the knuckleball work for them pretty much go "Don't ask me, I just throw it" rather than uttering deeply analytical explanations for why it works for them.

Hoyt Wilhelm was so much in the headlines on the sports pages at the end of the 1958 season and throughout the 1959 season that he almost made the knuckleball a major discussion point. He at least raised questions in the minds of the average fans, who were used to having sportswriters issue reasons for why things were as they were with their favorite team.

Even going back to August of 1958, when the Cleveland Indians essentially ditched Wilhelm, general manager Frank Lane's reasoning seemed odd to anyone listening. He said he placed Wilhelm on waivers because his catchers couldn't catch him. Now that's something you don't hear every day. However, since Wilhelm wasn't winning and the team wasn't really winning either, finishing 77–76, not much noise was made about the personnel move.

Then Wilhelm hurled a no-hitter, which made a very loud noise. And then he started the 1959 season handling every lineup in the American League. Then he made the All-Star team. Then he led the league in earned run average.

Obviously, something was up with this knuckleball thing. If kids had been running out to the playground begging their elders to teach them how to throw a knuckler, then it might have been said that the pitch was trendy. That was not the case. But it was quirky, tricky, eye-catching, and worthy of more intensive study. It became a sports topic of interest to non-experts the way once every four years some Olympic sport such as curling enjoys 15 minutes of fame.

13. Trying to Make Sense of It

The June 29, 1959, issue of *Sports Illustrated* (its timing inspired by Wilhelm's hot streak) took on the task of trying to explain the knuckleball to the masses. The publication that would grow into the finest sports magazine in American history was only five years old at the time. It sought a niche among discerning readers by often highlighting sports that were not as popular as the most followed professional teams in a city. *SI* ventured out of the usual spaces, checked out amateur and professional athletes and covered their achievements. A perfect example of this thinking outside the box was the cover of this issue featuring the knuckleball. It had a photograph of a golden eagle in flight, "a thrilling spectacle of nature."[1] The bird was not related to the knuckleball, but heralded another story in the magazine.

Some might have said the knuckleball fit into a similar category of being not as well known. The magazine sought to explain the pitch, consulting athletes and even scientists to inform readers why Hoyt Wilhelm was doing these Hoyt Wilhelm things that no other pitcher seemed capable of pulling off. Indeed, the first words of the story were all about Wilhelm before it veered off in directions that suggested it could serve as some higher education student's science project.

The story began, "One of the pitching sensations of the 1959 Major League season is a 35-year-old cotton farmer from North Carolina who throws a baseball for the Baltimore Orioles in such a way as to make strong batters weep with frustration and to cause his own star catcher to fall on his reddened face in frequently futile efforts to perform his primary duty, i.e., catching the baseball."[2]

Almost immediately, the story refers to the knuckleball as an "excruciating pitch" with less reliance on the knuckles than people may think and how it was producing "diabolic success." Rocky Bridges, then playing shortstop for the Detroit Tigers and hitting uncharacteristically well given the overall sample of his career stats, said, "It's like swinging at a goofy ball. I just close my eyes and hope."[3]

This was one time in *Sports Illustrated*'s history that the second word in the title, "Illustrated," was applicable and not by photographs, although there were some with the piece, sketch illustrations that resembled Albert Einstein's jottings when he was trying to work his way around to $E=MC^2$.

Views of the knuckler included Wilhelm's hand positioned on the baseball, the drop of the pitch when it was working well, up or down compared to a batter standing in the box, and a baseball following a squiggly path. There was also one "scientific diagram" that could not be deciphered in a glance; it showed long strands of what could be wires or spaghetti trailing from the ball as it made its way to the plate. Mainly, batters' brains unraveled trying to figure out how the ball would move as it approached.

The illustrations sought to show readers why the batter developed a headache trying to make contact. "It's a fingertip ball, not a knuckler," Wilhelm said.[4]

This was not a heyday of knuckleball pitching that would provoke *Sports Illustrated* into going to all of this explanatory trouble. Except for that brief period in the 1940s when the Washington Senators had a surplus of knuckleball throwers in the rotation, four at once, knuckleballers tended not to congregate in one place or during one era.

Besides Wilhelm, there were other pitchers of the 1950s and early 1960s who used the knuckler, but some retired just before they reached the majors and few had big-time success beyond short stretches.

Gene Bearden helped the Cleveland Indians win the World Series in 1948 but was out of the majors by 1953. Wilhelm's by-proxy instructor Dutch Leonard retired after that year too. Wally Burnette was in the majors between 1956 and 1958. Al Papai was a big-league knuckleball thrower between 1948 and 1955. Bob Purkey reached the majors in 1954 and lasted through 1964, but he mixed the knuckler with other pitches. And that was about it at the moment. Wilhelm essentially stood alone temporarily as the symbol of knuckleball success. He had really spawned no successors.

Coming soon, in the 1960s, before Wilhelm retired, however, came the Niekro brothers, Phil in 1964 and Joe in 1967. The Niekros learned how to throw a knuckler when they were youngsters from their father, also named Phil, while playing catch in the backyard of their Lansing, Ohio, home. They own the record for most victories by two brothers, 318 by Phil and 221 by Joe, for a total of 539 wins combined.

Phil played catch with his dad in the yard and said one day his father just tossed him this throw that bobbed and weaved. The son said, "What's that?" Little did he know that he himself would someday make a generation of big-league hitters (and catchers) ask the same question.[5]

Niekro said his father kind of chuckled when he made that first toss, as if he secretly knew it was about to open a can of worms for his son to deal with.

"He showed me how to hold it and we just started throwing it," Phil

13. Trying to Make Sense of It

said. "I just got hooked into it. It was something we did every day in the backyard, just throwing knuckleballs to each other."[6]

In that sense, like Wilhelm, the Niekros' introduction to and appreciation of the knuckleball was sui generis. They did not purposely set out to learn about it and they did not use it because their ability to throw a fastball waned due to a sore arm.

Regardless of how the rare big-league pitcher who used the knuckler came to the pitch, there never were many who built their livelihood around it. Whether it was in the earlier days of the game when their parent clubs went into the hinterlands to find prospects, or later, when they watched well-known high school or college players, or later still when they studied young throwers on film, scouts were always on the prowl for strong arms. They didn't seek out or recommend to their bosses pitchers who threw 65 mph. Everyone was looking for heat, the young arm that could fire between 90 and 100 mph or throw a curve that could make knees shake—not someone with a pitch that would stymie batters.

As Wilhelm told *Sports Illustrated*, the knuckler was about a fingertip grip, not a knuckle grip. He showed that he grabbed the ball with his right thumb and index and middle fingers and basically threw side-arm to the plate. Wilhelm also had a distinctive tilt to his head as he pitched and sometimes when he was just walking around, but that had little to do with the knuckler's release.

"From that point on neither he, nor the batter, nor his own catcher, knows what course it is going to take," the story read. "For most of the 60 feet, 6 inches of its journey to the plate the ball does nothing much but float easily and almost enticingly toward the expectant batter. This, as it turns out, is only a sly come-on, for suddenly it begins to bob and weave like Floyd Patterson [at the moment boxing's heavyweight champion] moving in to throw a left hook, it wobbles, it flutters, it dances and dips. And then, finally, it darts dizzily off in one direction or another—sometimes down, sometimes sideways, occasionally even up—while the batter bludgeons the air and the catcher makes his frantic lunge."[7]

As exhausting as it was to follow that itinerary, imagine the batter's eyes trying to communicate with his mind. In the early years of the 20th century, before there were radar guns and admiration had to suffice to measure the speed of a pitcher's fastball, Walter Johnson and Smoky Joe Wood were deemed the fastest of them all. Johnson got the nod among many because he was the second-winningest pitcher of all time with 416 victories, but he himself said "no man alive" threw faster than Wood. Wood's hummer was sometimes described as hissing as it approached the plate. If that was in the realm of apocryphal, then perhaps in contrast the knuckleball muttered as it reached a batter. It may have been saying, "Ha, ha, fooled you again."

Or was still fooling them, given that Wilhelm was having a big year and continued to pitch for many more years. Paul Richards, the manager of the Baltimore Orioles who gave Wilhelm the opportunity to start more often than anyone else had, believed Wilhelm's long-time reliance on the pitch, throwing it over and over for years and years, paid dividends.

Back to the science. Committing to due diligence, *Sports Illustrated* did search for scientists with baseball expertise who could expound on the whimsy of the knuckleball. The magazine settled on Dr. Stanley Corrsin, chairman of the Johns Hopkins University mechanical engineering department who specialized in air turbulence. Corrsin happened to be an eyewitness of Wilhelm's no-hitter against the New York Yankees the previous year and admitted he had been trying to teach his son the knuckleball ever since. Perhaps in case the youngster couldn't earn a scholarship to Johns Hopkins?

An aerodynamicist, Corrsin said he wished he could get one of his graduate students interested in doing research on the knuckleball, but that hadn't happened, and he said he would love to undertake such a project himself if only he had the time.

To satisfy his own curiosity or "educated conjecture," Corrsin did some minor experiments outside the serious environment of a laboratory as to why a knuckleball knuckles the way it does. He dropped ping-pong balls into a 10-foot-long tube with air being pushed upward to create a wind tunnel. When the ping-pong balls were fed into the tube, they stayed straight for a short while and then began diverging, going to the right side or the left side. The strength of the artificial breeze affected how the ping-pong balls moved. "They behaved just like Wilhelm's [knuckle] balls," Corrsin said.[8]

While that was the conclusion, Corrsin used far more complicated language and supporting scientific data to prove his point. So as not to cause readers' eyes to glaze over, it was stated his reference to "the Magnus Force, Venturi Force, Bernoulli's equation, angular velocity and drag coefficient" were left out of the story's explanation of what happened when Wilhelm pitched the knuckler into the wind.[9]

Obligingly, Corrsin set up a fresh demonstration with his ping-pong

13. Trying to Make Sense of It

balls at his campus building. This time he set free some ping-pong balls at the top of a staircase going down three stories to the basement. "As Dr. Corrsin predicted, the ping-pong balls put on quite a show," the story stated.[10] Bounding down the first two flights of stairs, the balls stayed pretty much in a straight line. Then, much as had occurred in the mini–wind tunnel, they began shifting and going off to one side or the other.

Contrary to what baseball manufacturers might insist, Corrsin noted, no sphere was perfectly round and tiny differences could make a difference with a pitch. "Actually, the knuckleball may never break as much as some of the hitters seem to think. But, make no mistake, it breaks. The problem here is one of optics. The human eye is used to certain things and it can easily be fooled. However, since it [the knuckler] does not spin, there is no way to plot its course accurately."[11]

This was a more high-falutin' way to say pretty much what Wilhelm had been telling sportswriters for years when asked how he got the knuckleball to do what it did for him. He basically admitted that he did not know where it was going to go, but inwardly (and this proved the argument), he attributed "air pressure" to the knuckler's shifts. Even in the course of this story, Wilhelm never hinted that he was the master of his own fate. Could he determine the break of the ball? "Heck, no," he said. "I wish I could." Not even after he let it fly? "Nope, not even then."[12]

No story on the knuckler would have been complete without a discussion of the hardships produced by the knuckleball for a catcher. Wilhelm's most frequent partner behind the plate at the time was Gus Triandos, who periodically moaned about the assault the knuckleball made on his performance. His complaints did increase over time and his own mental block about cleanly catching the pitch developed, or perhaps it should be said deteriorated, over the next few years as Wilhelm's teammate. But by 1959, even when things had been going well overall, he was already being disturbed by his woes.

Sports Illustrated described Triandos' approach to catching the knueckleball "a lunge and a prayer," and when he was approached to detail how he handled the knuckler, the first thing Triandos said was, "I don't know. The best thing I've found is just to wait until the last minute and then grab for it. If you get your glove up there too early, thinking it's going to break in one direction, you blank out the ball and then you're in trouble. It usually ends up going somewhere else."[13]

When that occurred, a catcher was likely to be charged with a

Hoyt Wilhelm

passed ball by the official scorer, embarrassing the catcher because by definition of the words he should have had it. Triandos was an all-around good player who made four All-Star teams and eight times reached double figures in home runs in a season. He was also a very popular player in Baltimore. Those passed balls ate at him. Wherever Hoyt Wilhelm played, passed balls were sure to follow. Triandos had many topics he preferred to talk about within and beyond the game of baseball than catching the knuckleball.

At this point, with Wilhelm being one of the hottest pitchers in the sport, and Triandos being the Orioles' everyday catcher, they were stuck with one another.

Their boss, Paul Richards, made his move to use Wilhelm more as a starter than a reliever based on his own years of baseball experience. He was well aware of how few knuckleball pitchers registered great success. In his mind, trying Wilhelm in the role was common sense, not some wild idea. He understood that even if the knuckler seemed possessed of magical properties or some hocus-pocus characteristics, or would likely be the pitch of choice by the Houdinis of the world or Las Vegas showmen, it was grounded in some type of baseball logic.

"Nobody can hit a good knuckleball," Richards said. "Heck, hardly anybody can even catch one. So, if you get it over the plate, you get them out. That's what Hoyt has been doing."[14]

Richards did not need a scientific experiment carried out by a professor at Johns Hopkins University or a *Sports Illustrated* magazine story to explain it to him. It was all fundamental. If Hoyt Wilhelm threw a pitch to the plate, no matter its name or its speed, and the opposition couldn't hit it, Richards was all in on giving him another start a few days later.

Richards never forgot how his gamble on Wilhelm paid off, either. Later in his own administrative career, as he moved from team to team, he played a role in converting Phil Niekro from a relief pitcher to a starter, and he supervised the Chicago White Sox when Wilhelm, Wilbur Wood and Eddie Fisher, knuckleballers all, were vying for spots on the roster.

Oh yes, the man with the long memory and the daring thought process in a conservative sport, was an executive with the Atlanta Braves in 1967 and quite willing to bring in an aging Hoyt "Old Folks" Wilhelm for a last shot at a big-league roster even as he closed in on 50 years of age.

Richards was one of the baseball people who did not fear the

13. Trying to Make Sense of It

knuckleballer but wondered what a pitcher with an ageless arm could do for one of his teams. As always, for him, it was about getting hitters out. It should also be noted that during his own playing career, Richards was a catcher. So he had sympathy for catchers like Gus Triandos and their rocky relationship with the knuckler. For his next idea the next year, 1960, in Baltimore, Richards sought a cure for that problem.

14

Out of Control

Catchers may have gritted their teeth and put on a false happy face when they were called upon as a receiver for their team on the days that Hoyt Wilhelm pitched. They knew they had to keep their concentration levels high and their muscles limber when knuckleballs sailed their way.

Still, it might not matter. The pitch with a mind of its own might embarrass them. Or possibly injure them. Although they were stationed as the second in line with catchers in front of them, home-plate umpires might also be required to stay on their toes and be ready for an out-of-control knuckleball headed in their direction.

Nobody told a more vivid knuckleball-gone-awry tale concerning an umpire than former player Eddie Robinson when he was a coach for the Baltimore Orioles in 1958. The victim in the story was long-time umpire Larry Napp. Napp was an American League umpire between 1951 and 1974 and was on the job for four World Series and four All-Star games.

Robinson was already a player-coach for Baltimore for his final games in 1957 and moved right onto manager Paul Richards' coaching staff the next season. The disaster for Napp happened during a regular-season game against the Boston Red Sox. Robinson was likely referring to the September 7 game at Memorial Stadium. Wilhelm threw three innings of relief in a 6–5, 10-inning Boston victory with Napp calling balls and strikes.

"In the middle of a hot day game a Red Sox batter fouled a knuckleball off the plate into Napp's private parts," Robinson wrote in his autobiography. "He went down like a wet rag, and the trainers rushed out and bounced him up and down on the ground and got him ready to umpire again. Two pitches later, the same thing happened again. The trainers rushed out and revived him again. Napp stayed in the game behind the plate, although one of the base umpires offered to take over for him. Two innings later, the same thing happened a third time. This

14. Out of Control

While Hoyt Wilhelm (left) was the oldster on the staff, many of his Baltimore Orioles pitching teammates were, like Steve Barber, in their early 20s. Wilhelm and Barber were teammates with Baltimore between 1960 and 1962 (National Baseball Hall of Fame Library, Cooperstown, N.Y.).

time, the trainers just grabbed a stretcher, ran out, loaded Napp on it, and took him to our training room."[1]

Although Robinson referred to the contest as a mid-season game, this was the only time that season Wilhelm pitched against the Red Sox with Napp behind the plate. He also pitched a complete game 3–2 loss versus the Red Sox a week earlier, but Napp was not on the crew.

Given Paul Richards' personal background on the field, his affinity for Hoyt Wilhelm, and his appreciation of Gus Triandos, it seemed somewhat logical he would try to create a formula, invent equipment, or do something that could maximize the effectiveness of the knuckleball for his Orioles.

As a player, Richards was a catcher for the Brooklyn Dodgers, New York Giants, Philadelphia Athletics and Detroit Tigers between 1932 and 1946, so he definitely understood the requirements of that job. He managed the Chicago White Sox twice (wrapped around his stint with the Orioles) and into the 1970s was general manager of the Orioles,

Hoyt Wilhelm

Houston Colt .45s–Astros when the expansion team was founded, the Atlanta Braves and the White Sox.

Richards' lifetime batting average was .227, but he did win a World Series ring in 1945 with the Tigers. Although the phrase was not popular when he managed, Richards' managerial style relied on "small ball," stressing pitching, defense and aggressive base-running.

Often, especially when he was manager-general manager, Richards worked overtime to out-think opponents. He was a GM at the same time as Frank Lane, aka "Trader Lane," was on the job with various teams, but Richards pulled the trigger on a 17-player deal that is the largest in baseball history. He also argued for his side so vociferously as a manager he led the American League in being ejected from games by umpires for 11 straight years. Richards was boss of the Orioles when he engineered the massive trade in 1954 with the Yankees and among his gets was Triandos, probably the best player in the whole bunch.

Since he came to the effort honestly through his own background, Richards took pride in helping to improve the fielding skills of catchers he managed, Triandos prominent among them.

Baseball has evolved in many dramatic ways since the National League was founded in 1876 and the American League was birthed as a second major league with staying power in 1901. That includes not only the invention of the knuckleball but also other pitches, including going way back to the credit allotted to Candy Cummings for inventing the curveball when he played in the 1870s.

Baseball bats themselves evolved from large, heavy cudgel-like bats to lighter-weight bats. By the 1890s, it was obvious that catchers were the most vulnerable of players on the diamond, more likely to be injured by a thrown or batted ball or sliding runners than other fielders. There was always an awareness for catchers, as well as for batters stepping into the box and umpires behind the plate, that a high-velocity fastball could injure them. It is somewhat miraculous that in 145 years of big-league play only one hitter has been killed by a pitched ball. Cleveland Indians second baseman Ray Chapman was struck in the head by a Carl Mays fastball in 1920 and died several hours later.

By the 1870s, catchers began realizing their bodies were at the mercy of too many types of incidents that could do them harm behind the plate. The protection adopted was a mouthpiece, the idea borrowed from boxing. George Wright, one of the founders of the original Cincinnati Red Stockings, introduced it. The first face mask was worn by a Harvard man in college play.

14. Out of Control

In the 1890s, some catchers attached old newspapers or leather padding to their lower legs for defense against bruises. It was in 1907 that Roger Bresnahan gained fame—and originally some ridicule—for inventing shin guards.

Baseball gloves were totally different across the sport in the early days compared to their growing sophistication after World War II and in the present day. For starters, really starters, ball players competed barehanded. Gradually, gloves were adopted, but they were unlike gloves of the future in that they were smaller and fit tighter on the hand; they had flatter hunks of leather with fat finger holders instead of deep pockets. They did not feature high webs or any webbing to ease the grabbing of a line drive when it was smoked and a fielder jumped for it.

A strong influence on the expansion of the use of gloves by more players stemmed from Albert G. Spalding. Spalding was first a pitcher, became a manager and the president of the Chicago White Sox, and then lent his name to the sporting goods manufacturing company that still endures. Besides being a pioneer of the game, Spalding was quite a good pitcher, with a record of 252–65. He is a member of the National Baseball Hall of Fame.

Spalding became an early proponent of the glove to help protect bare flesh, and his namesake company sold millions of them. The fielder's glove that is seen today really took a more efficient and recognizable form in 1920.

Bill Doak, a 13-year big-league pitcher who once led the National League in earned run average and who employed his own trick pitch—the spitball—was throwing for the St. Louis Cardinals when he devised an idea to improve the glove. Doak suggested webbing be inserted between the thumb and index finger, only he brought the idea to Rawlings, not Spalding, to make the first ones.

Essentially, all kinds of fielders' gloves grew up together, but none was more important to performance than the catcher's mitt. No one handled the ball more frequently under pressure than a catcher. The catcher had to be able to grab out of the air fastballs, slow balls, or any other balls thrown by pitchers. If they could not catch what their pitchers threw, the game could devolve into a farce.

Hard to fathom, but in the first days of professional baseball, catchers did go into battle with bare hands seeking to catch those offerings. Broken fingers were not unheard of, and the combination of one injury and, indeed, the elusiveness of Candy Cummings' new curveball created circumstances leading to the very first protective hand covering behind the plate.

The Cincinnati Red Stockings had a backstop named Doug Allison playing with an injured left hand on June 28, 1870, and he worried he would not be able to prevent Cummings' curves from bouncing away. So Allison cut the fingers from a pair of buckskin mittens and played the game with better traction for his catching hand.

The idea of a catcher's glove started catching on and grew slowly, if steadily, in popularity. These were very thin-layered mitts. A catcher named Harry Decker patented an actual catcher's glove with padding in 1890. Decker played for several teams, including the Philadelphia Phillies and Detroit Wolverines, over a handful of years in the National League.

While one of the primary roles of a catcher is to prevent opponents from stealing bases, Decker was apparently a real criminal when not playing ball, including stealing a horse, stealing a bicycle and stealing from his own teammates. It was known that he spent time in jail, including San Quentin. There were also suggestions his behavior could be summarized as that of someone who had lost his mind, perhaps because he had been hit in the head with a baseball while catching.

Nonetheless, Decker is credited as being someone who knew his stuff when it came to good catching equipment. As with all other gloves' manufacture over the passage of time, companies developed higher-quality catchers' mitts, with deeper pockets, more leather and better gripping capability.

In modern baseball, fielders' gloves are in the range of 12½ inches in size, but catcher's mitts are generally around 33 inches. The actual Major League rule on maximum size is 38 inches, or 15½ inches from top to bottom.

For the existence of that rule, baseball catchers can thank Paul Richards, Clint Courtney, Gus Triandos and Hoyt Wilhelm. As the 1960 season was beginning, Richards figured that if his catchers were having so much difficulty keeping track of Wilhelm's shifting knuckleballs, they should have better equipment to fight back.

Hence, the origin of the first 42-inch (then larger) catcher's mitt, which in its own way was so big compared to commonly used models that it seemed as if it belonged to a clown for an act on stage.

Of course, by that season Triandos had been vocal about how much aggravation the Wilhelm knuckleball caused him. He didn't complain all the time, but when any sportswriter asked him about the challenge, he didn't hold back.

14. Out of Control

Trianados was an established, All-Star player. He recognized being traded to Baltimore was a good career move, because the Yankees had Yogi Berra and Elston Howard ahead of him at catcher and he wasn't beating them out. His penance, his payment for being able to play every day, was catching Hoyt Wilhelm's knuckleball.

"Catching Hoyt was such a miserable experience," Triandos said long into his retirement. "I just wanted to end the game."[2]

Wilhelm told others, though, that Triandos was the best catcher he worked with in his ability to catch the knuckler. When Triandos was told that, however, he had trouble believing it.

"I think he was kidding about me being the best catcher for the knuckleball," Triandos said. "The more you caught him, the worse you got."[3]

To say Triandos was psyched about catching Wilhelm was a tremendous understatement. The big mitt, which was nicknamed "Big Bertha" by some, was designed to help him and his fellow Orioles catchers, but he was of two minds about it, saying, "At first I didn't need the big mitt, but later I did."[4]

There was a good reason why the oversized catcher's mitt reminded some baseball people of the kind of accoutrement a slapstick entertainer would use in an act. That was because the idea truly originated in such fashion. Al Schact, first a three-year big-league pitcher and then a coach for the Washington Senators, was later called "the Clown Prince of Baseball" for his shenanigans as he brought his comedy act to ballparks.

Richards saw Schact employ such a big-glove prop and the light bulb went on over his head just as it would have in a comic strip. Richards contracted with Wilson Sporting Goods to make a special glove 42 inches in circumference at a cost of $400.

There was some irony in that when Richards and the Orioles introduced the glove to a big-league game against the New York Yankees at Yankee Stadium, it was adorning the hand of Courtney, not Triandos. Wilhelm was the starting pitcher, though, and went the distance in a 3–2 victory.

Courtney had a marvelously appropriate nickname for a catcher—"Scrap Iron." Courtney broke into the majors in 1951 and had a 11-year big-league career. His first full-time year was with the St. Louis Browns, and he won *The Sporting News* Rookie of the Year Award by batting .286. Courtney went with the team to Baltimore.

Triandos was the real No. 1 catcher for the team, but Courtney appeared in 83 games in 1960, so him trotting out for the May 27

Yankees game was not unusual. His glove was the surprise to everyone not connected with the Orioles.

As soon as members of the Yankees saw it, they flagged the glove, which loomed as large as a hubcap to them, and issued a protest to the umpiring crew. The American League's supervisor of umpires was Cal Hubbard. Hubbard is the only man elected to the College Football Hall of Fame, the Pro Football Hall of Fame and the Baseball Hall of Fame. He tackled this situation head-on. Hubbard said the rule book was on the side of the Orioles, at that time reading, "A catcher may wear a leather glove or mitt of any size, shape, or weight."[5]

That was pretty all-encompassing. The Yankees likely filed their protest on the basis of the glove looking funny or being out of the norm, which it was. There had never been anything like it as a counter-weapon for catchers. Big Bertha seemed to work as an aid for Baltimore catchers. That day, when it made its debut, Courtney caught cleanly. There were no passed balls charged to the Orioles coming on throws by Wilhelm.

This was viewed as significant because to that point in the season, in 51⅓ innings thrown by Wilhelm, Baltimore catchers had committed 11 passed balls, a very high rate indeed. A third catcher on the Orioles, Joe Ginsberg, watched Courtney's performance unfold and how he handled the big mitt and said, "The damn thing really worked, except for one thing."[6] That one thing was the unwieldy nature of the glove when it came to trying to dig low pitches out of the dirt.

A little bit later in the season, again against the Yankees, Courtney was wearing the oversized mitt and dropped a foul pop that led to a New York rally. This raised the question of the value of the glove for other uses besides blocking knuckleballs. Still, it seemed, on balance, a plus for the Orioles.

A little while later, when Casey Stengel, dumped by the New York Yankees after winning 10 pennants in 12 years, was managing the hapless expansion New York Mets to the worst record of the 20th century, he expounded on catchers in his own Stengelese.

"You've got to have a catcher or you'll have a lot of passed balls," Stengel said.[7] Stengel was not blessed with many first-rate catchers during his stint with the woeful Mets, and even though he didn't have a knuckleball artist like Wilhelm on his staff, his catchers would probably have been helped by a big mitt anyway.

Despite his other success, Triandos was shadowed by his knuckleball experiences with Wilhelm. He once half-jokingly told a story about

14. Out of Control

one game catching the knuckle king when three of Wilhelm's pitches skittered away from him but Triandos also hit two home runs.

"At least I drove in more runs than I let in," Triandos said. "Sure, knucklers drive me crazy. It's gotten so that Richards doesn't let me know in advance anymore when Wilhelm's going to pitch. He wants me to get a good's night sleep and not worry about that crazy knuckler."[8]

Still, Triandos admitted that his biggest thrill in baseball was catching Wilhelm's no-hitter, though he didn't believe a catcher should take too much credit for a pitcher's good game or a pitcher issue blame to a catcher if the thrower had a bad game. Praising how Richards repeatedly gave him fine-point observations to improve his fielding, Triandos thought one example of Richards' smarts was making Wilhelm a regular starter when no one else had done so.

"Paul isn't afraid to experiment," Triandos said. "Look at what he did with Wilhelm. Hoyt was a relief pitcher for so many years, and then Paul gets him and makes him one of the best starting pitchers in the league."[9]

Richards said he believed he was getting a bargain when he claimed Wilhelm for $20,000 off waivers from Cleveland based on what he had seen from the man at his best in games directly against him.

"I like to get men who hurt me on my side and I dreaded Wilhelm ever since we saw him in exhibitions in Arizona," Richards said of Wilhelm's initial forays in the American League. He said he was "lucky" to obtain Wilhelm.[10]

Up and down, back and forth it went with Triandos discussing the Wilhelm knuckler. Richards praised his ability to handle it. Triandos often disparaged his own efforts. He seemed to become blunter the deeper into retirement he got, the farther removed he was from being a knuckleball catcher.

In 1982, 17 years into retirement, Triandos was asked by a writer about catching two no-hitters during his career, a perfect game thrown by Hall of Famer Jim Bunning and the one with Wilhelm on the mound. Perhaps thinking that because Wilhelm threw a slower pitch it would have made things more comfortable, he asked Triandos which was easier to catch.

"Are you kidding?" Triandos said. "Did you ever try to catch a knuckler?"[11]

At least Triandos was employed by a team featuring a manager who seemed to care and not really penalize his catchers for being flummoxed by the knuckleball. The sporting goods manufacturer labeled the big catcher's mitt the Wilson Model 1050CL, but by all rights it should simply have been labeled "the Paul Richards Mitt."

The "Big Bertha" name appended to the big mitt followed the naming of a German World War I howitzer. Much later, certain golf clubs, drivers, were called Big Berthas. It is not clear just how many Big Bertha 40-plus-inch baseball catcher's mitts were made, but not even a search on eBay or other Internet sales locations could produce one. The likelihood is that if one showed up it would be pricier than the $400 Richards paid Wilson for the first one.

15

Hanging Tough with the Orioles

The big mitt brought more notoriety to Hoyt Wilhelm and his knuckleball. After all, who else had a throwing repertoire that prompted catchers to try out new equipment?

This was not a subtle change. A mitt that measured 42 inches, 45 inches or 48 inches in circumference looked big. In fact, when an Orioles catcher posed holding up the glove for a picture, depending on the angle, it could obscure his face. It was like a big-fin Oldsmobile 88 of that vintage compared to an average-sized sedan.

The strangest thing of all was this alteration was simply for one man's best pitch. There may have been others flirting with the knuckleball, but no one else at the time was so identified with it as Wilhelm. And you didn't see their coaches, managers or teams shopping for Big Berthas.

Compared to 1959 when Wilhelm was pretty much a sensation, 1960 was not really special. His record was 11–8, down from 15–11, though he also had seven saves. His earned run average of 3.31 climbed substantially from his league-leading 2.19 in 1959. Wilhelm's workload was split between starting and relieving in 41 appearances. His number of innings pitched dropped from 226 to 147. Manager Paul Richards had a crew of young, up-and-coming starters breaking in and he needed Wilhelm more coming out of the bullpen to help them out.

The Orioles were actually making a big move for the first time since coming to Baltimore from St. Louis and changing their name. Their record was 89–65, second in the American League to the New York Yankees. Attendance was up to 1,187,849.

The promise was read in the arms of the young rotation. Chuck Estrada, who won 18 games, was 22. Milt Pappas, who was 21, won 15. Jack Fisher, who won 12 games, was 21. Steve Barber, who won 10, was 22

Hoyt Wilhelm

years old. General managers around baseball would have paid dearly for their futures in the trading market. Jerry Walker, 21, was also in the mix, though he was just 3–4 that season.

Wilhelm was 37 that season. But there was one additional irony about the composition of the staff in 1960 that stood out.

Harold "Skinny" Brown, who was 35 and went 12–5 with a 3.06 earned run average, was somewhat like the second coming of Wilhelm. He could start and relieve—and he also threw a knuckleball. Brown had been with the Orioles since 1955, a contributor, but this marked the most victories he compiled in 14 years in the big leagues.

Richards had managed Brown in the minors in 1950 at Seattle of the Pacific Coast League. He was not a knuckleballer only, but he could dish it. At least the big mitt didn't sit unused when Wilhelm wasn't in the game.

Hoyt Wilhelm shows off his knuckleball form from his first days in the majors with the New York Giants in the early 1950s. He played with the team 1952–1956 (National Baseball Hall of Fame Library, Cooperstown, N.Y.).

It should be noted that besides having a larger circumference, Big Bertha was heavier than the standard mitt, 30 ounces to 27 ounces. Richards was exasperated by his catchers' inability to handle Wilhelm's knuckler. In fairness, the glove may have been the brainchild of Richards, but coach Harry Brecheen did the on-site planning with Wilson on the instructions of Richards. So he could be said to be blamed for the specs, too, although he is hardly ever mentioned in connection with the introduction of the special glove.

There was never any question about Gus Triandos being the team's number one catcher, but Joe Ginsberg's playing time suffered when Courtney came over from the Washington Senators in an April 1960

15. Hanging Tough with the Orioles

trade. Triandos then incurred an injured thumb. "You know, Courtney is about three times better a catcher than anyone has ever given him for being. He hops around out there, but he gets the job done," Richards said.[1]

Richards was responding to an image Courtney had of not being a terribly sound catcher. Courtney did not lack for confidence. He spoke with a Southern accent and was quoted at the time as saying, "Ah got a hunch Ah'll play more than a lot of people think. Ah can hit and Ah ain't as bad a catcher as a lot of people think."[2]

Courtney's start with the big glove was premeditated because it was a scheduled Wilhelm start for that May 27 game. When the contest was over, Courtney seemed satisfied with himself. "I don't know how many pitches would have jumped past me with a regular glove." Courtney said. "This was the first time I ever caught [Wilhelm]. Boy, is he rough to catch. I don't see how anybody ever hits him."[3]

Although the other Baltimore players in the field were not directly involved in the use of the experimental glove, they were very interested in the results since they were affected by any passed balls scored against their catchers allowing foes to advance bases or score runs. The initial reviews were positive. "Clint was lower to the ground," said Orioles slugging first baseman Jim Gentile. "Ol' Scrap Iron, he'd get back there with that big glove on, and he'd just pounce on it."[4]

For the time being, the Richards-Brecheen innovation paid solid dividends for the Orioles, though Triandos never seemed to get over the traumatizing effects of Wilhelm's knuckleball.

As for Wilhelm, never again after the 1960 season did he experience any team really counting on him to fill a role as a starting pitcher. The next season, 1961, Baltimore started him in just one game, and during the 1963 season, he started three games. By then he was playing for the Chicago White Sox.

In 1961, Wilhelm returned to his familiar job as an ace out of the bullpen and he excelled at it as the team rolled to a 95–67–1 record, outstanding yet still 14 games behind the Yankees, who were driven by the Roger Maris–Mickey Mantle home-run chase of Babe Ruth's single-season record.

Wilhelm's record was 9–7, compiled over the 51 games he pitched in, and his earned run average had dropped down again, this time to 2.30. He was selected to the American League roster for both All-Star games of 1961. The double selection for that season made Wilhelm a four-time pick and he would add more.

Hoyt Wilhelm

Wilhelm benefited from the few-year stretch when the majors conducted two All-Star games per summer. He was on the AL roster for the first game of 1961, played July 11 in Candlestick. Some of Wilhelm's teammates were Whitey Ford of the Yankees, who was the American League starter, his Baltimore mate Brooks Robinson at third base, and other Hall of Famers including Mickey Mantle, Yogi Berra, Harmon Killebrew, Nellie Fox and Al Kaline. Outfielder Jackie Brandt was another Oriole in the mix.

Warren Spahn, the esteemed left-hander, was the starting pitcher for the National League and other Hall of Famers in the other dugout were Eddie Mathews, Willie Mays, Orlando Cepeda, Sandy Koufax, Hank Aaron, Roberto Clemente and Frank Robinson.

Candlestick Park was known for its high winds because of its inconvenient location. It was often said that playing baseball in San Francisco in summer was as cold as winter in other places. Appropriately, the most memorable aspect of this game, won 5–4 by the National League, was slightly-built Giants relief pitcher Stu Miller being blown off the mound by a strong breeze mid-windup, causing the umpires to slap a balk call on him.

Less remembered is the fact that Miller was the winning pitcher in relief of the 10-inning game and the loser was Wilhelm. Wilhelm was the sixth pitcher of the game for the NL, following Ford, Frank Lary of the Detroit Tigers, Dick Donovan of the Washington Senators, Jim Bunning, also of the Tigers, and Mike Fornieles of the Boston Red Sox.

Things did not go very smoothly for Wilhelm. He entered for the bottom of the ninth inning in a tie game with the score 3–3. The first National League batter was Don Zimmer, later more famous as a manager, and he grounded out shortstop to first. Smoky Burgess, the hard-hitting catcher renowned for his pinch-hitting prowess, was next up. Burgess grounded out, third to first. He was followed to the plate by the St. Louis Cardinals' Ken Boyer, who drew a walk from Wilhelm. Boyer represented the potential winning run.

At this point, American League manager Paul Richards removed Berra from the lineup as catcher and inserted Elston Howard. It was not clear if this was a judgment call by Richards or a request from Berra based on the gut feeling Howard could better cope with Wilhelm's knuckler. It was said, though, that Berra was not comfortable fielding Wilhelm's knuckleball when there were men on base in a big situation.

Boyer was picked off first base by Wilhelm, but first baseman Jim Gentile, Wilhelm's own Baltimore teammate, made an error. The

15. Hanging Tough with the Orioles

ball got away and Boyer ran to second safely, putting a man in scoring position.

However, the Los Angeles Dodgers' Maury Wills, the base-stealing star of his era, popped out to second to end the threat and the inning.

Miller, who endured his infamous moment with the balk due to the wind in the previous inning, was still hurling for the NL. Dick Howser led off for the American League but was caught looking on a third strike for the first out in the top of the 10th. Gentile, who had a great power swing, hitting 46 homers that year and leading the league with 141 runs batted in, had a chance to redeem himself but also struck out.

Fox, the tobacco-chewing, diminutive second baseman of the Chicago White Sox, did what he did best, coaxing a walk to reach base. His sharp eye—and his hustle—paid off. Kaline was up next and he hit a grounder to third base. But the throw went awry, Fox came all of the way around to score and Kaline reached third. This could have been a fatal National League error, but Maris, who was on his way to a memorable 61-homer season, stuck out, stranding Kaline.

Still, Wilhelm took a 4–3 lead into the bottom of the 10th with an excellent chance to provide the victory for the AL. But he could not contain the National League's murderers' row.

The end-of-the-game adventure began with Hank Aaron, years shy of becoming the all-time home-run king, pinch-hitting for Miller, certainly a no-brainer move by NL manager Danny Murtaugh of the Pittsburgh Pirates. Aaron singled to center field. Willie Mays came to the plate and alas, for Wilhelm, and Richards' substitution move, one of the knuckleballer's throws became a Howard passed ball, advancing Aaron to second base.

Berra was right to worry about the circumstances. Actually, the entire rest of the league was aware of what might happen to a catcher with Wilhelm on the mound. Wherever Wilhelm played teams set records for passed balls. The Cleveland Indians mishandled 35 pitches officially in 1958 and just six the next year. Only once between 1952 and 1967, the teams Wilhelm pitched for failed to lead their league in passed balls.

After that commotion, Mays dug in anew and promptly belted a double to left field, a shot that scored Aaron and tied the game, 4–4. Cincinnati slugger Frank Robinson (who not so far in the future would become a Baltimore Oriole) was hit by a pitch. The NL had runners on first and second and had not yet run out of superstars to send to the batter's box. Roberto Clemente followed with the game-winning single to right field, Mays tallying the winning run.

Hoyt Wilhelm

Wilhelm's losing pitching line was 1⅔ innings, three hits allowed and two runs given up, one walk and one strikeout. The curtain came down on those numbers.

The second All-Star game of 1961 was played at Fenway Park in Boston on July 31. The same managers were in charge and many of the same players participated. The score was different, however. For the first time, the game ended in a tie, 1–1, rather than going into extra innings.

Rocky Colavito of the Tigers hit a first-inning home run for the American League. The National League scored a lone run in the sixth inning, Bill White driving home Eddie Mathews with a single. Three pitchers, Bunning, also representing Detroit, Don Schwall of the Red Sox, and Camilio Pascual of the new Minnesota Twins, hurled three innings apiece. Wilhelm did not get off the bench for this one.

For the 1962 season, given all of those young, strong arms the Orioles were developing, and no doubt wondering how much longer Wilhelm, then 39 (or 40) could go on, the team used Wilhelm only out of the bullpen 52 times. Although his record slipped to 7–10, Wilhelm finished 44 games and saved 15. His earned run average improved to 1.99 in 93 innings.

The AL still couldn't hit him and that year Wilhelm was again selected twice for the All-Star roster. That was the last season Major League Baseball held the two All-Star games in one summer.

The first All-Star game of 1962 was held in Washington, D.C., on July 10. The National League won, 3–1, with the victory going to Juan Marichal of the San Francisco Giants and the loss going to Pascual. The AL used four pitchers this day, but none of them was Wilhelm who had a good seat but no activity.

The second All-Star game took place at Wrigley Field in Chicago on July 30. The American League won this one, 9–4, with the victory registered to Ray Herbert of the White Sox in his only 20-win season. Wilhelm was again a spectator, not urgently needed in relief although four pitchers for his side did get into the game, including Baltimore teammate Milt Pappas, who also threw relief in the summer's first All-Star game.

This was pretty much the end of an era for the Orioles. Paul Richards abruptly quit the team in September of 1961 despite the club's 95-win season and there was a new man in the dugout for 1962 in Billy Hitchcock. The Orioles immediately slumped, dropping to 77 wins, a losing mark, and a seventh-place finish. Upper management began shaking things up and one of the players exiting was Wilhelm.

15. Hanging Tough with the Orioles

Despite his double All-Star selection and all-around sound performance, the team took a look at Wilhelm's listed age (never mind his true age) saw a number that began with a four and figured the old man couldn't have too much left. It was not the first, and definitely not the last time, such an assessment was made about Wilhelm. Overlooked each time was his durability based on his knuckleball specialty. Unlike the flamethrowers, Wilhelm's right arm did not age as naturally or steadily, if at all.

"Hey, I threw 85 mph, I threw less than that, 70 mph, and I got people out," Wilhelm said, "so it's not how hard you throw. Unless you're Nolan Ryan or Goose Gossage, I ain't taking anything away from those guys because it's great to have an arm like that."[5]

Wilhelm knew he did not possess a super-strong big-league arm. He owned a super big-league pitch, had experience and savvy, and played to his strengths. He also kept himself in good enough shape to keep playing as he aged. In the modern game, there are workout fanatics who consult with strength coaches and lift weights and adopt specific routines for the off-season and rely on nutritional advice.

That was basically unheard of in Wilhelm's prime years and he was someone who did enjoy eating. In fact, one of his pleasures in life was going out to dinner with his wife Peggy. Yet he maintained a good weight of around 190 pounds on his six-foot frame.

Wilhelm did some walking during his off-seasons, though not on a treadmill or anything like that. He was an avid bird hunter and fisherman and he walked in the woods during the appropriate outdoors seasons when he was home in North Carolina, while living in Columbus, Georgia, and later when he moved to Sarasota, Florida.

"I was never one, I never believed in off-season athletic workouts," he said. "I did a lot of hunting and walking and keeping my legs in shape, but I wasn't one who believed in messing with the baseball. I never messed with the baseball until spring training and I never did any extra to get in shape for spring training because regardless of what you're going to do on your own, you're still not going to use muscles that you use in baseball. My theory was that I went to spring training and it took me about two weeks [to get in playing shape]. A week to get soreness in. A week to get it out and that was it. I had to go through that regardless of what I did before. That's just the way I did it."[6]

It was a good enough strategy to keep Wilhelm in good enough shape to continue as a big-league pitcher long after 99 percent of all hurlers throughout history had retired. Still, without Richards—off to

Hoyt Wilhelm

Houston—in his corner with the Orioles, and the team slumping rather than ascending, it seemed only a matter of time before the leftover administrators lost faith in him.

Really, they had other problems. In 1960, Baltimore had the most promising young rotation in baseball. The club seemed set for years with the young arms of Chuck Estrada, Jerry Walker, Jack Fisher, Steve Barber and Milt Pappas. As a group they were nicknamed the "Baby Birds." What a bright future they had. Yet it did not turn out that way for most of them.

Estrada's 18 wins led the AL and he was named the Sporting News Pitcher of the Year. His career lasted seven years, he compiled 50 wins, and he was out of the majors at 29. Although he became a pitching coach, Walker never won more than 11 games in a season and he was out of the majors at 25 with just 37 total wins.

Fisher pitched for 11 seasons, twice led his league in losses, finished more than 50 games under .500 and was out of the majors at 30. Barber did better, winning 20 games for the Orioles in 1963, staying in the majors for 15 seasons and winning 121 games overall.

It was Pappas who outshined all of the others, going 209–164 with a lifetime 3.40 ERA in 17 seasons. He never won more than 17 games in a season but was a three-time All-Star. A member of the Orioles' Hall of Fame, in 1972 Pappas pitched a no-hitter for the Chicago Cubs against the San Diego Padres, but came within one pitch of twirling a perfect game. He walked a hitter on a 3–2 count and always contended the pitch was a strike.

The remarkable aspect of this collection of promising young arms is how little the Orioles gained from their performances before they either retired young from injury or were swapped to other teams.

In five seasons, as the beneficiary of the two All-Star games per season, Wilhelm represented Baltimore six times in an American League All-Star uniform.

On January 14, 1963, Wilhelm figured into a major trade as the Orioles felt compelled to make those changes following the dismal 1962 season. The team bartered with the Chicago White Sox for future Hall of Fame shortstop Luis Aparicio and outfielder Al Smith, sending Ron Hansen, Dave Nicholson, Pete Ward and Wilhelm to Chicago.

The White Sox got Hansen as a replacement for Aparicio, some slugging power, and the question mark of what value Wilhelm's signature knuckleball still retained. To the surprise of many, Wilhelm was nowhere close to being finished.

15. Hanging Tough with the Orioles

Once, long before, his hometown *Charlotte Observer* had opined that Wilhelm had no future in baseball, actually saying he threw like a washer woman, deriding that knuckleball's slow-motion pace. Now, even as he passed 40 years of age and threatened to pitch until he was 50, no one could claim Wilhelm was yet washed up.

16

Good Company

When Hoyt Wilhelm was traded from the Baltimore Orioles to the Chicago White Sox for the 1963 season, he didn't realize he was joining what turned out to be a knuckleball fraternity or an island of knuckleballers. Throughout his career he had pretty much been on his own.

Actually, that wasn't the immediate circumstance in Chicago but a gradual evolution. Wilhelm stayed with the White Sox through the 1968 season. Eddie Fisher, another pre-eminent knuckleball thrower and a great admirer of Wilhelm's, was already there, with the club since 1962. Wilbur Wood, who was about to make his own waves with the knuckler, joined the team in 1967.

That made for three overlapping knuckleball specialists, the greatest collection of pitchers relying on that pitch since the Washington Senators of the mid–1940s and probably the best grouping of hurlers who could make the pitch work for them of all time.

The White Sox were strong contenders. Chicago won the American League pennant in 1959, though the Los Angeles Dodgers prevailed in the World Series. It was the White Sox's first league conquest in 40 years, the first since the besmirching Black Sox scandal of 1919. The team was managed by Al Lopez, ultimately selected for the Hall of Fame, but in his playing days, like Paul Richards, he was a catcher.

Lopez could not afford to be indifferent to the knuckleball like so many other managers, because it was too large a presence in his professional life. As for the catchers on his roster, however, they were about as concerned how the pitch would define them as Gus Triandos had been with the Orioles. One by one, White Sox catchers tried to cooperate with Wood, Wilhelm and Fisher and they felt the stress of passed balls mounting.

No one suffered more than J.C. Martin, a prospect from Virginia who was signed as an infielder and for a couple of years played very sporadically at first base or third base before being retrained as a catcher

16. Good Company

in 1962. Perhaps if Martin could hit better than his lifetime average of .222, he might have been able to resist the fielding change, but he struggled with big-league pitching. Martin made the move for opportunity at Lopez's suggestion. Veteran star backstop Sherm Lollar was nearing the end of his career and the farm system had no up-and-comer.

Martin did make it back up to the majors in his new role, but the flutterball tormented him. Martin committed 24 passed balls in 1964 and 33 the next year. The 1965 total was a record that lasted for 22 years.

"It wasn't very pleasant," Martin said in a 2014 interview about trying to balance the tricks of

The right-handed Wilhelm broke into the majors with the Giants before they moved to San Francisco and won a National League earned run average title with the club. He pitched for the team from 1952 to 1956 (National Baseball Hall of Fame Library, Cooperstown, N.Y.).

the three men, though not more than two of them per season with the White Sox. "Nobody really wanted that job. It was a rogue pitch. It created havoc. I didn't have to fight for that job. Everyone shied away."[1] Nice to know the guy was on those pitchers' side.

Wilbur Wood said that Martin pretty much deserved a Purple Heart or the Congressional Medal of Honor because of the physical beating he took from the knuckleballs flying his way in the 1960s. Martin had his own way of describing what the scene looked like from inside the mask.

"It was exciting because you never knew where the ball was going," Martin said. "Seriously, it could do a 90-degree break and then double back. If you didn't wait, you couldn't see it. You'd have to snatch it when it was right on top of you."[2]

Hoyt Wilhelm

Years later, after all of the individuals were retired, Martin included, he said of the three knuckleballers he caught with the White Sox, Wilhelm had the best one.

"Hoyt had the most consistent pitch," Martin said. "The other guys had good ones, but every so often they'd throw one that would spin and then they'd get hit. Hoyt's always worked."[3]

That actually had to be an overstatement, otherwise Wilhelm would have compiled a 0.00 earned run average. Yet over the long run, he did prove that his knuckleball was superior to the one thrown by almost anyone else who ever had the pitch.

Although Wilhelm's won-loss record was nothing to brag about in 1963, his overall work performance was excellent for the White Sox, showing once more that even at 40 he was young for his age and it was too soon for ballclubs to give up on him and push him toward retirement. Hoyt finished 5–8, but his ERA was a fine 2.64. While appearing in 55 games (three of them starts), Wilhelm accumulated 21 saves. He was still someone to be reckoned with coming out of the bullpen. He was on the mound to finish 40 games, basically one-quarter of the time when the last out was recorded for Chicago.

Although not the hardest hitting of teams, this White Sox edition fared well, going 94–68 in 1963. Players who came with Wilhelm in the big trade made contributions. Third baseman Ward smacked 22 home runs, drove in 84 runs and batted .295. Hansen hit 13 homers with 67 RBIs, though his average was a lowly .226. Nicholson may have hit 22 home runs with 70 runs batted in, but his .229 average reflected striking out 175 times, one of the major problems in his career.

The ace of the staff was southpaw Gary Peters at 19–8 and Juan Pizarro went 16–8. Eddie Fisher was there, the complementary knuckleball thrower whose record was 9–8 with a 3.95 earned run average. Wilhelm tossed 136⅓ innings and Fisher 120⅔. Fisher was then 26 years old, 14 years younger than Wilhelm, and he did make semi-regular starts, 15 times in 33 games, even if he was primarily a reliever and spent more time time in that job. It was a rare occasion, particularly compared to the modern era, when two top-notch knuckleballers came out of the bullpen to throw so many innings.

Wilhelm adjusted quite easily to the White Sox way of life. He just kept doing what he had always done, counting on his out pitch as his every pitch, the knuckler that had carried him so far.

A Chicago newspaper story pointed out that only Early Wynn and Warren Spahn were other hurlers in the majors in the 40-plus age

16. Good Company

category. Although it was not known at the time, all three of them would end up being elected to the Hall of Fame. Wilhelm's achievements were starting to be noticed, and by Jerome Holtzman, the legendary baseball writer and baseball historian, who said, "He has as distinguished a record as any big-league pitcher in the modern era."[4]

Accomplishments such as being the only pitcher to lead both leagues in earned run average and a career posting of a 2.74 ERA being the lowest of any pitcher since the end of the Deadball Era in 1920 were highlighted. Holtzman asked Wilhelm to reflect on his career and he noted how Leo Durocher and the New York Giants turned him into a bullpen cure in 1952.

"I was it," he said of filling the need for Durocher. "Then I had the big year and I was a relief pitcher from then on. If I had just been fair in relief, maybe I would have been a starting pitcher all these years and everything would have been different."[5]

Wilhelm was self-aware enough to realize throwing the knuckler is what provided his longevity because the lack of strain on his arm. That was why, even as he watched other pitchers age out of the game, he did not yet feel threatened by aging.

"I haven't given any thought to quitting," Wilhelm said. "Why should I? I don't see why I can't pitch three or four more years, barring injury. I throw now as hard as I ever did. Anyway, it's not how hard you throw, but what the ball does. I still don't know which way it's going to go, but I can throw it for strikes."[6]

Ballplayers reading Wilhelm's comments probably chuckled at his mention of throwing as hard as he ever did since the running joke with his stuff was about how slowly it traveled. But Wilhelm didn't mean it as a joke, only an observation of reality.

Unlike his knuckleball partner Wilhelm, Eddie Fisher got his first sniff of the majors when he was just 22, almost 10 years younger than Wilhelm was when he got called up. Fisher broke in with the San Francisco Giants in 1959, coming off a one-hitter thrown for minor-league Phoenix. It was common knowledge he threw a knuckler, and when he was brought up from the lower level in June, he was asked to talk about it.

"It has no pattern," Fisher said. "The wind determines the break of the knuckler. Sometimes it breaks in. Another time it darts down and out. I throw it like a fastball, but off the nails of the first two fingers. So far, I've had good control of it."[7]

His words pretty much echoed what Wilhelm had been telling

people for years. It was almost as if they had attended the same lectures at school.

Also shades of Wilhelm, in his wake Fisher left a trail of wounded catchers—both physically and mentally—as he rose to the majors. Al Stieglitz, who was a catcher handling the Fisher knuckler in minor-league clubs Corpus Christi and Phoenix, was bloodied by Fisher more than once, almost as if he was a sparring partner taking punches.

Fisher explained that during the playoffs the year before one of his knucklers "took off and caught Al above the right eye. It took 15 stitches to close the cut. Poor guy." More recently, before being brought up from Phoenix, Fisher had unfurled a knuckler that ripped open one of Stieglitz' index fingers for five more stitches. "He's still recovering," Fisher said.[8]

Despite paying his dues and playing with pain, Stieglitz never advanced beyond AAA to make an appearance in the majors. On the assumption he would make the jump to the majors, Topps, the maker of baseball cards, did issue a 1960 cardboard image of Stieglitz, heralding him as a rookie star.

Appropriately enough, Fisher said he was inspired to adopt the knuckleball by Wilhelm's success with it. Before turning pro, Fisher pitched at the University of Oklahoma, but he said he was prohibited from using the knuckler at the time.

"I kept working with it," Fisher said. "Actually, it came pretty easy for me. But my college coach wouldn't let me use it. He called it an old man's pitch."[9] Now that was an insult that had been in the minds of many over the years, until they swung and missed at it.

Despite getting that early opportunity with San Francisco and being heralded upon his arrival in the bigs, Fisher had a somewhat messy beginning. Following a pleasant debut, a win over the Pittsburgh Pirates in which he threw his knuckler 25 percent of the time, Fisher's good vibes faded pretty quickly.

Fisher, who had gained renown nationally as an American Legion star for throwing six no-hitters in high school, including a perfect game, was already conversant with the knuckler, but he had not completely harnessed it after all, going 2–6 with a 7.88 earned run average that season.

Fisher spent most of 1960 in the minors, going just 1–0 for the Giants. A year later, in a little bit more action, he went 0–2 in 15 games. None of that seemed to impress San Francisco. On November 30, 1961, the Giants sent Fisher and three others, including a player to be named

16. Good Company

later, to the White Sox for Don Larsen and Billy Pierce, two throwers with much bigger names.

Turning 25, Fisher began to blossom with the White Sox during the 1962 season, finishing 9–5 with a 3.10 ERA, a vast improvement. He was used in 57 games and finished 19 out of the bullpen, his stock rising with his new team.

On December 2, 1963, a few months after the first collaborative season shared by Wilhelm and Fisher with the White Sox, the Major League Baseball Rules Committee met and one of the votes taken phased out the Paul Richards oversized catcher mitt designed to aid knuckleball hurlers. The new rule took effect for the 1965 season.

Since Richards and Wilhelm were no longer affiliated with the Orioles, where all of the first attention was focused, it mattered not to the Baltimore franchise. Richards had decamped to Houston, where as general manager he was trying to build an expansion team's foundation.

Houston actually employed a couple of guys who used the knuckler some of the time, including Ken Johnson, who went 11–17 in 1963 though he had better success in ensuing years. The other was Bobby Tiefenauer, who passed through in 1962 only. That season, Houston catchers, who did employ the outsized glove, still committed 25 passed balls and were victimized by 74 wild pitches, so it didn't do them much good.

Eventually, the very first Big Bertha glove was sent to the National Baseball Hall of Fame in Cooperstown for its permanent collection.

When Wilhelm learned the big glove could no longer be used, he did not sound particularly upset. It was easy enough to read his thinking. Even if the original was introduced for his benefit in theory, it was utilized in reality to help catchers. The knuckler did what it wanted to do.

The new rule restricted the catcher's mitts to 34 inches.

"I don't know what their idea is," was Wilhelm's first reaction. "We'll just have to wait and see. What possible harm can the big mitt do?" Even though Al Lopez responded with disappointment and said it could deprive his man Hoyt of making a living, Wilhelm did not react quite so strongly. "I don't think it will be that bad. I've only been throwing to the big mitt for almost three years and I had some good years before it came along."[10]

Indeed, Wilhelm noted one of his best seasons was recorded in 1959 when he won 15 games for the Orioles and won the AL earned run average title, and that was the year before Richards introduced the bigger glove.

Richards was steamed when he heard of the Rules Committee's ban, much angrier than Wilhelm.

"Now what's wrong with a catcher using a bigger glove to catch a knuckleball?" Richards said. "From the time Abner Doubleday invented the game [the popular thought on the sport's origins for a time], there never was anything in the rules limiting the size of a catcher's glove. And now that a bigger mitt is necessary because of a new type of pitch, they restrict the size of it. It just doesn't make sense. Actually, the size of the catcher's glove for knuckleball pitching would take care of itself. No catcher will use a glove that's too big for him to handle."[11]

Intriguingly, Wilhelm offered some thoughts about the passed ball in general in baseball, not something that had been widely discussed over the years, but understandable because it had become such a nemesis for him, his catchers and his teams.

"I don't see what a team proves when it scores on a passed ball," he said. "I think that when a man strikes out, he should be out. It's OK for runners to move up on a passed ball, but I can't see why they give a man first base when he strikes out. If they're going to give the batter the advantage, why don't they just put him on first base to start with."[12]

He did not really see the elimination of the big mitt as a real game-changer, though he admitted catchers probably were able to better stifle potential passed balls with it than with a regular mitt.

"There probably will be a few more passed balls," Wilhelm said. "But what harm does a passed ball do if the other team doesn't score on it? Just think how many games are won and lost on errors each year."[13]

At different times, catchers who effectively used the Big Bertha glove to help them block knuckleballs admitted the sheer size of the mitt got in the way of some other tasks. Even Wilhelm agreed the biggest of the over-sized gloves may have been too big.

"Sometimes our catchers did have trouble getting the ball out of the glove and it made stealing easier," he said.[14]

Wilhelm did observe the White Sox already had big mitts on hand before he joined the club, and knuckleballer Eddie Fisher had been throwing to catchers using them.

The mere presence of Wilhelm on the same team was very helpful to Fisher in his own development of the knuckleball he already had but which needed maturing. He said being around the veteran,

16. Good Company

watching his preparation, the way he threw, and how he reacted to different situations in games, improved his own knuckleball use. It was not only observation of a man who was the acknowledged leader of the knuckleball world, but it was also spending time with Wilhelm during spring training, during the season, in workouts, in the dugout, and in the clubhouse that helped. Sessions were part of a long-form tutorial and Fisher was a sponge soaking up the Wilhelm's knowledge.

"Just being around a guy who is that successful with the knuckler has helped a lot," Fisher said. "I came to the White Sox with an average knuckleball. I thought it was pretty good, but nothing like Hoyt's. I learned how to use the knuckler by watching Wilhelm in a game. I go with the pitch more now. When it's working, I will use it 75 to 80 percent of the time."[15]

Fisher showed steady improvement with his knuckler during the 1964 season, going 6–3 in 59 outings and scoring nine saves for the White Sox while dropping his earned run average during the second half of the season. He was about to get better yet, the next two years in a row leading the American League in appearances and in 1965 winning a career-high 15 games.

Wilhelm used the knuckler even more often than Fisher did, often 90 percent of the time in games, and his long usage of it added up too. One of Wilhelm's regular victims was outfielder Jimmy Piersall, a natural right-handed batter who said he could not make safe contact with Wilhelm's ball swinging his normal way. "My one chance against a knuckler is to bat left-handed," Piersall said. "When I bat left-handed, Wilhelm gets mad. Maybe he'll walk me."[16]

The besieged catcher, J.C. Martin, who probably abhorred the thought, was asked if the knuckleball was so hard to hit, why didn't everyone throw it.

"A pitcher can't acquire a knuckler just like that," Martin said. "He has to work on it and then work on it some more. If he starts to get hit, the manager tells him to get rid of the pitch."[17]

Martin was probably right about that. Since there were so few knuckleball specialists and even fewer really successful ones, it was hard to get a manager to trust a knuckleballer, especially coming out of the bullpen when men were on base.

Al Lopez actually yanked Fisher from a 1962 game when the pitcher showed doubt over his knuckler. Trying to throw a slider past slugger Rocky Colavito that resulted in a three-run homer got Fisher

Hoyt Wilhelm

ousted. "He should have thrown the knuckler," the boss said. "That's his out pitch."[18] Apparently, Lopez was all in on the knuckler from Fisher.

Lopez was clear about being all in with his support of Wilhelm and his knuckler, a man with a longer track record of success.

"I was so darned tired of trying to beat Wilhelm when he pitched for Baltimore that we went out and traded for him," Lopez said.[19]

17

Wilbur and Hoyt

Wilbur Wood came to the church of the knuckleball late compared to Hoyt Wilhelm and others who were grounded in the pitch early in their throwing days.

Wood was a pitcher who showed great promise. He had a multitude of weapons and skills, and none of the pitches on his personal-use list was the knuckler. While Wilhelm began throwing the knuckleball in his teens, Wood only turned to the knuckler out of desperation, a late attempt to salvage a big-league career that was turning sour.

It always seemed to be one extreme or the other for the successful knuckleball guys. The Wilhelm way called for early-in-life commitment. The Wood way came about when living on the edge and hoping for the best.

During this stretch of the 1960s and somewhat beyond, the Chicago White Sox became an extraordinary haven for butterfly pitchers of renown with Wilhelm, Eddie Fisher and Wood following one another on the roster or overlapping on the roster.

Some baseball people with short memories or lack of awareness believe Wilhelm taught the knuckler to Wood and that it rescued his career. Not quite. They did not spend that much time together with the White Sox and Wood had already turned his attention to the knuckler and was switching his focus to it by the time he met Wilhelm. Wilhelm, however, was an influence on Wood's development.

Indeed, in some ways during his own unusual and at times spectacular career, Wood outshone Wilhelm and accomplished pitching feats that seem almost dream-like for starting pitchers in the 2020s.

A few things stand out. Wood had seasons when he pitched with two days' rest between starts. He had seasons when he won 20 games and lost 20 games. And one year he threw 376⅔ innings, a total not exceeded over the last 100-plus years and only rarely approached.

Wood first pitched for the White Sox in 1967 after struggles with

Hoyt Wilhelm

other teams. Wilhelm was a member of the team for one season after '67, so they did have those two seasons together as a knuckleball duo. Eddie Fisher was off to the Orioles in the middle of the 1966 season, so at no time did all three of them simultaneously inhabit the White Sox roster.

Born in 1941, Wood was from the Boston area, a high school star in Belmont who signed with the hometown Red Sox. A six-foot, 180-pound left-hander, Wood got his first taste of the majors briefly in 1961 when he was just 19.

A high school phenom who also played football and hockey, Wood received feelers from 50 colleges to play some sport. Although his go-to

Catcher J.C. Martin handled Wilhelm's knuckleball between 1963 and 1967. He sometimes felt as if he was going to war when he caught knucklers from Wilhelm and Wilbur Wood with the Chicago White Sox. They joked that he deserved a medal for all the flak he took (National Baseball Hall of Fame Library, Cooperstown, N.Y.).

pitches were the fastball and the curve, tellingly, and importantly for his future, his father, Wilbur Sr., who had been a semi-pro pitcher, taught him how to throw a knuckler. It just remained basically on the shelf.

The very beginning of Wood's big-league years followed the same pattern as his last teenaged year. The Red Sox would throw him in a small number of games, he would fail to emerge victorious, and he would mostly spend time at minor-league affiliates.

Between 1961 and 1964, small parts of four seasons, Wood made cameos for the Red Sox, appearing in a total of 36 games (25 in 1963). His record was 0–5 by then. In September of 1964, the Red Sox gave up on him and sold Wood to the Pittsburgh Pirates.

For the rest of 1964 and for the 1965 season Wood was property

17. Wilbur and Hoyt

of the Pirates. Though he saw more action in '65, pitching in 34 games, mostly in relief, he only sometimes flashed his original promise. Wood did finally win his first Major League game and his earned run average was a solid 3.16 in 51⅓ innings. Sent back to the minors in 1966, though, a demoralized Wood told his wife Sandy he was going to retire. But she talked him into giving his baseball career another try while stressing the knuckler and the Pirates swapped him to the White Sox for a player to be named later. The player was pitcher Juan Pizarro.

It was then, as a 25-year-old in Chicago, that Wood found himself, re-connected with his old self by choosing to cast his lot with the knuckleball. In 1967, he went 4–2 with a sparkling 2.45 ERA in 51 games. Gradually, over the next few seasons, Wood emerged as a star, first out of the bullpen and then as the busiest starter around. He appeared in more games than any other pitcher and started more games than any other pitcher in the league.

As had been mentioned by Wilhelm and other knuckleball specialists, grips differed between hurlers. Wilhelm was constantly trimming his fingernails to what he considered the proper length for the best way to hold the ball. Wood, it turned out, was like a youngster in his approach. He bit his nails, *The Sporting News* told the world, except for those on the first two fingers of his left hand.

Previously hesitant to go all-in on the knuckler, during his time away from the game, Wood completely adopted the tricky pitch and it was his entrée to steady work. First, he had that solid season out of the bullpen in '67. He followed up in 1968 with an even better year. Wood's record was 13–12. His earned run average was 1.87 in 159 innings. He finished 46 games but was used in a league-leading 88 games. Wood was so ubiquitous he received some votes for Most Valuable Player.

That same season Wilhelm finished 4–4 with a 1.73 ERA in 72 showings. They were quite the formidable 1–2 men in quelling rallies, Wilhelm and his quasi-protégé. The only problem was that there were too many rallies to shut down since the White Sox went 67–95 after being pennant contenders in 1967. It was a season of disarray, with Eddie Stanky, Les Moss, and then Al Lopez coming back, sharing big hunks of the season as manager. No one could blame Wood or Wilhelm for the team faltering from the previous season's 89 wins.

Interestingly, before Wood even showed up, it was Wilhelm and Fisher as the double knuckleballers for the White Sox potentially being affected by the Major League Rules Committee killing the specs for the oversized mitt of Paul Richards.

Hoyt Wilhelm

However, the team planned for the future. Under the direction of Al Lopez, in anticipation of the ban taking effect in 1965 when the maximum circumference would be restricted to 38 inches, the team had done some advance work to perhaps help their catchers. The White Sox went shopping, putting in an order with Wilson Sporting Goods, makers of the original big glove.

Over the decades, catcher's mitts had appeared somewhat flat. The new one Lopez sought had a much deeper pocket and more resembled the flexibility of a first-baseman's glove. That was the target Wilhelm and Wood were aiming at, another knuckleballing specialty.

"Actually, this mitt right now measures only 36 inches," Lopez said. "We had it made 38 inches, but when the lacing was added, it pulled the mitt in two inches. Now we're having another one made with the leather cut for 40 inches. When it's laced, it will come within the 38-inch maximum rule."[1]

While Wilhelm had expressed no particular worry about the elimination of the original big glove because of the change, he expressed enthusiasm about this new variation—on behalf of his catchers.

"This may even be better than the one Richards had made for Gus Triandos because it's more like a fielder's glove," Wilhelm said. "I know it's [the knuckler] hard to catch because you can't tell which way the ball is going to break. But then again, that's what makes it a tough pitch to hit. The only problem is to get it over the plate and then hope the catcher can at least knock it down. I've put a couple of catchers in the record book with passed balls."[2]

J.C. Martin seemed to have the best handle on Wilhelm's knuckler, but that was a relative term. One of Wood's main White Sox catchers was Ed Herrmann. In the minors, Herrmann was regarded as an excellent fielder and he was often praised for his skills in coping with the knuckler when he worked with Wood. Yet Herrmann still led the American League in passed balls four times. Hazard of the job.

Clearly, catchers were important partners for the knuckleball throwers, but the main responsibility always rested with the pitchers to put the ball where it could not be hit and it could be caught. Wood was a compadre of Wilhelm's, but they were not identical, either in background or at the stages of their career. Wood was a next-generation knuckleballer as Wilhelm turned 45 in 1968.

Perhaps because Wilhelm was 19 years older than Wood when they were teammates, there has sometimes been a misconception that the older hurler taught the knuckler to the younger one. Wood already

17. Wilbur and Hoyt

had knowledge of the knuckler and was making the switch to rely on it before he first teamed with Wilhelm. Wood always tried to draw that distinction.

"The question was always asked because of the overlap," Wood said in an interview in 2022. "My father did help me more than anybody else. When I switched to the knuckler, I thought, 'Either I'm going to make it or I'm going home.' I started using the knuckleball more and more. If you're going to throw the knuckleball, you've got to throw it and throw it and throw it. For me it was more than 90 percent of the time."[3]

Wood was grateful to Wilhelm in a general way, as a great example to follow, as proof someone tossing the knuckleball could achieve success, and as a role model right there in the same dugout. He understood how Wilhelm was sometimes given all the credit for Wood's knuckleball success, but he said that wasn't the truth, overlooking the fact that while he did not use it when he was young, he did have the background and had made the individual choice to give his dream one last run with the knuckler.

"I was ready to pack it in until the White Sox got me," Wood said. "Then I decided to give it one more try, to go with the knuckleball. If that didn't work, I was going to get into some other field."[4]

It is possible, since Wood said he could throw a knuckler as early as junior high but never used it in a game growing up, that he was even younger than Wilhelm when he became aware of the option. That was more a prelude to his origin story, since the knuckler wasn't doing him any good if he wasn't throwing it.

On the Hoyt-as-teacher part, Wood said, "That's the popular version, but it just isn't true. As I say, I'd been throwing knuckleballs for years. Hoyt did give me one big lift, though. He told me that in order to be effective, you had to throw the knuckleball more than 75 percent of the time and take your chances. I had nothing to lose, so I took his advice."[5]

Wood and Wilhelm had that one shared very fine year together in 1968, but Wood was still looking forward to a series of remarkable seasons that became the talk of the sport. The reason he was able to do what he did was his use of the knuckleball, but the kinds of feats he recorded defied several norms of the moment for pitchers of any kind. Especially given the way pitchers have become more protected with caps on their innings pitched, the comparative infrequency of their starts, and the way their arms are babied, Wood was such an outlier anyone in the present-day game would only reel in astonishment studying his career.

Hoyt Wilhelm

While their accomplishments stand on their own, and differ, and Wilhelm did not teach Wood the knuckler, it is possible Wood may not have had a team in his corner providing the opportunity to achieve what he did if Wilhelm had not come first or been present at the same time for some of it.

Wood retained deep respect for Wilhelm's longevity and deeds, with bonus points for how many of his games and innings were recorded coming into games in relief, with men on base and in scoring position.

"He had to have one of the best knuckleballs ever," Wood said. "Coming out of the bullpen as he did, he couldn't afford a mistake. That is the story right there."[6]

For a few years in the late 1960s and the early 1970s, Wood faced some of the same problems Wilhelm did. Wood was a reliever with a knuckleball and dealing with catchers who had to always be on their toes, big gloves, regular gloves, or whatever, to maintain control of the pitch as it crossed the plate.

In 1969, with Wilhelm gone elsewhere, Wood had a 10–11 record with a 3.01 earned run average. He led the AL by pitching in 76 games and he finished 50 of them. In 1970, Wood's record was only 9–13, but his ERA was 2.81 and for the third year in a row he led league pitchers in appearances with 77. He finished 62 games, also a league high.

Then, as had happened with Wilhelm, a manager got the idea of trying to use his most valuable pitching weapon as a member of the starting rotation instead of out of the bullpen. The 1970 season began with Don Gutteridge as manager, but sometimes it seemed as if only Wood was playing well for him. The team was 49–87 when he was ousted and Bill Adair (4–6) took over for 10 games before Chuck Tanner (3–13) wrapped up the dismal 56–106 season.

This was a totally lost season for Chicago. General manager Ed Short was fired in September. The team's attendance of 495,355 was 12th and last in the American League. Tommy John, he of the future famous arm surgery, was the leading starter at 12–17. There was some good hitting provided, including a .313 average by future Hall of Fame shortstop Luis Aparicio, who had come back from the Orioles. Third baseman Bill Melton hit 33 home runs.

The world changed dramatically for Wood during the 1971 season. He was hardly an unknown at this point after leading the league in outings for three straight seasons, but he was typecast as a reliever. During those three preceding years, Wood had thrown 159, 119⅔ and 121⅔ innings. He had not started a game in three seasons.

17. Wilbur and Hoyt

Welcome to the new Wilbur, a fresh version of the southpaw knuckleballer who baffled more hitters than ever, startled fans, and confused opposing management. His across-the-board statistics were viewed as outrageous for a guy turning his career around completely at age 29.

In 1971, Wood's won-loss record was 22–13. His earned run average was 1.91. His appearances dropped to 44, but 42 of those games were starts. He hurled 334 innings and was chosen for his first All-Star team. This was all done for a still sub-par (if slightly improved) 79–83 team.

When visiting sportswriters came to Comiskey Park, they wanted to talk to Wilbur. When the White Sox went on the road, sportswriters wanted to talk to Wilbur. Essentially, he was an overnight celebrity in the game and, naturally, the quirky knuckleball element made his story even more compelling.

In 1946, Cleveland Indians Hall of Famer Bob Feller led the AL with 371⅓ innings pitched. After that, the league leader in the category of most innings pitched per season trended mostly downward. Only one pitcher in the league, Bob Lemon, another member of the Indians in 1952, had broken 300 innings until Jim Kaat did it in 1965.

Then there was another uptick leading up to Wood's year, starting with Denny McLain with 336 innings pitching for the Detroit Tigers in 1968, McLain again, Sam McDowell and Jim Palmer also topping 300. In 1971, Mickey Lolich hurled 376 innings, the most in either the AL or NL since Grover Cleveland Alexander tossed 388 for the Phillies in 1917. It had been about 60 years since anyone in the American League topped that with the 393 innings hurled by "Big Ed" Walsh of the White Sox in 1912.

Lolich's effort became particularly relevant because the very next season, Wood bested that total by ⅔ of an inning. Wood's 376⅔ innings thrown in 1972 remains the highest number of innings pitched in Major League Baseball since Alexander's total 106 years ago. And that was just the second season of four in a row that Wood threw more than 320 innings in a season. It was no wonder people began to talk about him and wanted to learn more about him and the knuckler starting in 1971.

By the middle of that summer, baseball observers were taking note that Wood was doing some special things. A headline in the *New York Daily News* read, "Name's Wood, but his Arm Is Made of Rubber." By that time, he had won 12 games and one scribe compared him to "Iron Man" McGinnity, because he had just made a second straight start on only two days' rest. Even that early in his several-year streak of staying extremely busy, Wood had begun discussing his yearning to start both games of a doubleheader one day. "I just might let him do it," manager Chuck Tanner said.[7]

Even in the early 1970s, most pitchers started every fourth day. After his pace of starting every two days, Wood was not scheduled for three days and a sportswriter jokingly called that a veritable vacation. "It's as though Wood is gluttonizing to make up for lost time," a writer said, referring to his time devoted to shorter relief stints. "For years, he got only the crumbs. He was a reliever. He got lots of crumbs. One year, 88 of them, a record, but no starts."[8]

Once Wood realized the knuckler was his pitch and subscribed to the philosophy also espoused by Wilhelm, he felt it critical to throw as often as possible during the season. He didn't want to get stale and believed that only constant repetition with the strange pitch would produce good results.

"The only way to stay strong is to throw," Wood said. "You can run till the cows come home and the only thing that gets strong is your legs."[9]

There was no doubt Wood was thriving on more action and loving being a starter with predictability in his routine, not to mention the success. Still, that did not mean the knuckleball was obeying all commands from Wood all the time.

On the occasion of moving to 16–9 on the season with a 4–2 win over the Detroit Tigers, a complete-game decision, Wood commented that his knuckler may have proven effective that August 18 in Chicago, but it was a little bit deceptive. "This was one of the most strenuous games of my career," he said. "I couldn't control my knuckleball. It was going all over the place."[10] Yet he walked just two and struck out nine while allowing only seven hits and those two runs. There were no passed balls listed in the box score, which meant Herrmann must have performed extra sharp work behind the plate.

When Wood finished his season with 22 victories, that marked the most by a White Sox pitcher since Early Wynn's same total in 1959 when the team won the pennant. Wood ended up third in the Cy Young Award voting. Right to the end of the season, he was still surprising people who couldn't get over that he was not just a relief pitcher.

"I always knew I could do it," Wood said. "But nobody would listen."[11] Nobody but his wife Sandy, that is, and Wood did not overlook Wilhelm as a mentor contributing to this success.

"The conditions were perfect for me when I got to the White Sox," Wood said. "Hoyt was there. You couldn't ask for anything better. He

17. Wilbur and Hoyt

taught me more about the knuckleball in one day than I ever knew before. He took me aside in spring training and, in five minutes, he showed me why the knuckleball was good and why it was bad. I never can thank him enough. He helped me correct some flaws and kept harping at me, 'You've got to keep throwing it. Keep throwing it.'"[12]

If anyone believed Wood had just turned in a once-in-a-lifetime season, all they had to do was wait until the next spring training of 1972 as he resumed the same type of showing all over again, only slightly better. Wood's roll did not seem to know any calendar boundaries.

During the 1972 campaign, his record was 24–17, the number of wins leading the American League. He started a league-high 49 games. Although his ERA went up a little bit, it was still excellent at 2.51 and he was chosen for the All-Star team again. Most astounding was his durability, putting up those 376⅔ innings in a single season, just two-thirds more than Lolich had recorded.

Since Lolich had recorded his own high number just a year before, it was not likely at that time people thought Wood's total of innings pitched in a season would retain such longevity. The last time anyone in the American League was the circuit leader with more than 300 innings was 1977 when Jim Palmer of the Orioles threw 319 innings. In 1980, Steve Carlton threw 304 innings for the World Series champion Phillies. In the 2000s, even cresting 250 innings has become unusual.

Actually, in 1972, Wood threw so many innings with the arm some dubbed "Rubber Hose" he also led the American League in negative categories such as 325 hits allowed and 105 earned runs. But that didn't matter so much since he was on the mound more than other pitchers.

Wood acknowledged that he still dabbled with his fastball and curveball but they had become supplements to his knuckler and they had the reverse effect on hitters. When he was short of making the cut with the Red Sox and the Pirates, counting on those pitches to lead the way, he was falling just short. Once he emphasized the slower knuckler and mixed in the other pitches, they seemed to fool hitters with more regularity.

"The fastball is no faster," Wood said in the midst of his success in 1972, "and the curve doesn't break any sharper. They just look faster and seem to break sharper to hitters who have gone half nuts looking at knucklers."[13]

Wood was known for working quickly on the mound, even if his ball covered the distance to home plate slowly. He was the embodiment of the knuckleball starter who needed less rest than other hurlers who

Hoyt Wilhelm

threw their guts out with fastballs. In 1971, as he was establishing his new status as a starter, Wood started 14 times on just two days' rest. In the modern era, if a pitcher is sent to the mound in an extreme clutch situation, such as a World Series showdown, with only three days' rest, a hurricane of public opinion is unleashed on the manager: he has to be out of his mind for risking the player's career! Yet Wood conditioned his manager Tanner to think differently.

"We can get along with a rotation of three starting pitchers, if we have to," Tanner said. "Wood, two other guys, and Wood."[14]

He didn't really try it, but Tanner's remark spoke to Wood's new status and the fact that he had made true believers out of his employers. Wood kept telling everyone who asked, and many did, that he never got tired, that his arm was never weary, and because his pitch was the knuckler, that he never needed to take time off. He kept stressing what Wilhelm taught him about throwing every day.

"The only times I ever threw every day were in the bullpen," Wood said, even in the season when he set an appearance record with those 88 games. "Even there, I would sometimes miss a day if I had worked relief the day before. But then, with Hoyt's encouragement, I never missed a day, whether I worked long relief or not. And now that I'm a starting pitcher, I still don't miss a day."[15]

For a time during the 1972 season, it seemed possible Wood might match or exceed the modern (post–1900) record for most games started by a pitcher. The mark of 51 was set by Jack Chesbro in 1904 with the New York Highlanders. Chesbro won 41 games that year with a 1.82 earned run average. The National League record is 48 starts by Joe McGinnity of the New York Giants in 1903, which Wood topped, albeit in the other league. Wood may well have set a new record for the AL, except a week and a half of the season was lost to a Major League labor dispute between players and owners. The decision was made not to make up the games.

Wood was not boastful about his capability of pitching often on little rest, not feeling he was a one-of-a-kind guy, but the only one willing to give it a shot.

"Really, a lot of other pitchers could work on short rest if they tried," Wood said.[16] That was really speculation, because no other pitcher was clamoring to be used as a starter quite so often.

Since Wood set his appearance mark of 88 games in 1968, it has been matched or exceeded many times. The all-time record is 106 games by reliever Mike Marshall of the Los Angeles Dodgers in 1974. That is

17. Wilbur and Hoyt

one of 18 times Woods' 88-game standard has been equaled or surpassed. The most recent occasion was the 2010 season by Pedro Feliciano with the New York Mets, who threw in 92 games that year. No one besides Marshall has gone over 100 games. Kent Tekulve of the Pittsburgh Pirates surpassed Wood three times, with seasons of 94 games (1979), 91 (1978) and 90 (1987) with the Philadelphia Phillies.

Actually, it was neither Wood himself nor his manager Tanner who first contemplated the notion that the lefty could perhaps work on as little as two days' rest. It wasn't something Wilhelm thought up. The idea came from White Sox pitching coach Johnny Sain, himself a star pitcher for the Braves when they were still in Boston.

"He's an amazing man," Sain said of Wood. "Wilbur has tremendous poise. He doesn't let anything bother him."[17]

In 1972, the question regarding Wood following his extraordinary 1971 season was, "Can he do it again?" Well, he did do it again. The same question arose for 1973, and there was Wood, floating that darned knuckleball past hitters as well as ever and doing so with mound showings more often than any other starter again. That year, Wood matched his 24-win total of the prior year, though his record was 24–20 and his ERA rose a bit to 3.46. He again led the AL with 48 games started and with 359⅓ innings.

During the 1973 season, one of Wood's long-held wishes came true. He nagged, lobbied and begged enough that Tanner gave in and allowed him to attempt to pitch both ends of a doubleheader as a starter. Wood had long felt he could pull off the daunting assignment, though he did say the best-case scenario was that the first nine innings would speed by.

Events did not play out as anticipated on July 20 for two games against the New York Yankees in Yankee Stadium. It was a nightmare of a day for Wood. The Yankees beat the White Sox, 12–2 and 7–0, and Wood took the loss in both games.

Going for his 19th victory, Wood was clobbered, not getting out of the first inning before allowing six runs on four hits and a walk. He was relieved quickly by fellow knuckleballer Eddie Fisher, who didn't have the best day of his career either, permitting 10 hits and three runs over five innings. Wood fared only slightly better in the second game, lasting 4⅓ innings and giving up seven runs on five hits. Oops.

"He could have won the second game," Tanner said of Wood pitching on three and a half hours' rest instead of three days' rest. "He was pitching real well. In the first game, he just didn't have it."[18] It may have been a case of the law of averages catching up to Wood anyway, because he had beaten the perennial champion Yankees eight times in a row.

Wood got his chance at the doubleheader and experienced one of the tougher days on the mound.

"I'm not making any excuses," Wood said. "I had good stuff. My knuckler was breaking real good. The heavy air ought to have helped me, too."[19]

Overall, the season's results represented more of the same in 1974, with Wood recording his fourth straight season of at least 20 wins, this time going 20–19 and again leading in starts with 42. His innings pitched were at 320⅓. He made his third All-Star team. In 1975, while the flesh was willing and the time was invested, the results were slightly off. Wood's record was 16–20, the 20 defeats leading the league, and his ERA expanded to 4.11. His innings pitched were at 291⅓.

Over a five-season span, 1971–1975, Wood won 106 games for the White Sox with renewed pitching life due to his allegiance to the knuckleball, his own perseverance and the advice he always cited receiving from Hoyt Wilhelm.

Season after season new sportswriters—and some familiar ones—kept asking Wood how he was able to pitch so often when no one else could. The mystery was not that he was one of the finest knuckleball throwers of his or any era, but that the doubters just couldn't understand how a knuckler worked. He was asked the same questions often over the years.

He always insisted, and Wilhelm backed him up, that it was critical he had begun learning the knuckleball early. Why that made a difference, he couldn't say, nor could Wilhelm help him with that other than insisting it was so.

"He said he didn't know," Wood said. "I have long since learned that if he doesn't know, nobody does. He is not an authority on the knuckleball. He's *the* authority. No man, living or dead, ever knew as much about that pitch as Hoyt Wilhelm."[20]

18

White Sox and Still Going

Hoyt Wilhelm spent six seasons with the Chicago White Sox, at times teaming up with other knuckleball throwers like Eddie Fisher and Wilbur Wood, but at all times showing how it should be done.

After that initial 1963 season with the Sox, even as he passed age 40 and climbed toward 45 and beyond, Wilhelm repeatedly posted eye-opening, astonishing earned run averages that seemed frozen in time from the Deadball Era. Never mind other knuckleball hurlers; no pitchers were as consistent in holding opposing teams without runs.

If the White Sox had been better in the in the standings, Wilhelm's own won-loss record would have undoubtedly been better. But it is hard to imagine how much better his ERA could have been unless he was throwing to Little Leaguers. This is how Wilhelm's streak in Chicago stacked up:

    1963, 5–8, 2.64, 55 games
    1964, 12–9, 1.99, 73 games
    1965, 7–7, 1.81, 66 games
    1966, 5–2, 1.66, 46 games
    1967, 8–3, 1.31, 49 games
    1968, 4–4, 1.73, 72 games

For five straight seasons, Wilhelm did not allow as many as two earned runs a game for the White Sox. He also received no All-Star mention during that period. By the conclusion of that run, Wilhelm was still pitching at 45 years old, an age bracket reached by less than 1 percent of all Major League pitchers throughout history, or to put it another way, by hardly anyone else.

Among position players, notables who appeared in big-league games after the age of 45 include all-time hits leader Pete Rose, 45; Hall of Famer Minnie Minoso, who appeared in a few games once in a while as a stunt in cooperation with team owner Bill Veeck until he was 56;

Hoyt Wilhelm

In 1960, the Baltimore Orioles introduced the Big Bertha catcher's mitt to help the backstops better hold on to Wilhelm's knuckler. Clint Courtney (shown here) was the first on the team to use the oversized glove, which was eventually ruled illegal by Major League Baseball (National Baseball Hall of Fame Library, Cooperstown, N.Y.).

Artie Latham, Hughie Jennings, and Julio Franco, 49; Johnny Evers and Gabby Street, 48; Sam Thompson and Dan Brouthers, 46; and Carlton Fisk, Cap Anson and Ichiro Suzuki, 45.

More pitchers passed that milestone. The astonishing Satchel Paige pitched one inning for the Kansas City Athletics at 59 as part of a promotion, though ironically, for most of his life, Paige's true age was a mystery. He is the oldest individual to play in any Major League game. Jack Quinn, who won 247 games ending in 1933, made two appearances as a 50-year-old.

Other pitchers of some renown who tossed games in the majors after their 45th birthday included Jamie Moyer, Phil Niekro, Nolan Ryan, Charlie Hough, Randy Johnson, Ted Lyons, Tim Wakefield, Roger Clemens, Gaylord Perry and Red Faber. Niekro, Ryan, Johnson, Lyons and Perry are Hall of Famers and Clemens likely will be some

18. White Sox and Still Going

day. Niekro, Hough, Lyons and Wakefield all threw the knuckler. Moyer heaved the ball to the plate so slowly he might as well have.

Not that Wilhelm was retiring at 45. He was just looking for new employment after the White Sox. The team had no evidence he was "slowing down" due to age, or was being hit any harder at 45 than at 35, and let Wilhelm go to the Kansas City Royals in the October 15, 1968, expansion draft. It is possible Chicago felt no fledgling team would select a player of such an age and took the risk of making Wilhelm available to save another, younger body from being picked.

Just reviewing his statistics over his entire stay with the White Sox, the Royals did not have to be pushed too hard to take a flyer on Wilhelm. They didn't have much to lose and everything to gain. Who else on their staff was going to hold opponents to fewer than two runs per game? He could be an elder statesman and steadying influence on younger pitchers just starting out in the majors.

Wilhelm was just happy to stay in the game. When informed the Royals drafted him, he said, "I consider it an honor." He said he was a little bit surprised but wanted to help the expansion team get started. "I figured I would be on the expansion list, but I really didn't think anyone would claim me because of my age."[1]

Although it was likely that an expansion club would be doomed to losing for a while, Wilhelm pointed out that the White Sox hadn't been playing much better in recent years either, not reaching .500.

"Heck, the White Sox were playing for ninth place all season," Wilhelm said of 1967. "I don't see how it could be much worse than that. I think Kansas City could have a pretty good ball club. They've been doing a lot of scouting and everybody says they've got some young kids that can throw real hard."[2]

Wilhelm's wife, Peggy (maiden name Reeves), was from Columbus, Georgia, and at the time of his new affiliation with Kansas City, the family of five, including three children, lived in that town. At one point, Wilhelm had owned a printing business in Columbus, expanded it with a second location in Tampa, Florida, then briefly lived in Atlanta before returning to Columbus. Ultimately, the family settled in Sarasota, Florida.

Even when talking to old newspaper friends, Wilhelm was inevitably asked how long he could keep going at the highest level of baseball. He was the oldest pitcher playing, but he said he didn't think about retiring. He pointed to his recent record—the earned run average over the long haul better than anyone else's on the planet—as proof he still could be at the top of his game.

Hoyt Wilhelm

"Heck, I had a good season with the White Sox this year," Wilhelm said. "Why should I think about quitting as long as I'm going good? If I was getting shellacked, it would be a different matter. But I don't think I've lost any of my effectiveness. That's the fifth straight year I've been under two in ERA. I guess I've been real lucky."[3]

It was obvious the word lucky did not apply to such an extended body of work and Wilhelm did not appear to be speaking sarcastically, so he had to be joking.

In the middle of the summer of 1968, as Wilhelm was rolling toward making 72 appearances on the mound, he broke a 67-year-old Major League record previously owned by the venerable Cy Young, by most standards the greatest pitcher of all time.

Young, born in Ohio in 1867, lived until 1955. A right-hander, Young played for the old Cleveland Spiders and St. Louis Perfectos, plus the Boston Red Sox, the Cleveland Indians when they were called the Naps, and the Boston Braves (aka the Rustlers). He retired from a 22-year career in 1911 as the holder of many of the biggest and most enduring records in the game. Young won 511 games, the most, lost 315, the most, compiled a 2.63 earned run average, pitched the most innings, and importantly, in this instance, pitched in the most games, 906.

No one has ever approached Young's record for victories (Walter Johnson of the Washington Senators is second on the list with 416) and that is why baseball's most coveted pitching honor, the Cy Young Award, is named after him.

However, Wilhelm, while still hurling for the White Sox, etched his name into the record books alongside Young's in July of 1968. On their way to finishing in a tie for eighth place in the American League standings, the White Sox faced the Oakland Athletics, losing 4–0. Although Wilhelm did not absorb the defeat, he did pitch one inning, allowing two hits and a run.

This marked Wilhelm's 906th pitching appearance in a Major League game, tying Cy Young. It's interesting to note that also pitching for the White Sox earlier in the game were Don McMahon and Wilbur Wood, two other knuckleballers. The A's did most of their damage that day off starter Jack Fisher, Wilhelm's old teammate in Baltimore, and he was the one who took the loss.

Two days later, the White Sox met the Athletics again. In the second game of a doubleheader, also a 2–1 loss by Chicago, Wilhelm came to the mound. This time he allowed two hits and a run in ⅓ of an inning

18. White Sox and Still Going

and was slapped with the loss. However, it was the 907th appearance and it broke the Young record.

"I really wanted to break Young's record," Wilhelm said. "It was amazing to me that he had pitched 906 games as a starter. It was downright unbelievable."[4] In actuality, although 815 of his appearances were as a starter, Cy Young did throw some relief. Relief pitching was hardly employed during Young's era, especially not as it is now, and Young threw 749 complete games, also a record. It should also be stated that Young was 44 when he hurled his last game, an oldster himself, particularly for a guy who relied on a fastball, not a so-called junk pitch as Wilhelm's knuckler was sometimes termed.

Wilhelm was asked if someone else might come along to break his new record, which, of course, he kept adding to. If someone like himself could push aside a Cy Young, he wasn't discounting anything. What he was certain of, though, was that a future record-holder would more resemble his way on the mound than Young's in terms of how their longevity played out.

"Records are made to be broken," Wilhelm said. "But I think it will take someone with an off-speed pitch like the knuckler or the fork ball. It will probably have to be a relief pitcher, but a relief pitcher who relies on the fastball usually doesn't last more than five or six years."[5]

One guy Wilhelm knew very well was pretty much taking aim at that record already. Former teammate Eddie Fisher was having so much fun pitching so frequently he kept begging his managers for more work for his own knuckleball. In 1965, Fisher pitched in an American League–high 82 games with the White Sox, going 15–7. The next season, when he was swapped to the Baltimore Orioles after starting with Chicago, he threw in a league-high 67 games.

Over a 15-year career, Fisher moved around after his White Sox stay to Baltimore, to Cleveland, to the California Angels, back to the White Sox and finally to the St. Louis Cardinals, retiring in 1973 at 36 with a lifetime record of 85–70 with 690 appearances. He threw in as many as 67 games for the Angels, but he still felt under-utilized.

"To tell the truth, I think I can pitch 100 games a year," Fisher said.[6]

During his Angels days, Fisher routinely exceeded 100 innings in relief in a season, going as high as 130⅓ in 1970. When informed he was keeping up a potential record pace, Fisher responded, "I guess I should either ask for a raise, or be tired."[7]

As well-known as Fisher was as a big-league ballplayer, an elite profession in American society, and playing in a major market like Chicago, his name often caused confusion because he came to prominence at the same time as the well-known singer Eddie Fisher.

Eddie the Pitcher never made it off the sports pages. But Eddie the Singer was all over the front page and the gossip columns, not only because of his voice and appearances in movies. At one time he was married to actress Debbie Reynolds, who was best friends with Elizabeth Taylor, the premier screen star of the time. Together they had daughter Carrie Fisher of *Star Wars* fame. Eddie the Singer broke up with Reynolds and married Taylor. After five years of marriage, they divorced and he married singer Connie Stevens. Eddie the Pitcher's knuckleball could not compete with that for attention. He did say once in a while there was confusion over what he wrote when he signed an autograph for a less knowledgeable fan.

Long before hitters routinely strolled to the batter's box to selected walk-up music, the organist at Comiskey Park played an Eddie the Singer song when Eddie the Pitcher came on in relief.

By the time Fisher was in his mid–30s, quite unlike Wilhelm, his pace of pitching slowed way down. (As of 2022, he ranked 92nd on the all-time list of number of appearances with 690.) As solid a career as Fisher was able to amass using the knuckleball, he admitted his handling of the risky and tricky pitch could not equal Wilhelm's capabilities with the weapon.

He also admitted that if he tried to count on his best fastball to win the way Nolan Ryan was able to blow people away, his would not measure up.

"Mine would be like a Model A to a Rolls Royce," Fisher said of his speediest pitch.[8]

When Fisher first came to the White Sox, his knuckleball situation resembled Wilbur Wood's to some degree. He knew how to throw one, but he only used it intermittently, perhaps 20 percent of the time. It was joining up with Wilhelm on the Sox roster in 1963 that pushed him into the camp of the full-time knuckleball men.

"We'd be out there together in the bullpen almost every day," Fisher said, "and, as a couple of guys who threw the knuckler, we'd talk shop. He kept hammering away at me to throw the knuckler more. He insisted it was my 'out' pitch and he finally convinced me. When I first threw the knuckler in the minors, or even at the start in the majors, I'd use it only when I was ahead of the hitter. Now I use it in all circumstances. I've been blessed with a strong arm, which is essential to being a successful reliever."[9]

18. White Sox and Still Going

It was not as if Wilhelm taught classes in large lecture halls at universities on how to throw the knuckleball. He did work hard to teach teammates who already had some familiarity with the knuckler how to improve it. In that sense, pitchers like Fisher and Wood with the White Sox also continued Wilhelm's legacy with the club after he had moved on to another team.

Wood won 20 or more games four years in a row for the White Sox, and partially watching Wilhelm shrug off birthdays from afar, he was one player who thought he could pitch forever by using the strain-free knuckleball. He practically never felt the slightest twinge in his left arm from over-throwing, over-work, or any of the usual ailments associated with hard-throwing pitchers, so his confidence built on that front.

Only then he was blindsided. What ruined Wood's career was a totally different type of unforeseen injury. He threw and threw constantly, daily, as instructed by Wilhelm, and his arm only grew stronger, not wearier. He was the ultimate pitching machine in terms of not wearing down, with his volunteering to pitch same-day doubleheaders, on one day's rest, or regularly on only two days' rest. Nothing about that kind of workaholic approach on the mound fazed him.

Although Wood experienced an off-year in 1975 with his 16–20 mark, he began the 1976 season pitching like his usual self. By early May he was carrying a 2.24 earned run average and almost humorously and very Wilbur-like had started consecutive games for the White Sox in late April, although in this instance there were days between games.

On May 9, Wood got the call to start from manager Paul Richards, the same Richards who had invented the oversized catcher's mitt for knuckleballers. It was an afternoon game against Detroit at Tiger Stadium and Wood could not know his life would never be the same.

If "humming it" is the right phrase for a knuckleball pitcher, Wood was doing just that in the sixth inning with the Sox leading the Tigers, 2–0, and were on their way to a 4–2 triumph. That turned out not to be the big news of the day, however. In the home half of the inning, Wood induced Tom Veryzer and Gary Sutherland to swat consecutive grounders to shortstop for the first two outs.

Next up was outfielder Ron LeFlore. LeFlore tagged a pitch right back to the mound, a hard line drive that struck Wood in the left knee. The ball bounced away for a single, but Wood was down and out. Replaced on the mound by reliever Clay Carroll, Wood earned the victory that day, but he was in serious trouble. Wood immediately bent over in pain and then fell to the ground, rolling around in agony.

"It was a hell of a lick," Richards said. "He went down like a gored hog."[10]

The hard-hit ball shattered the kneecap. Wood was aided from the ballpark and promptly taken to a local hospital for X-rays, though he knew what the reading would say. Frustratingly, at the moment, Wood felt he was regaining his groove from two seasons earlier.

Though he probably wished he could block out the play, he very clearly remembered the moment of the swing and the contact.

"Ron hit me in the kneecap with a line drive, and it just blew it apart," Wood said. "He swung at a ball using an inside-out swing. That's always the toughest for a pitcher to pick up, because it looks like he's pulling the ball. Instead, he hit it right back up the middle. I never saw it. I wasn't trying to catch it. I was just trying to get out of the way."[11]

It was a debilitating injury, instantly season-ending. Wood went 4–3 that year in just seven appearances and knew it was going to be a hard road back to top form. He was never the same carefree, dominating pitcher. The hard drive not only affected him physically but also mentally. He admitted later it left permanent mental scars, affecting his mound approach.

"LeFlore's shot got to me," Wood said. "I pitched everybody inside, I wasn't going to let them get out on the ball and maybe hit another one back up the middle. It's hard to pitch that way."[12]

Wood did return to the White Sox for the 1977 season, but he was no longer sharp. He went 7–8 with a 4.99 earned run average in 24 games. He gave it another shot, trying to start fresh in 1978, going 10–10, but with an ERA of 5.20. That convinced him to retire at 36 after 17 seasons in the big leagues.

That age was fairly normal for retirement for most players, a good run, but it wasn't unusual for knuckleballers to go on much longer. Wood had planned to pitch until he was much older, maybe until he was pushing 50 as some of that small collection of major leaguers had done.

His final record, after his slow start with those other pitches, was 164–156 with a 3.24 earned run average.

Wood always had nice things to say about his relationship with Wilhelm, who was so helpful, and he remembered him as an all-around good guy.

"He was a great person and outside of baseball he was liked by everyone," Wood said of his old chum. "He had a lot of friends outside of baseball. He wasn't someone looking for the limelight, who presented

18. White Sox and Still Going

himself as 'I'm the greatest thing that ever walked.' He was a hell of a teammate."[13]

Wood was living proof of what could happen to a pitcher to end a career that didn't even stem from an arm injury. Another of Wilhelm's White Sox pitching teammates in the 1960s was a fellow who incurred perhaps the most famous arm injury—and repair—in history. A young Tommy John was on the staff with Wilhelm as a starter and the two men became good friends.

Wilhelm often talked about how his walks in the woods while hunting served a double purpose, as a hobby and as exercise. In fact, with then–White Sox teammate Gary Peters, one year Wilhelm traveled to Colombia in South America to hunt and they were filmed for the popular TV show *The American Sportsman*.

Usually, he hunted closer to home, wherever he was living, North Carolina, Georgia, or Florida, before eventually settling in Sarasota. Sarasota was a good place for golfing and fishing.

"He was an avid golfer," Wilbur Wood said of Wilhelm. "He was a good golfer. He played as much as he could when he had the free time." Wood also said Wilhelm loved to fish. Once, he and Peters "caught a bunch of fish," though he could not recall what kind, and Peters "packed them up and shipped them to Hoyt." The point was mild one-upmanship, showing off a little bit. The package Peters shipped to Wilhelm when he was living somewhere else arrived when he was on an extended trip. "He finally showed up and opened the package." The fish were not as fresh as they had been. "He sure didn't make any fish chowder out of it."[14]

John, from Terre Haute, Indiana, played for the White Sox between 1965 and 1971 and six times won at least 10 games for Chicago. He was a member of the Dodgers in 1974, with a 13–3 record, when he blew out the ulnar collateral ligament in his left elbow, his pitching elbow.

This was a Humpty Dumpty scenario at first. Not all of the doctors and their nurses thought they could put John back together again. However, he underwent experimental surgery and made a brilliant comeback after missing the 1975 season. He came to be called "the Bionic Man," but the operation that rescued his career was termed "Tommy John surgery," giving him a sort of immortality in the pitching fraternity.

The repair job worked beyond all medical professionals' and athletes' wildest dreams. John played parts of 26 seasons through 1989 and won 288 career games.

In his days with the White Sox, before he got hurt and before he

Hoyt Wilhelm

moved permanently to Sarasota, also Wilhelm's home, John said he met Hoyt at spring training. When a group of guys got together to play golf, he said, he was at first left out.

"Then I pitched my first good game at spring training, and he asked, 'T.J., are you going to play golf with us?' said John, who is now turning 80 years old. 'He wanted to see if I was good enough.'"[15]

John was a sinker-curveball pitcher mainly, but partly through his connection to Wilhelm and the example of his knuckler, he had quiet plans for his future after the surgery on his elbow. He was determined to return as a first-rate pitcher.

"I had given myself two years to come back," John said. And if he could not do so with his staple pitches, John said, he intended to turn to the knuckleball full-time as a weapon. "Then I'm going to go down to Sarasota, spend time with Hoyt and learn the knuckleball. I wanted to pitch again and if I couldn't pitch my way, I would throw the knuckleball. He threw it every day in the outfield, playing catch. Every day."[16]

John did recover after missing one entire season. Post-surgery, relying on his usual stuff, he won 20 more games three times for the Dodgers and Yankees.

Wilbur Wood chuckled and then turned serious, upon hearing that long-ago teammate John nearly became a member of the knuckleball fraternity.

"For his sake, I'm glad the surgery worked for him," Wood said. "But knowing the man, he would have had a good knuckleball."[17]

Especially if Hoyt Wilhelm did the teaching.

19

A Thousand Games

Hoyt Wilhelm said he was glad to be taken by the Kansas City Royals in the expansion draft when that franchise came into existence in October of 1968, took it as flattery that he was still wanted by somebody in the big leagues at age 45 as he was approaching his 46th birthday.

No major leaguer, no player, can afford to be terribly choosy at that age if he hopes to remain in the game. However, Wilhelm never actually pitched for the Royals. Turned out someone else was still interested in what work his arm could do for them. Not quite two months later, on December 15, Kansas City traded Wilhelm to the California Angels for Ed Kirkpatrick and Dennis Paepke. Kirkpatrick had a long career after that while batting .238. Paepke survived with a .183 average for a few years.

For Wilhelm, this quick switching of teams represented the beginning of the end of his big-league odyssey, being shuffled from team to team as a hoped-for final piece that might lead to a pennant. There always seemed to be a knuckleball–Hoyt true believer among the general manager fraternity who felt Wilhelm could be a quick fix for his bullpen.

Wilhelm came to be called "Old Sarge" within the sport, harkening back to his days as a World War II hero. But with the Angels, he was still very much an active figure in the bullpen when the 1969 season began. The Angels' hopes of making a good run in the American League fizzled as the season wound down and they finished 71–91–1.

By then Wilhelm was no longer with the club. He had performed well, appearing in 44 games with an earned run average of 2.47, though his record was just 5–7. One team willing to take a flyer on him to finish out the '69 season was the Atlanta Braves. Wilhelm was willing. He was traded with Bob Priddy to Atlanta for Clint Compton and Mickey Rivers and wrapped up the season by throwing in eight games for the Braves with a 2–0 mark and a sterling 0.73 ERA. So, at 46, he ended up 7–7 with an overall 2.19 ERA.

Hoyt Wilhelm

Pitchers did not pitch until they were 46 years old and they did not come back for more after that. For several seasons already, wherever Wilhelm tossed his knuckleball, the sportswriters marveled at his longevity, could not get over his continuing success. He began facing hitters half his age, young enough to be his sons, and he was still confounding them with his bread-and-butter pitch.

This commentary had been underway for some time. In 1963, while he was still in the employ of the White Sox, a headline in *The Sporting News* read, "Hoyt's 40 Now, and He Throws Knuckleball Sharper Than Ever."[1]

"The veteran knuckleballer certainly isn't a ham-and-egger and can stand alone," it was written. "He has as distinguished a record as any big-league pitcher in the modern era." Wilhelm was unimpressed to be informed he was in old-man company. He separated himself from the fastball specialists more likely to feel effects of aging in their arms than a soft thrower like him. "Anyway, it's not how hard you throw, it's what the ball does."[2] Wilhelm made similar statements several times.

And that pre-dated by several years Wilhelm's latest team-hopping as he not only passed 40 but also 41, 42, 43, and 44.

When Wilhelm joined the Angels, the team gleefully recounted his many accomplishments, noting he owned six Major League records, including appearing in the most games (937) and having the most victories in relief (111), plus a few more American League records. Then he was sent to the National League to the Braves.

There was a behind-the-scenes logic to the Braves' acquisition of Wilhelm—the general manager was his old friend Paul Richards, inventor of the oversized catcher's mitt. When Richards obtained Wilhelm, one of the first things he said was that the newcomer could well pitch for "four or five more years." The headline on the *Chicago Tribune* story read, "Hoyt Wilhelm Has a Future with Braves."[3]

All Wilhelm was really asking for after the Angels shipped him out was a present, not a future. Richards was pretty much offering a welcome-home greeting. Besides the 2–0 won-loss record, Wilhelm saved four games among his initial eight appearances for Atlanta. Richards had wanted Wilhelm for the post-season for the team that ended up 93–69 during the regular season, but when the Angels asked waivers on the thrower in August, the Dodgers and Giants jumped in, precluding a deal. Despite his flashy arrival in Atlanta, Wilhelm was ineligible to suit up for the National League West Division championship-winning

19. A Thousand Games

Braves in the playoffs unless the commissioner's office offered special permission as a replacement for an injured player.

Once again, when the old-timer got to town, he had to explain his rare ability to keep on chuckin' at such an advanced age. Wilhelm said he should be at his best by throwing 50 to 60 games a year, and said, "I've never felt better." He noted the knuckleball's big value allowing him to steer clear of arm problems. "With the kind of pitch I throw, there's no strain on my arm and as long as I can keep tossin' it up there, I'll keep pitching."[4]

It was a new home, not at all far from the Wilhelm family's off-season main abode in Columbus, Georgia, roughly 90 miles distant. There were only weeks left in the regular season when Wilhelm became a member of the Braves, but he was well-positioned for the next season, 1970, when he would turn 47. With Richards' estimation of perhaps five more seasons still in his arm, Wilhelm was reminded that the Major League baseball pension plan eligibility began at age 50.

"A man's got to work up until he starts gettin' his pension, doesn't he?" Wilhelm said.[5]

Unless he was blindsided by another trade, Wilhelm was poised to reach another milestone early in the 1970 season. From the time he surpassed Cy Young's record for most appearances as a pitcher, moving right along past 906, Wilhelm hoped to pitch in 1,000 Major League games. Each time he pitched beyond the 906 point he was breaking his own record, but there was something about that big round number that appealed to him.

There was even an off-season story about Wilhelm's thinking in the *New York Times* in December of 1969 looking ahead to the next year with the Braves. The headline read, "Wilhelm Continues Assault on Record."[6]

It seemed obligatory for writers to visit with Hoyt Wilhelm when he showed up for spring training. That was its own rite of spring, in essence. Yep, the old guy was still twirling, still in uniform, and here he was. The Braves worked out in West Palm Beach and that's where Wilhelm could be found in March of 1970, preparing for another season, not necessarily a last season. This was Wilhelm's 19th annual visit to a spring training camp and he was glad to be there.

"I don't remember being too nervous in my first spring training either," Wilhelm said with his usual calm while reflecting on the years gone by. "But I had played a couple of years in AAA and knew some of the guys, including Willie Mays."[7]

Hoyt Wilhelm

That was 1952, when he was hoping to make the jump from the highest level of the minors in Minneapolis to the New York Giants.

"I thought I could pitch in the big leagues, but I had to prove it then," Wilhelm said. "Now I can pace myself and just prepare myself to be ready by the time the season opens. I guess I did all right that first spring training. The first thing I knew, it was over, and I was in New York with the club."[8]

This was when manager Leo Durocher made a fateful decision to try Wilhelm coming out of the bullpen in relief instead of keeping him as a starter as he had been throughout his minor league journey to the top.

"They treated me well," Wilhelm said of the Giants' veterans. "I got tips, and, of course, Leo Durocher came up with the idea that I should be a relief pitcher. That was probably the best thing to ever happen to me in this game."[9]

Not that Wilhelm gave any hint that this might be his final season. He was thinking the same way as he always did, putting one foot in front of the other and throwing one pitch after another.

"This is my 19th spring training, going on 20," Wilhelm said.[10]

Just by keeping busy, by being on call during the normal course of events during the season, and, as Wilhelm always said, barring injury, this was merely about showing up for work. That meant one day Wilhelm would get the call from the bullpen and it would happen to be his 1,000th trek to the mound.

That day turned out to be May 10, 1970, when the Braves were playing the St. Louis Cardinals in a day game at home at Atlanta Stadium.

As the new decade began, Wilhelm's third in the majors despite his late start, he was once again on call to quench any fires by coming out of the bullpen. Wilhelm was summoned into the game, but unfortunately, marring the occasion, it was not one of Wilhelm's finer showings.

George Stone started for the Braves against St. Louis' Mike Torrez, who lasted six innings. He was followed by three Cardinal hurlers. Stone lasted eight innings, but when he was relieved by Bob Priddy, Wilhelm's partner in the trade, Priddy was touched for two runs without getting anyone out.

Wilhelm reported for duty in the ninth inning. He allowed one hit and one walk and was charged with a blown save. Outfielder Jose Cardenal cracked a key two-run single off Wilhelm as the Cardinals totaled four runs in the inning. Priddy took the loss and Jerry Johnson got the win for St. Louis in the 6–5 verdict. It was a day to remember for Wilhelm but not such a grand day to remember for Wilhelm.

19. A Thousand Games

"My arm felt all right," a disappointed Wilhelm said. "The knuckler was jumping pretty good. The guy bounced the ball for a hit [previous hitter Vic Davalillo off Priddy]. We've won some like that, too. That's baseball." Wilhelm actually erupted at reporters during this post-game session, accusing them of asking a "stupid question" when it was suggested perhaps Stone should have stayed in the game. "You can't blame Hoyt," Stone said. "I'm mad, too. I just don't show it like he does."[11]

Braves outfielder Rico Carty kept a 28-game hitting streak going but still felt badly about how things turned out. "I just wanted Wilhelm to win his 1,000th ... so it would be perfect for him," Carty said.[12]

Only the previous night, in outing number 999, Wilhelm had been superb as the Braves topped the Cardinals, 5–3. He hurled three shutout innings with five strikeouts. This was another day, another game, and Wilhelm wasn't as sharp.

Braves manager Luman Harris had tried to resist the idea of sending Wilhelm to the mound so soon after the previous appearance but felt he had to go with his best in the tight circumstances. He was second-guessing himself, was grumpy about the result, but he also said the special game for Wilhelm really had nothing to do with the results.

"I guess you gentlemen see why I didn't want to use Wilhelm today," Harris said after the game. "The 1,000 games had nothing to do with it. I had to. I had no choice. If I'd had anyone I thought could get them out, I wouldn't have brought him in. No, not because of the double pressure, because he pitched last night. No use kidding myself. He can't do it every day."[13]

He often had, though, and one game does not make a career. The record was in the appearance, not the performance, and the number stayed on the board of lifetime statistics.

Wilhelm was correct about one thing. His record for games pitched was surpassed. The mark is now held by Jesse Orosco, who appeared in 1,252 games as a thrower in 24 seasons. Wilhelm is sixth on the list now.

One special occurrence, an overlap in time and history, took place because Wilhelm spent time with the Braves. The long-time knuckleball artist was a teammate in late 1969 and in 1970 of Phil Niekro. Two of the all-time great knuckleball kings—the two greatest to most people—spending time together on the same roster was an unusual situation given the shortage of knuckleballers out there.

Niekro, born April 1, 1939, was from Ohio. Like Wilhelm, he learned the knuckleball at a young age, in his case from his father, Phil Sr. Phil's brother Joe was also an accomplished knuckleball thrower and together the siblings won 539 games, a big-league record. Phil, who won 318 games, was all in with the knuckler. Joe had a bit more variety in his pitching toolbox but still used the knuckleball, particularly after his big brother emphasized that he had to throw it all of the time.

When Wilhelm showed up on the Braves roster late in the 1969 season, Phil Niekro was completing a 23–13, 2.56 ERA campaign. Niekro slumped in 1970, ending up 12–18 and 4.27. By then Niekro was 31, but soon enough sportswriters and other baseball observers would be talking about him in the same manner they had come to speak of Wilhelm—as a Methuselah of the mound who was defying age, the law of physics and other commonplace circumstances for professional athletes.

Perhaps because all of the oldster nicknames had been gobbled up by Wilhelm ahead of him, Phil Niekro acquired a nickname describing what he did with a baseball. He was called "Knucksie." Niekro was a five-time All-Star and a five-time Gold Glove winner, and he was selected for the National Baseball Hall of Fame after he retired due to his mark of 318–274 with a 3.35 earned run average. Like Wilhelm, he also pitched a no-hitter, his coming on August 5, 1973. Also like Wilhelm, it seemed Niekro may have been capable of pitching forever at the big-league level.

Niekro did not pitch in his first Major League game until he was 25 in 1964 and he did not pitch in his last Major League game until he was 48 in 1987, giving him parts of 24 seasons in the majors. Four times Niekro led the National League in innings pitched, topping 300 each time. He won at least 20 games in a season three times in 864 games. That number is especially impressive because, unlike Wilhelm, he was mostly a starter, stepping to the mound to begin a game 716 times. His 3,342 strikeouts are the most by a knuckleball pitcher.

Yes, it did seem as if Niekro might pitch forever—just not for his beloved Atlanta Braves. From his time in the minors on through the 1983 season, Niekro had been a Braves fixture, and then the team cut him during the off-season when he was 44. Neither Niekro nor his arm felt it was time to retire and he immediately surfaced with the New York Yankees and won 16 games at 45 in 1984. Another misjudgment about a knuckleballer. He made the American League All-Star team for the Yanks that season.

Atlanta catcher Bruce Benedict, who had a mixed attitude about being on the receiving end of Niekro's knucklers, reacted strongly.

"Catching that knuckleball set me apart, made me feel kind of

19. A Thousand Games

special, and I think I became a better player because of it, and him," Benedict said. "I would miss a couple, and he would tell me that I was just making him look good, or he'd kid me that I was getting so good at catching it that he felt he was losing his stuff."

"I'll tell you what he meant to me," he continued. "I was in Omaha with my folks the day he announced he was leaving. I got on the next plane to Atlanta, went to the ball park and picked up the big glove we used. We put a lot of work in that mitt, and I wasn't about to let someone take it. I feel like carrying it around with me in a Brinks truck."

"I broke my fingers three times with his knuckleballs, and I've got all sorts of aches and pains because of that pitch," he said, "but the relationship I had with him will never be touched in my baseball career."[14]

Clearly, Benedict made the risk assessment and decided his relationship with Niekro and the knuckler was more valuable than the threat to his own health.

Another Braves catcher, Bob Uecker, who would have a more prominent career in acting and sportscasting than he did as a big leaguer, got a jump on his humor leanings by coping with Niekro's knuckleball. Perhaps the single funniest and most revealing comment made about the knuckleball spouted from Uecker's mouth when he was asked about his philosophy of catching it.

"I always thought the knuckleball was the easiest pitch to catch," Uecker said. "Wait till it stops rolling and then go to the backstop and pick it up."[15]

There was more from Uecker, who played in the majors between 1962 and 1967 and in most of one season was charged with 27 passed balls for the Braves. "Catching Niekro's knuckleball was great," said Uecker, a Hall of Fame announcer. "I got to meet a lot of important people. They all sit behind home plate."[16]

One quirky thing on Niekro's record was that when it came time to go for his 300th win he decided to see if he could pitch a whole game without throwing one knuckleball. The day arrived on October 6, 1985, and at the time, after being jettisoned because of old age by his reliable Braves, Niekro was pitching for the New York Yankees against the Toronto Blue Jays in Canada. When he was warming up, he told catcher Butch Wynegar of his secret game plan.

"I thought he was kidding," Wynegar said. "Hey, I was happy not to have to catch that thing."[17]

When things worked out well, Niekro cruising toward a complete game, he decided to give the last batter the knuckleball treatment. Had to do it and that's how he finished up.

Both Niekro and Wilhelm are in the Hall of Fame, Niekro because he won so many games as a starter, Wilhelm because he performed so well for so long as a reliever. Twice over a period of many years, Major League Baseball's website ranked the best knuckleball throwers, placing Niekro first and Wilhelm second.

Of Wilhelm, it was written, "The knuckleball was seen as something of a trick pitch that aging hurlers used to try to stay in the game before Wilhelm made it his primary weapon of choice."[18]

Once again, much like Wilhelm, Niekro could offer no rational explanation for why the knuckler behaved the way it did when he threw it. "All I try to do is make the ball do nothing," he said.[19]

Many say Niekro had the best knuckleball of them all. Not Niekro, who says the best knuckler belonged to Wilhelm, and even more significant to him, Wilhelm should be credited as the pitcher who uplifted the knuckler into the realm of somewhat more common usage in the modern era.

"There were some guys," Niekro said of players such as Jesse Haines and Gene Bearden. "But to me, Wilhelm is the start of the knuckleball."[20]

While it was probably expected that Wilhelm would be hanging around in Atlanta longer, before the end of the 1970, he was put on waivers by the Braves. In 50 appearances for the team, Wilhelm went 6–4 with a 3.10 earned run average and 13 saves.

That showing was good enough to gain Wilhelm his final career selection for an All-Star team, this time representing the National League. The NL won the July 14 game, 5–4, at Riverfront Stadium in Cincinnati, but Wilhelm was not used. Tom Seaver started for the National League and was one of five pitchers deployed. The winner was Claude Osteen in a game that ran for 12 innings.

The Braves did not even hold onto Wilhelm through the end of the regular season and the Chicago Cubs, hoping to pick off a pennant, grabbed Wilhelm on September 21. Wilhelm was hardly used by the Cubs and might have been in shock because of his quick change of addresses. He went 0–1 with a 9.82 earned run average, being hit well in three appearances spanning 3⅔ innings.

Hoyt Wilhelm was running out of chances in the big leagues, but he did not plan on retiring before the 1971 season. He was still convinced the knuckler could carry him through another season at age 48.

20

Running Out of Teams

In February of 1972, as spring training was revving up and Hoyt Wilhelm was still hanging around his Columbus, Georgia, home, he received a visit from a local newspaperman to gauge his mental outlook at what would be an ancient age for a professional baseball player. The headline on the story updating readers Wilhelm perfectly encapsulated his mood. It read, "At 48, Wilhelm Talks Like Rookie."[1]

Barely two months after the Chicago Cubs claimed Wilhelm on waivers from the Atlanta Braves in hopes of his giving them a jump start on a pennant, the Cubs traded him back to Atlanta for Hal Breeden. Breeden played parts of five seasons, mostly with the Montreal Expos, and batted .243.

This meant Wilhelm was headed back to spring training with the Braves for the 1972 season, a bit of a whirlwind series of events and location shifts.

"I feel great," Wilhelm said. "I don't think my arm is going to give me any trouble this spring."[2] This was a notable declaration because some months earlier—in a real rarity for him and any other knuckle-baller—he had been having stiffness in the throwing arm. To alleviate that issue and to shore up his belief that it would not recur, he had been throwing a lot to his son Jimmy, then a teenager, in the off-season.

When the Braves were ready to start the 1972 season, Wilhelm was with them. By then, he was gathering fans all across the baseball and sports world, simply by hanging around. This age admiration began to crop up when Wilhelm passed age 40 . It was one thing for the average fan to praise the superior athleticism of young players in their 20s and 30s, but quite another to appreciate those in their 40s at a time when their own legs and backs began creaking when they climbed out of bed.

In 1966, one newspaper story's headline read, "Like Ol' Man River, Hoyt Keeps Rollin' Along as Relief Ace."[3] In 1969, another headline read, "Hoyt Wilhelm Tabbed as Wonder of Baseball."[4] In 1970, still another

Hoyt Wilhelm

headline read, "Old Man Wilhelm a Hero to Every Fan Pushing 50."[5] It might be said Wilhelm was bucking to be named the American Association of Retired Persons' Athlete of the Year, though all he was seeking to do was keep himself alive in the marketplace as a pitcher.

The common theme was basically, "How does he do it?" Wilhelm was not enthusiastic about being too introspective on that front with explanations about how his body stayed in one piece better than most. He was not much more forthcoming than he was in offering seminars on why his knuckleball kept working. They both pretty much came under the umbrella viewpoint of just being glad the knuckleball did what it did and the body outlasted most athletic norms.

Wilhelm was "Ol' Man River" when he was 43, called "the ageless knuckleball wizard of the bullpen."[6] This was on the occasion of him pitching in his 803rd game, surpassing Walter Johnson for second place on the appearances list. Wilhelm's number of games being on the decline in 1966 was caused by a broken middle finger suffered in spring training. This had nothing to do with throwing the ball. He was in the batting cage at the time. In what might have been a minor incident for another player, Wilhelm lost a fingernail, an all-important element in his grip on the knuckler.

Manager Eddie Stanky provided a Wilhelm testimonial that sounded just like the pitcher after he appeared in seven games in eight days, including both ends of a doubleheader. "He may be 43, but he has a young arm," Stanky said. "There's no end in sight for him. He may be around a long time yet." Wilhelm loved the sound of that and it merely confirmed his own thinking. "Really," he said, "I'm as good now as I ever was."[7]

Wilhelm graduated from "Ol' Man River" to a "wonder" status when he was with the California Angels three years later and mention was made about him closing in on being able to claim his pension. Sure enough, Wilhelm made almost the identical comment about his ability. "I feel as if I am pitching as well now as I have for several years," he said. "As long as I can get them out, I won't think about retirement. I've said it many times, the knuckleball doesn't put too much strain on the arm. That's the reason pitchers who use it can continue for so long. But there are not too many who can throw it."[8]

Next thing you knew, Wilhelm was a role model to the rocking chair set. An Atlanta sportswriter discussed that newfound stature in print, inspired by overhearing two men in their 50s at a ballpark concession stand and their banter about Hoyt. "You know, every time that old guy gets somebody out, I get somebody out," one of them said. "Every time he throws a pitch, I do, too. If he wins, I win." The companion responded, "Yeah, I like to see him get those young guys out." If there was any doubt at all, the first guy replied by saying, "I guess we identify."[9]

One was not required to be an innocent bystander lining up for a hot dog, either, to consider Wilhelm in such terms.

"That Wilhelm is really something when you stop to think about it," said Braves infielder Clete Boyer, who was a 15-year veteran heading for more than 1,700 games in his career at that time, but he could not fathom a pitcher throwing in 1,000 games.[10]

At 48, for the 1971 season, Wilhelm was back with the Braves after his short interlude with the Cubs. But unlike the first time around, this was not really a happy reunion. Wilhelm pitched in just three games, covering 2⅓ innings and being lit up for a 15.43 earned run average. That was it for his time in Atlanta. On June 29, the Braves released Wilhelm, severing his affiliation with the team.

He was not happy about being dumped as the Braves made some personnel moves promoting players from AAA Richmond as they waved goodbye to Wilhelm.

"I'm not surprised," Wilhelm said. "This is the way they do things here. But what the heck, I sure wasn't doing anything around here. They might as well let me go." He wasn't giving in to the idea of forced retirement, however. "I think I can pitch if I'm given the chance. I believe I can catch on with somebody. I'll wait a few days and see what happens."[11]

About two weeks later, on July 10, Wilhelm found a new team. The Los Angeles Dodgers signed him. Wilhelm spent a brief period with the Dodgers' AAA Spokane team getting back into form and then appeared in nine games with a 1.02 earned run average and an 0–1 record for Los Angeles before the end of the year.

Near the end of the season, a newspaper sports section took a close look at the Dodgers' bullpen and did a double-take. The relief corps included knuckleballer Wilhelm, forkball thrower Jose Pena, screwball specialist Jim Brewer, and palmball hurler Pete Mikkelson. A headline writer took one peek at that crew and wrote a story summary reading, "Dodgers Bullpen Bulging with Freaks." Was that an insult or a compliment?

"Name a freak delivery and some Dodger has it," the story read while describing Wilhelm as the patriarch of the bullpen who could offer advice and assistance to those throwers and other inhabitants of

Hoyt Wilhelm

the bullpen such as Ron Perranoski and Phil Regan.[12] Joe Moeller was trying to improve a knuckler and Wilhelm seemed just the man to provide help.

Wilhelm still wanted to pitch more than tutor, though, and he wasn't heavily used. Time really was starting to run out on "Old Folks" in the majors this time. It was not about speculation but real life encroaching. The 1972 season with the Dodgers turned out to be Wilhelm's last spin around the majors. He appeared in 16 games, compiled a 4.62 earned run average, and had a record of 0–1 and just one save in 25⅓ innings. On July 21, 1972, the Dodgers released Hoyt Wilhelm.

It could be said one of the greatest relief pitching careers of all time ended with a whimper, not a bang, with Wilhelm probably still wishing and hoping a team would provide one more chance. That call never came and Wilhelm last pitched in a game 16 days before his 50th birthday. The 50-year-old fans buying concessions were no doubt still rooting for him.

Wilhelm spent 21 years in the majors and owned several records, including some that still stand nearly a half-century past his retirement when he ceased pitching. Wilhelm's lifetime record was 143–122. He has the most victories by a relief pitcher. His earned run average at the time of retirement—2.52—was the best by any other pitcher at retirement since Walter Johnson gave up the game in 1927. Wilhelm was the first reliever to 200 saves, accumulating 228, and the first pitcher to 1,000 games, concluding with 1,070 appearances. He remains the only pitcher to win the earned run average title in both the National League and American League.

Wilhelm also remains an icon to the knuckleball union, an inspiration to some who came after him. Some of the best knuckleball throwers followed his precepts of casting their fate with the pitch completely, and although they didn't surpass him in age in the majors, several came close.

Phil Niekro, of course, outdid Wilhelm in wins and losses with his career 318 victories, pitching for 24 seasons and staying in the game until he was 48.

The two were succeeded by some other remarkable knuckleball throwers. Charlie Hough played in parts of 25 seasons until he was 46 and won 216 games (while also losing 216). Hough was as much a starter as a reliever. Tim Wakefield won 200 games over 19 seasons before retiring at 44. He was a starter about two-thirds of the time while appearing in 627 games. R.A. Dickey lasted 15 years and won 120 games. His

20. Running Out of Teams

standout achievement came in 2012 when he finished 20–6 and won the National League Cy Young Award for the New York Mets. He was 37 at the time and pitched until he was 42. Tom Candiotti won 151 games in 16 seasons and retired at 42.

One fairly obscure late-in-life knuckleballer cheered for was Dan Boone, who insisted he was related to the original Daniel Boone, frontiersman, about eight times removed. For much of his pitching career, Boone kept coming up just an inch away time after time in sticking with a major-league club after being drafted five times, post–high school and every season at Cal State Fullerton.

Slightly built at 5-foot-8 and 132 pounds, Boone, born in 1954, made his first stop in the majors with the San Diego Padres in 1981 and went 1–0. The next year he split time between the Padres, who gave up on him, and the Houston Astros, going 1–1 before they too gave up on him.

Boone never gave up on himself, however, and in contrast to Wilhelm, added a knuckleball later in his career. Suddenly, at the end of the decade, he was a prospect all over again. In July of 1990, floating his knuckler past befuddled batters, Boone pitched a no-hitter in AAA for the Rochester Red Wings against the Syracuse Chiefs, winning 2–0 as part of a doubleheader. Of when he was getting close to finishing off the performance, Boone said, "My eyes started tearing up [in the dugout]. I knew what kind of feeling I'd have after the game. It's not every day a guy gets a chance to throw a no-hitter."[13]

Most remarkably, eight years after his previous big-league game, Boone resurfaced in the majors in 1990 for the Baltimore Orioles at age 36. His record was 0–0, but Boone pitched in four games over 9⅔ innings, with a 2.79 earned run average. The knuckler strikes again.

Although far better known than Boone, Jim Bouton, who won 21 games for the New York Yankees in 1963 when he still had a fastball and became the best-selling author of *Ball Four* in 1970, also made a comeback throwing a knuckler with a years-long gap. After eight years out of the bigs, Bouton pitched in five games for the Atlanta Braves in 1978, winning once. He was relying solely on a knuckler, which he only rarely threw in his prime.

As it turned out, Bouton said he actually was first exposed to the knuckler when he was a 12-year-old pitcher and saw a picture of knuckleball practitioner Dutch Leonard on a cereal box. Yes, that is the same knuckleball thrower who inspired Hoyt Wilhelm.

"It explained on the back of the box that the trick was not to throw it with your knuckles," said Bouton, who used a three-finger grasp of the pitch, one more finger than some other knuckleball men. "The idea was that you really need to throw it with your fingertips, without any spin."[14]

Bouton said he was fascinated with the cereal box instruction and thought it might give him the weapon he needed to succeed on the mound. He practiced throwing a knuckler for about 30 minutes a day for 10 days, his cooperative brother Bob acting as catcher. The knuckler wasn't doing what it was supposed to do initially—no one ever said it was easy to throw. Then on one throw, the ball did its butterfly thing, dodging out of Bob's reach and cracking him on the knee.

"And Bob's down on the ground moaning," Bouton said, "'Oh, what a great pitch!' I had maimed my brother and he was thrilled!"[15]

Jim Bouton, descendent of Dutch Leonard and Hoyt Wilhelm.

While most baseball experts believed there would always be someone around to carry on the knuckleball tradition, there were doubters and as the 2000s went on it became apparent that the knuckleball was indeed an endangered species.

Phil Niekro was always on call as a knuckleball doctor to help any team that reached out and asked for assistance with a young wannabe. For a time, a handful of years ago, the Baltimore Orioles had two such prospects in their minor league system, but they did not make the grade.

In 2013, 6-foot-2, 215-pound righty Steven Wright surfaced with the Boston Red Sox and went 2–0 as a next-generation knuckleballer. For the next few seasons, he had some good moments for Boston and then in 2016, Wright went 13–6 and made the American League All-Star team. However, the success didn't last. Wright played parts of a few more seasons but was suspended by Major League Baseball for 80 games for the use of performance-enhancing drugs. He tried a comeback with the Pittsburgh Pirates organization in 2021 but did not make the team and was released after a minor-league stint with Indianapolis. His lifetime record was 24–16.

It is possible the knuckleball has become extinct, despite the example of Hoyt Wilhelm and others showing what can be accomplished with it.

One of the great sportswriters, Pulitzer Prize–winning columnist Jim Murray of the *Los Angeles Times*, always had a fun time writing about Wilhelm. A master of language, Murray loved to play with words and he could string them together. Sometimes he did so in writing about Wilhelm.

In one column, Murray listed several nicknames players had

adopted for Wilhelm's knuckler as they swung futilely at it, including "The Moth," "The Iron Butterfly," "The Dancer," and "The Bat." He added, "It comes up to the plate just faster than a postcard." He noted the knuckleball was a misnomer because it was thrown with the fingertips. "Hoyt Wilhelm has the best one in the history of baseball."[16]

Murray added what catchers and hitters had long known, too: if the knuckleball pitcher is right and the ball behaves as intended, they are all at a loss.

"Everybody knows it's coming," Murray wrote. "But it's like knowing an atom bomb or an earthquake is coming. There's not much you can do about it when it gets there."[17]

After a lifetime spent in baseball as a pitcher, reluctant retiree Wilhelm made a quick switch to the other side of the lines. He became a minor league manager and then a long-time pitching coach.

Wilhelm's first post-playing-days job was managing the Greenwood Braves of the Western Carolina League in 1973. His team finished 61–66 in his single season at the helm. In 1975, he managed the Atlanta Appalachian team to a 33–33 mark. Most notably, Wilhelm spent 22 years as a minor-league pitching coach for the New York Yankees. One thing Wilhelm did not do in that role was try to convert players to the knuckler, but he did take on special requests to help players already in the majors who tried to make the switch to the knuckler. He spent time with Joe Niekro and Jeff Reardon.

That first season off the mound, Wilhelm's time with Class A Greenwood in South Carolina offered some free time to drive golf balls. The itch to continue pitching seemed to have been quelled.

"When I got out of baseball last July, I hadn't thought much about managing," Wilhelm said. "But I knew if you get out for several years, they forget about you. I'll tell you what this job has done for me. It's given me something so that I didn't miss playing. I feel I got all the pitching out of me. I don't regret leaving. Besides, I still throw batting practice quite often."[18]

As Wilhelm hit the road with his minor-league teams, sportswriters found a new topic to quiz him about regularly, taking the place of those routine questions about his age. They all wanted to know if he was teaching young pitchers the knuckleball and he always said the same thing: Nope. He believed the same thing throughout his hurling career and he hadn't changed his mind. A pitcher had to take it up young or stay clear. Indeed, he said, neither management nor young pitchers were asking him for that kind of instruction.

Hoyt Wilhelm

"You can't teach the knuckler," Wilhelm said. "I just picked it up myself. Nobody taught it to me."[19] At that time, 1977, only Phil Niekro, Wilbur Wood and Charlie Hough were even throwing it. Wilhelm said the Yankees had one guy at West Haven in the minor-league system giving it a try. Larry McCall earned just a taste of the majors, going 2–2 over parts of three seasons with the Yankees and Texas Rangers.

Despite trying his hand at managing, Wilhelm said he preferred the role of pitching coach. He felt he best knew the strengths and weaknesses of those guys. He believed he could be most useful if a pitcher was struggling. "Then, you can adjust his delivery, his drive [off the rubber]. The most important thing is still talent and control. I look for good control in a reliever. I was always in one-run situations."[20]

From Ted Williams, the Boston power hitter, to Yogi Berra, the Yankees' Hall of Fame catcher, from Jim Murray, the superstar wordsmith, to John Steadman, the Baltimore columnist who watched Wilhelm perform his magic with the knuckleball during his years with the Orioles, many close baseball observers and players reached the same conclusion about the man who at various times was anointed simply the King of the Knuckleball.

Hoyt Wilhelm, they agreed, threw the best knuckler of any pitcher who ever lived.

21

A Call from the Hall

When Hoyt Wilhelm retired as an active player in July of 1972 after years of being called "Old Folks" or "Old Sarge" and teasing headlines about whether or not he was living the relaxed life of a shuffleboard player, he was putting the period on a 21-year big-league career that began late and ended late. And it was still to come that the baseball world would learn he was actually a year older the whole time it was making fun of his age.

He was a unique figure in baseball, having set records for most wins in relief and most games pitched while compiling the lowest earned run average in 45 years. And all of this while employing a knuckleball as his primary pitch.

There were those who said that when they made Hoyt Wilhelm they broke the mold, but like any cliché, there was truth in the observation.

Wilhelm finished with a won-loss record of 143–122 in 1,070 games, with an earned run average of 2.52. For five seasons, between 1964 and 1968, Wilhelm's ERA did not stray above 2.00. Along the way, one of his teammates joked that one year it might drop to a negative number. He also recorded 228 saves, the first reliever to top 200. Although known essentially as a relief pitcher, Wilhelm at times served as a starting pitcher, and he became the only hurler to lead both the National League and American League in earned run average in a season. Becoming a starter, at least temporarily, afforded Wilhelm the chance to throw a no-hitter, which he did in shutting down the New York Yankees in 1958. He was an eight-time All-Star, partially because some of his best years occurred during the brief period when the majors played two All-Star games a season.

Taken together, it was a remarkable resume, bulging with firsts and mosts, made more dazzling because Wilhelm was old for a rookie when he broke into the majors in 1952 and was very old for a player when he retired at 49, just shy of his 50th birthday. Wilhelm became a symbol of what older folks could accomplish and a model for aspiring knuckleball pitchers who saw his success and could aspire to their own.

Sports columnists who appreciated these nuances of success, much like a connoisseur of fine wine, began lobbying for Wilhelm's inclusion as a member of the National Baseball Hall of Fame in Cooperstown, New York. Not only did they suggest he was the best of his kind as a knuckleball king, but they also said that he was one of a kind.

It took until Wilhelm's eighth year on the Hall of Fame ballot before he was voted in—one needs 75 percent of the votes cast by the Baseball Writers Association of America. When Wilhelm was selected in 1985, he received 83.8 percent of the votes.

"In the back of my mind, when I became eligible, I thought I might make it," Wilhelm said after being chosen. "But it never really affected me and I never really campaigned."[1]

The previous year, Wilhelm came within 13 votes of being elected and this time around he led the ballot. Lou Brock, who reached stardom as an outfielder with the St. Louis Cardinals, was the only other player chosen. Nellie Fox, the Chicago White Sox star second baseman, missed out by two votes but was later selected for the Hall.

It was a time for reflection for Wilhelm, about how he languished in the minors for so long, perhaps a victim of anti-knuckleball prejudice.

Some of Hoyt Wilhelm's finest pitching was accomplished with the Orioles, including a September 1958 no-hitter against the New York Yankees. He joined the team late in the 1958 season and remained through 1962 (National Baseball Hall of Fame Library, Cooperstown, N.Y.).

21. A Call from the Hall

"Nobody wanted me," Wilhelm said. "Only thing I can say is maybe it was because I was a knuckleball pitcher. Nobody thought too much of me." When the New York Giants and manager Leo Durocher kept him on the 1952 roster, it was originally to be a reliever. "The bullpen, that's usually where they put old me. I'd have been happy to make the team as a water boy."[2]

Naturally enough, the passed balls came up in conversation, those catchers who were charged with four in a game or 25 or so in a season, all waving helplessly at knucklers that passed them by like the hitters who caught only the breeze when they took their swings.

"I can't remember too many games I ever lost on passed balls," Wilhelm said. "I used to tell the catchers, 'After I turn it loose, it's your responsibility.'"[3]

One time, a young White Sox teammate, trying to make his way to the big leagues as a catcher, seemed to underestimate the knuckler, figuring it must be easy to catch if it came in so slow.

"I remember once, when I was with the White Sox, riding a bus in spring training, some rookie catcher said he'd catch me without a mask." Big mistake. "Couple of days later, I was warming up to throw batting practice, and he was catching me. After about three pitches, I had it warmed up pretty good. Threw one that landed in his eye, just like you'd placed it there. By the time I got to him, his eye was swollen shut. After that, he used the mask."[4]

Of course, when it came to the passed ball making a difference in base runners advancing while a catcher was sprinting to the backstop to retrieve the rolling ball, Wilhelm had his own approach—the first line of defense for a pitcher.

"The trick is not to let them get on in the first place," Wilhelm said.[5]

Which is a critical philosophy for a relief pitcher who often is in jeopardy from the moment he is summoned to the mound. One mistake can be costly, whether it is a passed ball, a walk, or a hit allowed. Relievers, as a characteristic of their kind, should generally have low blood pressure and a slow pulse.

"I never went into a game and got all flustered up," Wilhelm said. "I try to take a close game and men on base in stride. I've always thought baseball was just a game and I enjoy it. And ever since I was a boy and learned the knuckleball, I've thrown it with a lot of determination."[6]

Wilhelm's performance also earned him fans among other pitchers, including White Sox teammate Billy Pierce. "Hoyt was one of the few pitchers who seemed to be virtually unhittable," said Pierce, who won 211 Major League games and an earned run title himself.[7]

As is to be expected, Wilhelm, who was said to be 61 at the time, although really 62, was graciously pleased when first informed he had been voted into the Hall of Fame.

"That's great," he said. "I think that's the ultimate for any player that's played a few years in the big leagues. It's a great thing."[8]

This really was a time when it was appropriate for compliments to flow Wilhelm's way, with many baseball people acknowledging just maybe he possessed the best knuckleball of all time, though they didn't want to get in an argument about Phil Niekro's knuckler.

It wasn't as if Wilhelm was out of baseball, either, doing his long stint as a minor-league pitching coach for the Yankees. He always found time to play golf when the weather and time allowed during the warmer months of the year. He also liked to go fishing and hunting, especially bird hunting. His exercise, as always, came from walking in the woods more than going to a gym. He called a reliance on weight training "a change in the times." Regardless, and he was about in the middle of his Yankees stint when he became a Hall of Famer, Wilhelm did not see the different methods of training doing anything more to help stop the incidence of pitcher injuries. "I don't think anybody knows what the answer is," Wilhelm said. "I mean, if somebody could come up with the real bona fide way to prevent injuries, they would make a million dollars. I mean, it's just things that happen and I don't see—it doesn't seem like the conditioning really makes that much difference."[9]

Wilhelm's arm stayed healthy despite the limited amount of physical exercise he did. He was just a superb technician in terms of getting the knuckleball to do what he wanted it to do more often than the knuckler did what it wanted to do.

Long-time baseball executive Pat Gillick, who himself was later chosen for the Hall of Fame, gave Wilhelm his vote as the most outstanding knuckleballer.

"I went to spring training in '62 with him," Gillick said. "He didn't do any physical work at all. He just threw in the bullpen and sat in the training room and got treatment on his shoulder. Over a time frame of 40 years or so, the myth builds up. But I think he had one of the best knuckleballs I ever saw. Wilbur Wood had a good one and so did Charlie Hough and Eddie Fisher. But Hoyt had three or four different ones and he could throw them for strikes."[10]

21. A Call from the Hall

Hoyt Wilhelm was inducted into the Baseball Hall of Fame on July 28, 1985, in a ceremony that also honored the Cardinals' Lou Brock and Enos Slaughter and shortstop Arky Vaughan of the Pittsburgh Pirates, the latter two chosen by the Veterans Committee. The Hall had broadcaster Brent Musburger handle introductions.

Each living inductee is given the opportunity to make a speech to the thousands of spectators who gather in Cooperstown for the annual event that is regarded essentially as a holiday in the small upstate New York community. Often, speakers tear up, fight to hold onto their composure, and much like recipients of Oscars at the Academy Awards ceremonies, spend a large portion of their speaking time thanking others who helped make their moment possible.

Sometimes speeches make the audience laugh. Other times they are so heartfelt they produce more somber emotions. Wilhelm was neither funny nor overtly serious, though he was sincere. Members of his immediate family, wife Peggy and children Jim, Patti and Pam, were present. While reflective about his time spent on the diamond, ironically enough, Wilhelm made no mention of the knuckleball, the pitch he was so strongly identified with and which brought him his fame and success.

The beginning of Wilhelm's speech to the fans was as simple as it gets. "Ladies and gentlemen, fellow Hall of Famers, baseball fans everywhere," he began. "Today, I'm honored to stand up here, something that I never dreamed of when I started playing baseball way back in Huntersville, North Carolina. First of all, on this beautiful day here in Cooperstown, I would like to thank the Lord for making this honor possible today. I give Him all the praise, all the honor and all the glory for this day. After all, the Hall of Fame that He selects is the all-important one for all of us."[11]

No matter what the weather, hurricane-force winds, rain, or snow, anyone being inducted into the Hall of Fame could call it a beautiful day. While Wilhelm did speak of the Almighty on this day, he had never been one of those players who cited religion in his post-game analysis over the years, so that was a departure.

Wilhelm said from the moment he learned of his selection to the Hall of Fame months earlier in January he wondered what emotions would run through his mind and he learned that he was as nervous as he anticipated he might be. "I think I would probably be more calm facing Yankee Stadium before a full house. In fact, I know I would."[12]

Hoyt Wilhelm

Actually, he had been calmer against the New York Yankees when hurling a no-hitter in 1958 when pitching for the Orioles.

"I've been asked many times what being elected to the Hall of Fame means to me and that's a tough question to answer," Wilhelm said. "When you consider all the players over the years and years [that] have played the game of baseball, and then you think of the number … that have been elected here, that really makes you start thinking."[13]

What Wilhelm thought most about was how close his dream had come to ending so close to the beginning, when he was cut from a Class D ball club in the minors before World War II, yet still fought to reach the majors, pitch for two decades and be elected to the Hall of Fame.

"That's just unreal and it's pretty hard for me to contemplate," Wilhelm said.[14] In his role as a minor-league manager and pitching coach, Wilhelm said he had to face the tough decisions and tough messaging that came with telling a young player he had been released, and he said he told the player his own story as a way of encouragement, as a boost to the psyche suggesting he not give up.

As part of the speech, Wilhelm was able to introduce his wife, his children and their spouses, his grandchildren and several of his siblings who made the journey from North Carolina to be there for him. He said six of his sisters alone were in the audience. He thanked his kids for being adaptable enough to attend multiple schools a year and putting up with moving around.

Wilhelm also put in a plug for baseball wives. Peggy Wilhelm, he said, was a baseball fan before they met, but she was his support crew, especially when there was doubt about his future when he was just making his way with the New York Giants.

"I was in a lot of tough games early in my career," Wilhelm said, "and I tried not to bring the game with me when I had a problem and got beat. But I got home and I'd be worried about losing the game or something, and she's the kind of person, I guess she sees good in everything, and she'd always find something good about the game. After a while, she'd have me thinking I had won a tough game. So, it was a good thing to be around a person like that and have the encouragement that she gave me over the years."[15]

Wilhelm referred to having good coaches and managers. As a group his big-league managers were men who distinguished themselves in the sport, from Leo Durocher to Paul Richards to Fred Hutchinson to Walt Alston. He thanked Durocher for giving him a chance and Richards for giving him the opportunity to be a starting pitcher.

21. A Call from the Hall

"There was a man that I figured and consider to this day one of the greatest pitching coaches that I have ever run into," Wilhelm said of Richards. "He was a catcher and maybe that's where he learned. But he had a knack of taking older pitchers, and he did it with several of them, he'd take older pitchers that were kind of over the hill maybe, or a little bit down, and rehabilitate them and get them to go and get several good years out of them. And I give Paul Richards a lot of credit for turning my career around. It could have been the end of the road the way I was pitching in Cleveland."[16]

Also, in Atlanta, Richards summoned him again. The Braves were looking for help and so was Wilhelm.

"I will never forget the first words that he said to me when I made that call to him," Wilhelm said. "He said, 'Hoyt, can you still throw it?' I said, 'Yes.' He said, 'Well, get on the next plane to Atlanta. We made a deal for you. I want you here as quick as you can get.'"[17]

Wilhelm failed to mention Richards' development of the Big Bertha catcher's mitt, another example of his boss looking out for him.

Surely everyone else in the crowd remembered the big glove and certainly everyone else there thought about the knuckleball. When he cited memories from the sport, Wilhelm said it was a thrill to play for a World Series winner, to be chosen to represent his leagues in the All-Star game, to pitch a no-hitter, and to be standing there as a new member of the Hall of Fame.

He let others ponder the meaning of the knuckler, much as he had done throughout his long career, and the humor inherent in the big glove. Inside the National Baseball Hall of Fame these days, more than 25 years after Wilhelm was enshrined, a visitor can see one of his White Sox uniform jerseys in a glass case, read his name in some statistical categories, spot one of those old oversized catcher's mitts, and above all, if they are looking for evidence of Hoyt Wilhelm the great pitcher, read the plaque that adorns the wall in the building's special gallery honoring all of those chosen as the crème de la crème of the sport.

The image on the plaque has Wilhelm looking out with concentration as if he is studying what a batter is bringing to the plate. With his full name James Hoyt Wilhelm, the plaque lists all of the teams the right-hander pitched for, as briefly as some of the pit stops were, in addition to the teams like the New York Giants, Baltimore Orioles, and Chicago White Sox which he starred for.

In addition to many standout lifetime statistics lauded on the plaque, Wilhelm is called "Baseball's Premier Relief Pitcher." It also

Hoyt Wilhelm

casually notes for younger generations that he "used knuckle ball" to win his games and produce his notable statistics.[18]

"Used knuckle ball" is probably the grandest understatement of all that could be applied to Hoyt Wilhelm's baseball career. It might be more accurate to say the man was the epitome of the knuckleball.

Epilogue

When Hoyt Wilhelm died in 2002, it turned out he had one more trick to pitch to the masses, one better than all of his knuckleball throws combined and at least as elusive. His birth certificate showed Wilhelm was born one year earlier than everyone thought.

All of those years when sportswriters and baseball officials kept exclaiming about how old he was, Wilhelm was actually a full year older. It was ironic and somewhat humorous, given that his age was probably written about more than any of his contemporaries, or maybe more than any other in history except for possibly Satchel Paige.

Certainly, Wilhelm was aware of the incorrect age appearing next to his name year after year in newspaper story after newspaper story, but he never felt any urgency to correct it. After all, everyone was talking about how old he was for a professional athlete, so why help along the narrative about him being too old to persevere?

Wilhelm's youngest surviving sister, Viki Hager, knows for a fact the truth was uncovered. She has no idea how the numbers were jumbled in the first place, if Hoyt played any role in altering his age or just went with it.

"Old Folks" was actually 80 years old when he passed away in Sarasota, Florida, his retirement home over the last stretch of his life, on August 23, 2002. Wife Peggy gave the reason as heart failure. In a quote first published in the Sarasota newspaper but used by the Associated Press and other news outlets, she said of Wilhelm, "My husband always thought it was the greatest thing in the world that he could make a living at doing what he loved best."[1]

Wilhelm had a lifelong passion for the game and he was able to make it a lifelong career, first making his way through the minors for pay, then for 21 years visiting mounds for nine teams in the majors, then managing and coaching in the minors for the New York Yankees. He may have held odd jobs as a young man during the off-seasons of his

Epilogue

playing days, but basically for decades, his main source of income was professional baseball. He was one of the lucky handful who had baseball in his blood and could teach and coach for years and years after he could no longer make a team's roster.

At the time of his passing, Wilhelm was survived by six sisters of the original 11 siblings which included two brothers; all but Hager have since passed away. At the time of his death, Wilhelm also had 12 grandchildren and three great-grandchildren.

Hoyt Wilhelm's plaque in the National Baseball Hall of Fame gallery. He was elected in 1985 and inducted the following summer (National Baseball Hall of Fame Library, Cooperstown, N.Y.).

Epilogue

As befitting a Hall of Famer, Wilhelm's death was noted by publications all across the country, even highlighted in sports pages in cities where he never played a minute. Tribute was paid in numerous local articles, sportswriters reaching out to teammates he shared clubhouses and fields with over the course of his career. Thus, a new trove of Hoyt stories appeared for fans who had missed his astonishing pitching career, which had concluded 30 years earlier.

"He was a great teammate and obviously an outstanding pitcher," said longtime player and manager Bobby Valentine upon Wilhelm's death. "He had humor, work ethic and camaraderie that I will always remember. He was good to the young guys. We really liked that."[2]

The *Charlotte Observer*, Wilhelm's original hometown paper, did not catch the age discrepancy and said he passed away at age 79, as did other newspaper reports. The North Carolina story did take note of Wilhelm's picking up the knuckler from Dutch Leonard.[3]

The compliments about Wilhelm's skill with the knuckler—both he and Phil Niekro shied away from applying the word "mastery" when it came to the pitch because of its unpredictability—mounted up.

"Wilhelm's knuckleball did more than anyone's," said baseball executive Roland Hemond, who spent time with the White Sox. "No one could predict what it was going to do."[4] This appeared in the *Chicago Tribune*, which also had the well-known but incorrect birth year for Wilhelm in its story.

Perhaps the most memorable comment that appeared in Wilhelm stories of the time was one uttered by Ron Hansen, a teammate of Hoyt's both with the White Sox and the Baltimore Orioles, who was joking when it was made but upon Wilhelm's death learned how close to the truth it was.

"We used to kid him about his age because he never told anybody," Hansen said. "We'd kid him, saying we'd find out how old he is when he went to collect his pension or Social Security check."[5] He was not far off the mark. The teammates had to wait until Wilhelm's death certificate was released.

Different catchers had different reactions to trying to catch the Wilhelm knuckleball. Many were losers in the exchange in the sense that they committed more passed balls as a battery mate of his than at any other time during their careers.

Although he had his greatest success in a 10-year big-league stint with the Cleveland Indians, All-Star John Romano was in a second go-around with the White Sox when he overlapped with Wilhelm.

Epilogue

Romano was almost driven into retirement by the knuckler when he was inserted into a game, because two other catchers with better success working with Wilhelm were injured. The first two knucklers flummoxed Romano and rolled away from him. When the third straight pitch did the same, Romano stood up, began stripping off his catcher's gear and headed to the dugout. Manager Eddie Stanky intercepted him and had to cajole him to go back out on the diamond.

It was easier to admire the knuckler from afar, or no worse a vantage point than the batter's box, than just about from any angle besides squatting behind the plate.

"Hoyt was a good guy and he threw the best knuckleball I ever saw," said first baseman Bill Skowron, who starred with the Yankees and also played with the White Sox. "You never knew what Hoyt's pitch would do. I don't think he did either."[6] And Hoyt admitted that very thing quite regularly.

Many batters admitted how often Wilhelm and his knuckler fooled him. In a way they were like Romano, only with a stick of wood trying to catch up to the twists and turns of the pitch.

"The toughest pitcher for me was a teammate of mine in Baltimore for a few years," said Bob Boyd, a first baseman who hit just shy of .300 and might have made it if he never faced Wilhelm. "I always hated the knuckleball, a real tough pitch for me to hit. I remember one time I was facing Wilhelm and he threw the knuckler with two strikes. I swung and missed and the ball hit the toe of my right foot, my front foot. So, it went in the books as a strikeout when I should have been hit by the pitch. But that was the knuckler. Like I said, I always hated it."[7]

Although he was of another generation, too young to catch Wilhelm, Chris Widger, who was born in 1971 and spent parts of 10 years in the majors, offered one of the most vivid yet imaginable scenarios to describe the way a knuckleball moves.

"If you've ever been on a plane with a lot of turbulence and you're shaking all over, that's what a knuckleball looks like coming in," Widger said. "That's why we call a plane [ride] like that a 'knuckleball express.' You don't know where it's going to go, or when it's going to go up and down."[8]

Although there is no evidence Wilhelm made such a comparison, only Muhammad Ali in the sports world gave so much publicity to floating like a butterfly as the knuckleball.

When Wilhelm was voted into the Hall of Fame along with base-stealing guru Lou Brock and they met for the first time in

Epilogue

connection with Hall business, Wilhelm figured Brock was going to tell him about the time he got a hit off of him since that's what all hitters he met did. Brock said he didn't remember ever facing Wilhelm, so probably not.

Besides highlighting Wilhelm as a member of the Baseball Hall of Fame—and emphasizing that he was the first relief pitcher so honored—many of the obituaries did stress that he was a war hero from World War II, winner of a Purple Heart.

Included were several notable numbers, Wilhelm's 143 victories on the mound, his 1,070 appearances in games, and his glittering 2.52 earned run average.

It was Wilbur Wood, taking a last opportunity to thank Wilhelm for his savvy advice, to let all things ride on the knuckleball, who offered the most heartfelt of baseball player comments.

"It was a great privilege and honor for me to be a teammate and friend of his," Wood said.[9]

Yet it was the succinct observation offered by his wife Peggy that summed up the link between Hoyt Wilhelm and the sport, him realizing just how fortunate a man could be to possess the talent and the will, and also be blessed with opportunities, to make America's game a way to make his mark in this world and to make a living for all those decades.

And also, to realize—in a sense having a long, last laugh on skeptics—that such a peculiar, often overlooked, periodically snubbed tricky pitch with the unlikely name of "knuckleball" could be at the root of so much good for him across a long life.

Notes

Preface

1. Phil Niekro, personal interview, April 2014.

Introduction

1. Dave Clark, *The Knucklebook* (Chicago: Ivan R. Dee, 2006), p. 27.
2. Phil Niekro, personal interview, April 2014.

Chapter 1

1. Viki Hager interview, October 4, 2022.
2. *Ibid.*
3. *Ibid.*
4. (No byline) *Charlotte News* photograph, March 14, 1941.
5. Hoyt Wilhelm oral history interview, National Baseball Hall of Fame and Museum by Rod Roberts, February 26, 1988.
6. Hoyt Wilhelm, "Gary Beddington's Baseball in Wartime," *The Sporting News*, June 10, 1953.
7. (No byline) "Dutch Uses Finger Tips," *Charlotte News*, May 5, 1938.
8. Ed Sainsbury, "Dutch Leonard Keeps Throwing His Knuckleball," *The Alva* [OK] *Review-Courier*/United Press International, June 11, 1952.
9. *Ibid.*
10. Dutch Leonard and Stanley Frank, "Too Old to Pitch? Don't Make Me Laugh!" *The Saturday Evening Post*, July 4, 1953.
11. *Ibid.*
12. *Ibid.*
13. Bill Libby, *Star Pitchers of the Major Leagues* (New York: Random House, 1971), p. 96.
14. *Ibid.*, p. 103.

Chapter 2

1. (No byline) "First Ball Game," *Charlotte Observer*, April 14, 1940.
2. (No byline) "Wilhelm Hurls No-Hit Battle," *Charlotte Observer*, April 12, 1941.
3. Brett Honeycutt, "The Lost Baseball Years of Hoyt Wilhelm," National Baseball Hall of Fame Library archives, Hoyt Wilhelm player file.
4. "Gary Bedington's Baseball in Wartime: Baseball's Greatest Sacrifice," https:///www.baseballinwartime.com, June 9, 2007.

Chapter 3

1. William C. Kashatus, *One-Armed Wonder: Pete Gray, Wartime Baseball, and the American Dream* (Jefferson, NC: McFarland, 1995), p. 3.
2. Winston Churchill, House of Commons, January 18, 1945.
3. Paul Zsoldra, "Surrounded. Low on Supplies. Freezing. The Nazis Demanded his Surrender. He replied, 'Nuts!'" https://taskandpurpose.com, December 22, 2020.
4. *Ibid.*
5. *Ibid.*
6. *Ibid.*
7. (No byline) "Wounded," *Charlotte Observer*, April 7, 1945.
8. Brett Honeycutt, "The Lost Baseball

Notes

Years of Hoyt Wilhelm," National Baseball Hall of Fame Library archives, Hoyt Wilhelm player file.

9. Viki Hager interview, October 4, 2022.

10. *Ibid.*

Chapter 4

1. Ira Berkow, *The Corporal Was a Pitcher: The Courage of Lou Brissie* (Chicago: Triumph, 2009), p. 93.

2. Bill Libby, *Star Pitchers of the Major Leagues* (New York: Random House, 1971), p. 98.

3. *Ibid.*

4. *Ibid.*

5. Hoyt Wilhelm oral history interview, National Baseball Hall of Fame and Museum by Rod Roberts, February 26, 1988.

6. Eddie Allen, "Jim Mitchell Is Visitors' Villain," *Charlotte Observer*, August 8, 1948.

7. (No byline), *Tampa Times*, Associated Press, May 31, 1949.

Chapter 5

1. Joe Hendrickson, "Sports Views," *Minneapolis Star-Tribune*, May 3, 1950.

2. *Ibid.*

3. *Ibid.*

4. *Ibid.*

5. Bob Beebe, "Favorable Wind Big Aid," *Minneapolis Star-Tribune*, June 11, 1950.

6. *Ibid.*

7. (No byline) "'I Like to Beat Those Cocky Guys'—Wilhelm," *Minneapolis Star-Tribune*, September 16, 1950.

8. Dick Cullum, "Cullum's Column: Syracuse Is in Finals on Merit," *Minneapolis Star-Tribune*, April 14, 1950.

9. Dick Cullum, "Cullum's Column," *Minneapolis Star Tribune*, March 10, 1951.

10. (No byline), "Kropf Set; Outfield Job Open," *Minneapolis Star Tribune*, March 21, 1951.

11. Halsey Hall, "It's a Fact," *Minneapolis Star Tribune*, March 24, 1951.

12. Dick Cullum, "Cullum's Column," *Minneapolis Star Tribune*, April 10, 1951.

13. Bob Beebe, "Katt Joins Wilhelm, 'Dan' in Cuba," *Minneapolis Star-Tribune*, September 12, 1951.

Chapter 6

1. Hoyt Wilhelm oral history interview, National Baseball Hall of Fame and Museum by Rod Roberts, February 26, 1988.

2. Paul Dickson, *Leo Durocher, Baseball's Prodigal Son* (New York: Bloomsbury, 2017), p. 212.

3. Bill Libby, *Star Pitchers of the Major Leagues* (New York: Random House, 1971), p. 99.

4. Richard A. Johnson, *The Knuckleball Club: The Extraordinary Men Who Mastered Baseball's Most Difficult Pitch* (Lanham, MD: Rowman & Littlefield, 2016), p. 71.

Chapter 7

1. Jim McCulley, "Rhodes' HR Beats Bucs in Rain, 4–3," *New York Daily News*, August 3, 1952.

2. Dick Young, "Chuck Eyes Giants, Saves Erskine for Series Opener," *New York Daily News*, August 11, 1952.

3. Bill Libby, *Star Pitchers of the Major Leagues* (New York: Random House, 1971), p. 101.

4. Hoyt Wilhelm oral history interview, National Baseball Hall of Fame and Museum by Rod Roberts, February 26, 1988.

5. *Ibid.*

6. *Ibid.*

7. Johnson, *The Knuckleball Club*, p. 65.

8. *Ibid.*, p. 67.

9. Judith Testa, *Sal Maglie: Baseball's Demon Barber* (DeKalb: Northern Illinois University Press, 2007), p. 205.

10. Roberts interview.

11. John Drebinger, "Wilhelm Clouts Triple in Beating Redlegs at Polo Grounds, 11 to 3," *New York Times*, June 5, 1953.

Notes

Chapter 8

1. Gene Schoor, *The History of the World Series: The Complete Chronology of America's Greatest Sports Tradition* (New York: William Morrow, 1990), p. 240.
2. Viki Hager interview, October 4, 2022.
3. Red Smith, "Views Of Sports" (syndicated column), September 11, 1954.
4. *Ibid.*
5. (No byline), "Katt's Passed Ball Mark Draws Much Sympathy," *New York World-Telegram and Sun*, September 11, 1954.
6. *Ibid.*
7. *Ibid.*
8. Gene Fehler, *When Baseball Was Still King* (Jefferson, NC: McFarland, 2012), p. 131.
9. Schoor, *The History of the World Series*, p. 240.
10. *Ibid.*
11. Dan Carditz, "Never Hit Ball Harder, Wertz Said," *Cleveland Plain-Dealer*, September 30, 1954.
12. Author source missing
13. Jimmy Cannon, "Jimmy Cannon Says" (syndicated column), October 1, 1954.
14. *Ibid.*
15. Bob Broeg, "Antonelli Is Relief Hero In Final Rout of Indians; Lemon, Newhouser Kayoed," *St. Louis Post-Dispatch*, October 3, 1954.

Chapter 9

1. Hoyt Wilhelm oral history interview, National Baseball Hall of Fame and Museum by Rod Roberts, February 26, 1988.
2. *Ibid.*
3. *Ibid.*
4. Frank Bilovsky, "Giants of '54 a 'Fame' team," *Rochester [NY] Democrat and Chronicle*, July 26, 1985.
5. *Ibid.*
6. Frederick G. Lieb, "Giants' Sweep Rivaled Game's Greatest Upsets," *The Sporting News*, October 13, 1954.
7. Brent Kelley, "Wes Westrum: New York's Other Catcher," *Sports Collectors Digest*, April 13, 1990.
8. *Ibid.*
9. *Ibid.*
10. Warren Corbett, "Bob Purkey," Society for American Baseball Research, no date.

Chapter 10

1. Jim McCulley, "Whitey Returns to Giants; Wilhelm Goes to Cards," *New York Daily News*, February 27, 1957.
2. *Ibid.*
3. *Ibid.*
4. *Ibid.*
5. Johnson, *The Knuckleball Club*, p. 76.
6. (No byline), "How Hoyt Wilhelm got traded to Cardinals," Cardinals History Behind the Box Score, February 8, 2017.
7. *Ibid.*
8. Hoyt Wilhelm oral history interview, National Baseball Hall of Fame and Museum with Rod Roberts, February 26, 1988.
9. *Ibid.*
10. *Ibid.*
11. Eddie Robinson and C. Paul Rogers III, *Lucky Me: My Sixty-Five Years In Baseball* (Dallas: Southern Methodist University Press, 2011), p. 127.
12. *The Inside Pitch with Bob Wulf*, TV show, 1958.
13. *Ibid.*
14. *Ibid.*
15. *Ibid.*
16. *Ibid.*
17. *Ibid.*
18. *Ibid.*

Chapter 11

1. Joe Falls, "Gus Grins Again—No Butterflies to Bug Him," *The Sporting News*, March 23, 1963.
2. Alex Coffey, "Hoyt Wilhelm Pitches No-Hitter Versus Yankees," Baseball Hall of Fame and Museum Inside Pitch Series (no date).
3. *Ibid.*

197

Notes

4. Mike Klingaman, "Wilhelm's Gem Gave City Hope," *Baltimore Sun*, September 20, 2008.
5. Lou Hatter, "Hoyt's Wife Gets Big Gift," *Baltimore Sun*, September 21, 1958.
6. *Ibid.*
7. *Ibid.*
8. (No byline), "Hoyt Wilhelm No-Hits Yankees," *Arizona Daily Star/ United Press International*, September 21, 1958.
9. *Ibid.*
10. Bob Maisel, "Wilhelm Hurls No-Hitter as Birds Beat Yanks, 1–0," *Baltimore Sun*, September 21, 1958.
11. Klingaman, "Wilhelm's Gem Gave City Hope."

Chapter 12

1. Warren Corbett, *The Wizard of Waxahachie* (Dallas: Southern Methodist University Press, 2009), p. 203.
2. Brooks Robinson and Jack Tobin, *Third Base Is My Home* (Waco: Word Books, 1974), p. 112.
3. *Ibid.*, p. 113.
4. Lew Freedman, *Knuckleball: The History of the Unhittable Pitch* (New York: Skyhorse, 2015), p. 70.
5. *Ibid.*, p. 71.
6. Lou Hatter, "Wilhelm's 4-Hitter Stops Yanks as Orioles Win, 5–0," *Baltimore Sun*, May 29, 1959.
7. Norman L. Wetzler, "American Viewpoint," *Baltimore Sun*, May 15, 1959.
8. Ernest B. Furgurson, "Beauty Queen Abdicates, Crowns Lady-in-Waiting," *Baltimore Sun*, July 2, 1959.
9. *Ibid.*
10. Lou Hatter, "Hoyt's 1959 Win Streak Stops at 9," *Baltimore Sun*, June 16, 1959.
11. (No byline), "Orioles Visit Crippled Group," *Baltimore Sun*, July 2, 1959.
12. (No byline), "The Orioles," *Baltimore Sun*, June 16, 1959.
13. Corbett, *The Wizard of Waxahachie*, p. 218.

Chapter 13

1. Cover, *Sports Illustrated*, June 29, 1959.
2. Roy Terrell, "Nobody Hits It," *Sports Illustrated*, June 29, 1959.
3. *Ibid.*
4. *Ibid.*
5. Freedman, *Knuckleball*, p. 132.
6. *Ibid.*
7. Terrell, "Nobody Hits It."
8. *Ibid.*
9. *Ibid.*
10. *Ibid.*
11. *Ibid.*
12. *Ibid.*
13. *Ibid.*
14. *Ibid.*

Chapter 14

1. Robinson and Rogers, *Lucky Me*, p. 128.
2. Mike Klingaman, "Gus Triandos, Beloved Ex-Orioles Catcher, Dies at 82," *Baltimore Sun*, March 29, 2013.
3. Rich Marazzi, "Lumbering Gus Triandos Was an All-Star Catcher for Some Top-Flight Orioles Clubs," *Sports Collectors Digest*, April 4, 1997.
4. Corbett, *The Wizard of Waxahachie*, p. 228.
5. *Ibid.*
6. *Ibid.*
7. *Ibid.*, p. 266.
8. (No byline), "Hero in Baltimore: Catcher Gus Triandos," *Baseball's Best Magazine*, 1960.
9. *Ibid.*
10. Joe King, "Thanks to Triandos, Hoyt Has 6–0 Record," *New York World-Telegram and Sun*, May 28, 1959.
11. Edward Kiersh, "Whatever Happened to Gus Triandos," *San Francisco Chronicle*, April 19, 1982.

Chapter 15

1. (No byline), "Clint Courtney Big Help in Oriole Drive," Associated Press, June 3, 1960.
2. *Ibid.*

Notes

3. (No byline) "Catcher's Mitt Helps Orioles Win," Associated Press, May 28, 1960.
4. John Eisenberg, *From 33rd Street to Camden Yards: An Oral History of the Baltimore Orioles* (New York: Contemporary Books, 2001), p. 101.
5. Hoyt Wilhelm oral history interview, National Baseball Hall of Fame and Museum with Rod Roberts, February 26, 1988.
6. *Ibid.*

Chapter 16

1. Freedman, *Knuckleball*, pp. 97–98.
2. Mark Liptak, "J.C. Martin," *Baseball Almanac*, Player Interview Series, May 2002.
3. *Ibid.*
4. Jerome Holtzman, "Hoyt's 40 Now, and He Throws Knuckleball Sharper Than Ever," *Chicago Sun-Times*, August 10, 1963.
5. Freedman, *Knuckleball*, p. 132.
6. Holtzman, "Hoyt's 40 Now."
7. Curley Grieve, "Sports Parade: Eddie Fisher's Knuckler Could Make Difference," *San Francisco Examiner*, June 19, 1959.
8. *Ibid.*
9. *Ibid.*
10. Paul Cox, "Ban on King-Sized Mitt Fails to Upset Hoyt," *Columbus* [Georgia] *Enquirer,* January 18, 1964.
11. Edgar Munzel, "Richards Raving at Rules Ban on His Baby—King-Sized Mitt," *Chicago Tribune*, December 26, 1964.
12. Cox, "Ban on King-Sized Mitt Fails to Upset Hoyt."
13. *Ibid.*
14. *Ibid.*
15. Brent Musburger, "Life Begins at 30 for Fisher, White Sox Flutterball Expert," *Chicago American*, May 15, 1965.
16. *Ibid.*
17. *Ibid.*
18. *Ibid.*
19. *Ibid.*

Chapter 17

1. Edgar Munzel, "New Mitt Designed to Handle Knuckler," *Chicago Tribune,* April 10, 1965.
2. Wilbur Wood, personal interview, October 4, 2022.
3. *Ibid.*
4. Tim Horgan, "It Was Almost a Pipe Dream," *Boston Herald*, August 26, 1972.
5. *Ibid.*
6. Wood, personal interview.
7. Dick Young, "Name's Wood, but His Arm Is Made of Rubber," *New York Daily News*, July 30, 1971.
8. *Ibid.*
9. *Ibid.*
10. (No byline), "Wilbur Wood Reveling in Starting Pitcher Role," *Boston Record-American*/United Press International, August 20, 1971.
11. Ed Rumill, "Knuckleball Ace," *Christian Science Monitor*, October 9, 1971.
12. Jerome Holtzman, "Workhorse Wood-King of White Sox Hurlers," *The Sporting News*, October 2, 1971.
13. Al Hirshberg, "Wilbur Wood & The Art of the Knuckleball," *Sport Magazine*, August 1972.
14. *Ibid.*
15. *Ibid.*
16. Jerome Holtzman, "Iron-Man Wood," *The Sporting News*, May 13, 1972.
17. *Ibid.*
18. (No byline), "Wood's 2 Good 2 Be True," Associated Press, July 21, 1973.
19. *Ibid.*
20. Hirshberg, "Wilbur Wood & The Art of the Knuckleball."

Chapter 18

1. Paul Cox, "Hoyt Is Happy with Royals," *Columbus* [Georgia] *Enquirer*, October 24, 1968.
2. *Ibid.*
3. *Ibid.*
4. *Ibid.*
5. *Ibid.*
6. Dick Miller, "Angels' Fisher Is Busiest Reliever in A.L. History," *The Sporting News*, July 29, 1972.
7. *Ibid.*
8. *Ibid.*
9. Edgar Munzel, "Eddie Fisher Show-

Notes

Stopper of Chisox," *The Sporting News*, July 10, 1965.
10. Bob Logan, "Wood's Kneecap Broken in 4-2 Win," *Chicago Tribune*, May 10, 1976.
11. Mark Liptak, "A Conversation With: Wilbur Wood," *Sports Illustrated*, November 28, 2019.
12. Ibid.
13. Wilbur Wood, personal interview, October 4, 2022.
14. Ibid.
15. Tommy John, personal interview, July 18, 2022.
16. Ibid.
17. Wood, personal interview.

Chapter 19

1. Holtzman, "Hoyt's 40 Now."
2. Ibid.
3. Richard Dozer, "Hoyt Wilhelm Has a Future with Braves," *Chicago Tribune*, October 3, 1969.
4. Ibid.
5. Ibid.
6. (No byline), "Wilhelm Continues Assault on Record," *New York Times*/Associated Press, December 20, 1969.
7. Wayne Minshew, "19th Major Spring Camp, Hoyt Still Recalls His First," *The Sporting News*, March 28, 1970.
8. Ibid.
9. Ibid.
10. Ibid.
11. Charlie Roberts, "In 1,000th, No Smiles for Hoyt," *Atlanta Constitution*, May 11, 1970.
12. Ibid.
13. Ibid.
14. Steve Wulf, "Knucksie Hasn't Lost His Grip," *Sports Illustrated*, June 4, 1984.
15. Matthew Waxman, "Catching a Knuckleball," *Sports Illustrated*, July 31, 2006.
16. (No byline), "Hall of Fame Pitcher Phil Niekro, Famous for Signature Knuckleball," ESPN News Services, December 27, 2020.
17. Bud Shaw, "Niekro Wins No. 300," *Atlanta Constitution*, October 7, 1985.
18. Matt Kelly, "Speed Limit? Baseball's Slowest Pitches," www.mlb.com, June 21, 2020.
19. Wulf, "Knucksie Hasn't Lost His Grip."
20. Freedman, *Knuckleball*, p. 140.

Chapter 20

1. Paul Cox, "At 48, Wilhelm Talks Like Rookie," *The Sporting News*, February 12, 1972.
2. Ibid.
3. Edgar Munzel, "Like Ol' Man River Hoyt Keeps Rollin' Along as Relief Ace," *Chicago Tribune*, September 17, 1966.
4. (No byline), "Hoyt Wilhelm Tabbed as Wonder of Baseball," *Boston Record*/United Press International, May 14, 1969.
5. Wayne Minshew, "Old Man Wilhelm a Hero to Every Fan Pushing 50," *The Sporting News*, May 15, 1970.
6. Munzel, "Like Ol' Man River Hoyt Keeps Rollin' Along as Relief Ace."
7. Ibid.
8. (No byline), "Hoyt Wilhelm Tabbed as Wonder of Baseball," *Boston Record*/United Press International, May 14, 1969.
9. Minshew, "Old Man Wilhelm a Hero to Every Fan Pushing 50."
10. Ibid.
11. (No byline), "Hoyt Unhappy Over Release," *The Sporting News*, July 10, 1971.
12. Bob Hunter, "Dodger Bullpen Bulging with Freaks," *Los Angeles Times*, September 4, 1971.
13. Patti Singer, "Boone No-Hits Syracuse," *Rochester Democrat and Chronicle*, July 24, 1990.
14. Tyler Kepner, "Jim Bouton Opened Up the Major Leagues to Everyone," *New York Times*, July 11, 2019.
15. Ibid.
16. Jim Murray, "Wilhelm's Knuckler Gives Batters Butterflies," *Los Angeles Times*, October 7, 1967.
17. Ibid.
18. Norman Arey, "Down on the Farm: Hoyt Wilhelm—A Specter of Summers Past," *Atlanta Journal*, August 7, 1973.
19. Bob Snyder, "Do as I Say, Not

Notes

as I Did: Hoyt Wilhelm's Philosophy," *Syracuse Herald*, June 30, 1977.
20. *Ibid.*

Chapter 21

1. Stan Hochman, "Knuckleball, Nerves of Steel, Put Wilhelm in Cooperstown," *Philadelphia Daily News*, January 8, 1985.
2. *Ibid.*
3. *Ibid.*
4. *Ibid.*
5. Thomas J. Lueck, "Hoyt Wilhelm, First Reliever Elected to the Hall of Fame," *New York Times*, August 26, 2002.
6. *Ibid.*
7. Bill Gleason, "Control of Knuckleball Made Wilhelm King of the Relievers," *The Sporting News*, January 21, 1985.
8. *Ibid.*
9. Hoyt Wilhelm oral history interview, National Baseball Hall of Fame and Museum with Rod Roberts, February 26, 1988.
10. Fran Zimnuich, *Fireman: The Evolution of the Closer in Baseball* (Chicago: Triumph, 2010), p. 39.
11. Hoyt Wilhelm Hall of Fame speech, July 28, 1983.
12. *Ibid.*
13. *Ibid.*
14. *Ibid.*
15. *Ibid.*
16. *Ibid.*
17. *Ibid.*
18. Hoyt Wilhelm National Baseball Hall of Fame plaque.

Epilogue

1. (No byline) "King of Knuckleballers, Hoyt Wilhelm Is Dead," *Press and Sun-Bulletin* (Binghamton, NY)/Associated Press, August 25, 2002.
2. *Ibid.*
3. Stan Olson, "Hall of Famer Wilhelm, an N.C. Native, Dies," *Charlotte Observer*, August 25, 2002.
4. Johnny Rosenstein, "Hoyt Wilhelm, 1923–2002, Ex-Sox, Hall of Famer, the Knuckleball King," *Chicago Tribune*, August 25, 2002.
5. (No byline), "Wilhelm First Reliever Elected to Hall of Fame," Associated Press, August 25, 2002.
6. Rosenstein, "Hoyt Wilhelm, 1923–2002, Ex-Sox, Hall of Famer, the Knuckleball King."
7. Lee Heiman, Dave Weiner, and Bill Gutman, *When The Cheering Stops* (New York: Macmillan, 1990), p. 154.
8. Dave van Dyck, "Flotation Advice," *Chicago Tribune*, May 10, 2006.
9. Rosenstein, "Hoyt Wilhelm, 1923–2002, Ex-Sox, Hall of Famer, the Knuckleball King."

Bibliography

Books

Berkow, Ira. *The Corporal Was a Pitcher: The Courage of Lou Brissie*. Chicago: Triumph, 2009.
Clark, Dave. *The Knucklebook*. Chicago: Ivan R. Dee, 2006.
Corbett, Warren. *The Wizard of Waxahachie*. Dallas: Southern Methodist University Press, 2009.
Dickson, Paul. *Leo Durocher, Baseball's Prodigal Son*. New York: Bloomsbury, 2017.
Eisenberg, John. *From 33rd Street to Camden Yards: An Oral History of the Baltimore Orioles*. New York: Contemporary, 2001.
Fehler, Gene. *When Baseball Was Still King*. Jefferson, NC: McFarland, 2012.
Freedman, Lew. *Knuckleball: The History of the Unhittable Pitch*. New York: Skyhorse, 2015.
Heiman, Lee, Dave Weiner, and Bill Gutman. *When the Cheering Stops*. New York: Macmillan, 1990.
Johnson, Richard A. *The Knuckleball Club: The Extraordinary Men Who Mastered Baseball's Most Difficult Pitch*. Lanham, MD: Rowman & Littlefield, 2016.
Kashatus, William C. *One-Armed Wonder: Pete Gray, Wartime Baseball, and the American Dream*. Jefferson, NC: McFarland, 1995.
Libby, Bill. *Star Pitchers of the Major Leagues*. New York: Random House, 1971.
Robinson, Brooks, and Jack Tobin. *Third Base Is My Home*. Waco: Word Books, 1974.
Robinson, Eddie, and C. Paul Rogers III. *Lucky Me: My Sixty-Five Years in Baseball*. Dallas: Southern Methodist University Press, 2011.
Schoor, Gene. *The History of the World Series: The Complete Chronology of America's Greatest Sports Tradition*. New York: William Morrow, 1990.
Testa, Judith. *Sal Maglie: Baseball's Demon Barber*. DeKalb: Northern Illinois University Press, 2007.

Interviews

Viki Hager
Tommy John
Phil Niekro
Wilbur Wood

Magazines

Baseball's Best Magazine, 1960
Saturday Evening Post
Sport Magazine
Sporting News
Sports Collectors Digest
Sports Illustrated

Newspapers

Alva [OK] Review-Courier
Atlanta Constitution
Atlanta Journal
Baltimore Sun

Bibliography

Boston Herald
Charlotte News
Charlotte Observer
Chicago American
Chicago Sun-Times
Chicago Tribune
Christian Science Monitor
Cleveland Plain-Dealer
Columbus [GA] *Enquirer*
Los Angeles Times
Minneapolis Star-Tribune
New York Daily News
New York Times
New York World-Telegram and Sun
Philadelphia Daily News
Rochester [NY] *Democrat and Chronicle*
St. Louis Post-Dispatch
San Francisco Chronicle
San Francisco Examiner
Syracuse Herald-Journal
Tampa Times

Online Sources

Baseballinwartime.com
ESPN
MLB.com
Taskandpurpose.com

Index

AARP (American Association of Retired Persons) 174
Aaron, Hank 128, 129
Abreu, Bryan 90
Adair, Bill 148
Adams, Ace 53
Adams, Bobby 64
Alabama 68
Alexander, Grover Cleveland 46, 91, 149
All-America Football Conference 30
Allison, Doug 120
All-Star game 2, 13, 50, 58, 59, 74, 75, 78, 92, 93, 94, 106, 108, 114, 116, 121, 127, 128, 130, 131, 132, 149, 151, 154, 170, 178, 181, 187, 191
Alston, Walt 186
American Airlines 8
American Association 4, 34, 35
American League 13, 17, 24, 30, 35, 36, 46, 58, 67, 72, 75, 76, 83, 88, 94, 100, 104, 105, 106, 116, 118, 124, 127, 128, 129, 130, 132, 141, 148, 149, 151, 158, 165, 166, 176, 181
American Legion 138
The American Sportsman 163
Anderson, South Carolina 29
Anson, Cap 156
Antonelli, Johnny 66, 70, 72, 74, 78, 106
Aparicio, Luis 132, 148
Ardennes Offensive on the Western Front 25
Associated Press 189
Atlanta 157
Atlanta Braves 118, 165, 166, 167, 168, 169, 170, 172, 173, 175, 187
Atlanta Stadium 168
Atrium Health 8
Auburn, Illinois 10
Augusta, Georgia 34
Averill, Earl 49
Avila, Bobby 67, 69, 71, 72

Ball Four 5, 177
Baltimore Block 106
Baltimore Colts 99, 102
Baltimore Inner Harbor 106
Baltimore Memorial Stadium 84, 88, 104
Baltimore Orioles 2, 24, 49, 84, 86, 88, 89, 91, 92, 93, 94, 95, 96, 97, 98, 99, 100, 101, 104, 105, 106, 109, 112, 114, 116, 116, 117, 118, 120, 122, 125, 127, 128, 129, 130, 132, 134, 139, 142, 148, 159, 177, 178, 186
Baltimore Sun 103, 104, 106
Bank of America 8
Banks, Ernie 106
Barber, Steve 125, 132
Barbieri, Jim 67
Baseball Hall of Fame 1, 2, 5, 19, 22, 36, 40, 42, 44, 46, 48, 49, 50, 54, 57, 67, 78, 90, 95, 96, 106, 119, 122, 123, 128, 134, 137, 139, 148, 155, 156, 170, 172, 180, 182, 184, 186, 187, 191, 192, 193
Baseball Writers Association of America 182
Bastogne, Belgium 26
Battle of the Bulge 25, 27
Bauer, Hank 89, 91, 92, 93, 95
Bearden, Gene 5, 77, 110, 172
Belgium 25
Bender, Chief 90
Benedict, Bruce 170, 171
Berlin 26
Berra, Yogi 21, 22, 67, 90, 94, 96, 102, 121, 128, 129, 180
"Big Bertha" (oversized catcher's mitt) 121, 122, 124, 125, 126, 139, 140, 187
Black, Frederick H. (general) 25
Black, Joe 47
Black Sox 4, 134
Blyleven, Bert 91
Boone, Dan 177

Index

Boone, Daniel 177
Boston (Bees) Braves 17, 21, 32, 48, 49, 50, 52, 58, 62, 153, 158
Boston Red Sox (Naps) 11, 17, 21, 31, 35, 45, 56, 64, 97, 101, 104, 116, 117, 128, 144, 151, 158, 178
Bouton, Bob (brother) 178
Bouton, Jim 5, 177, 178
Boyd, Bob 90, 91, 94, 192
Boyer, Clete 175
Boyer, Ken 128, 129
Bradley, George Washington 90
Brady, Bob 37
Bragan, Bobby 86
Branca, Ralph 42
Brandt, Jackie 80, 128
Brecheen, Harry 126
Breeden, Hal 173
Bresnahan, Roger 35, 119
Bridges, Rocky 109
Brissie, Lou 29, 30
Brock, Lou 182, 185, 192, 193
Brooklyn Dodgers 4, 11, 13, 17, 36, 38, 42, 43, 47, 48, 52, 53, 58, 60, 61, 62, 66, 75, 76, 80, 91, 117
Brouthers, Dan 156
Brown, Ben 56
Brown, Dick 86
Brown, "Skinny" Hal 126
BUD BERMA PRO-JAC 103
Bunning, Jim 91, 123, 128, 130
Burgess, Smoky 128
Burnette, Wally 78, 110
Busby, Jim 93, 94
Busch, Kyle 8

Cal-State Fullerton 177
Camp Croft (military base) 23
Camp Maxey (military base) 23, 24
Campanella, Roy 42, 48, 66, 75
Canada 25
Candlestick Park 128
Candiotti, Tom 5, 177
Cannon, Jimmy 70
Cardenal, Jose 168
Carolina League 33
Carolina Panthers 9
Carroll, Clay 161
Carty, Rico 169
Castleman, Foster 90, 93, 94
Cepeda, Orlando 35, 128
Chapman, Ray 118
Charlotte, North Carolina 7, 8
Charlotte Hornets 9

Charlotte Motor Speedway 9
Charlotte News 9, 10
Charlotte Observer 16, 27, 133, 191
Chase, Ken 10
Chesboro, Jack 152
Chicago 159
Chicago Cubs 11, 12, 13, 17, 52, 61, 62, 75, 88, 132, 172, 173, 175
Chicago Sun Times 45
Chicago Tribune 191
Chicago White Sox 2, 4, 17, 58, 75, 77, 100, 103, 114, 117, 118, 119, 127, 129, 130, 132, 134, 135, 136, 139, 140, 141, 143, 145, 146, 147, 149, 150, 153, 154, 155, 157, 158, 159, 161, 163, 166, 172, 182, 183, 187, 191, 192
Churchill, Winston 25
Cicotte, Ed 4
Cincinnati 58
Cincinnati Reds (Redlegs, Red Stockings) 17, 49, 52, 58, 59, 62, 63, 64, 65, 78, 82, 118, 120, 172
Clark, Will 49
Clarkson, John 90
Clemens, Robert 5, 156
Clemente, Roberto 128, 129
Cleveland Indians 5, 17, 20, 21, 36, 67, 68, 69, 71, 72, 75, 77, 83, 84, 85, 86, 87, 88, 100, 108, 110, 118, 123, 129, 149, 158, 187, 191
Cleveland Spiders 158
Cleveland Stadium 71
Colavito, Rocky 130, 141
College Football Hall of Fame 122
Collins, Andy (Wilhelm grandson) 97
Cologne, Germany 27
Colombia, South America 163
Columbus, Georgia 131, 157, 167, 173
Columbus, Ohio 19
Columbus Red Birds 38, 40
Comiskey Park 149, 160
Compton, Clint 165
Concord, North Carolina 20
Conlan, Jocko 65
Cooper, Walker 82
Cooperstown, New York 50, 139, 182, 185
Corcoran, Larry 90
Cornelius High School (North Carolina) 9, 16
Corpus Christi, Texas 138
Corrsin, Dr. Stanley 112, 113
Courtney, "Scrap Iron" Clint 39, 120, 121, 122, 126, 127

Index

Cox, Billy 48
Crippled Children and Adults' Sheltered Workshop (Baltimore) 104
Crosley Field 52, 58
Cuba 39, 40
Cullum, Dick 39
Cummings, Candy 118, 119, 120
Cy Young Award 5, 150, 177

Dallas, Texas 81
Damn Yankees (stage show) 106, 107
Dandridge, Ray 36, 39, 40
Dark, Alvin 57, 69, 71, 80, 82
Davalillo, Vic 169
Davidson, North Carolina 19
Davidson College 19
Deadball Era 137, 155
Decker, Harry 120
Des Moines, Iowa 19
Detroit Tigers 18, 21, 57, 82, 101, 104, 109, 117, 118, 128, 130, 149, 150, 161
Detroit Wolverines 120
Dickey, R.A. 5, 176
Dickson, Murray 58
DiMaggio, Joe 21, 29, 30
Doak, Bill 119
Dobbs Ferry (New York) 73
Doby, Larry 36, 67, 69, 71, 72
Donovan, Dick 128
Doubleday, Abner 140
Dressen, Chuck 35, 53, 58
Duren, Ryne 78
Durocher, Leo 42, 44, 47, 48, 50, 51, 53, 60, 61, 65, 68, 69, 71, 72, 77, 78, 137, 168, 183, 186

East Baltimore Street (Baltimore) 106
Ebbets Field 42, 48
Eckersley, Dennis 91
Edison, Thomas 4
Edward VIII 103
Einstein, Albert 109
England (Great Britain) 24, 25
Erskine, Carl 48, 53, 75
ESPN Sports Center 34
Estrada, Chuck 125, 132
Europe 25, 29
Evers, Johnny 156

Faber, Red 156
Feliciano, Pedro 153
Feller, Bob 21, 22, 29, 31, 54, 90, 149
Fenway Park 130
Fisher, Carrie 160

Fisher, Eddie (pitcher) 5, 100, 114, 134, 136, 137, 138, 139, 140, 141, 142, 143, 144, 145, 155, 159, 160, 161, 184
Fisher, Eddie (singer) 160
Fisher, Jack 125, 132, 158
Fisk, Carlton 156
Forbes Field 51, 106
Fornieles, Mike 128
Ford, Whitey 106, 128
Fowler, Art 33, 64
Fox, Nellie 128, 129, 182
France 24
Franco, Julio 156
Fred Hutchinson Cancer Research Center 82
Furillo, Carl 75

Galvin, Pud 90
Game of the Week 96, 97
Garcia, Mike 67, 71
Gardner, Billy 90, 93, 94
Gedeon, Elmer 29
Gentile, Jim 127, 128, 129
Germany 21, 25, 26, 27, 28, 37
Gibson, Bob 91
Giles, Warren 60
Gillick, Pat 184
Ginsberg, Joe 126
Glynn, Bill 71
Gomez, Ruben 57, 66, 71
Gordon, Joe 86
Gossage "Goose" Rich 131
Gray, Pete 24
Great Depression 17
Greenberg, Hank 21, 29, 57
Greengrass, Jim 65, 66
Greenville (South Carolina) Spinners 34
Greenwood (South Carolina) 179
Griffin, Mike 49
Griffith, Clark 36
Grissom, Marv 69
Groat, Dick 47
Gutteridge, Don 148

Haefner, Mickey 11, 12
Hager, (Wilhelm) Viki (sister) 7, 9, 28, 61, 62, 189, 190
Haines, Jesse 5, 90, 172
Halladay, Ray 91
Hanlon, Ned 95
Hansen, Ron 132, 136, 191
Harris, Bucky 67
Harris, Luman 169
Hartford Dark Blues 90

Index

Harwell, Ernie 95
Havana, Cuba 39, 40
Hearn, Jim 43, 44, 48
Hemond, Roland 191
Herbert, Ray 130
Herrmann, Ed 146
Hickory, North Carolina 20
Hitchcock, Billy 130
Hodges, Gil 42, 48, 75
Holtzman, Jerome 45, 137
Hooper, Bob 33
Hoover, Dick 48
Hough, Charlie 5, 64, 156, 157, 176, 180, 184
Houk, Ralph 67
Houston Astros (Colt .45s) 90, 118, 132, 139, 177
Houtteman, Art 67
Howard, Elston 89, 91, 92, 94, 121, 128, 129
Howser, Dick 129
Hubbard, Cal 122
Hubbell, Carl 91
Hudson River 42
Hudson, Sid 10
Hughes, Jim 95
Huntersville, North Carolina 7, 8, 19, 20, 28, 96, 185
Hutchinson, Fred 82, 186

Indianapolis 38
Indianapolis 500 3
The Inside Pitch 84
Irvin, Monte 35, 36, 42, 44, 57, 69
Italy 3

Jackson, Larry 82, 83
Jacksonville Tars (Florida) 33, 35
Jansen, Larry 42, 43, 44, 48, 52, 53, 57, 66
Japan 21
Javier, Christian 70
Jennings, Hughie 156
Joe Gibbs Racing 8
John, Tommy 148, 163, 164
Johns Hopkins University 112, 114
Johnson, Ken 139
Johnson, Randy 91, 156
Johnson, Walter 54, 90, 110, 158, 176
Joss, Addie 90
Judge, Aaron 49

Kaat, Jim 149
Kaline, Al 128, 129

Kansas City 38
Kansas City Athletics 78, 101, 104, 156
Kansas City Monarchs 66
Kansas City Royals 157, 165
Katt, Ray 40, 63, 64, 65, 66, 77, 80
Keeler, "Wee" Willie 95
Killebrew, Harmon 128
Kirkpatrick, Ed 165
Knoxville Smokies (Tennessee) 33, 35
Korean War 56
Koufax, Sandy 75, 90, 128
Kuenn, Harvey 104

Labine, Clem 75
Labonte, Bobby 8
Landis, Kennesaw Mountain 17, 21, 23
Landis, North Carolina 20, 32
Landrith, Hobie 82
Lane, Frank 82, 86, 108, 118
Lanier, Max 52
Lansing, Ohio 110
Larsen, Don 89, 91, 92, 93, 139
Lary, Frank 128
Lasorda, Tommy 78
Latham, Artie 156
Lauer, Walter F. (general) 25
Lavarnway, Ryan 64
Law, Vernon 78
Lawrence, Thompson (general) 25
Lazzeri, Tony 46
LeFlore, Ron 161, 162
Lemon, Bob 67, 69, 71, 91, 149
Lennon, Bob 63
Leonard, "Dutch" Emil 5, 9, 10, 11, 12, 13, 14, 54, 55, 110,, 177, 178, 191
Leonard, "Dutch" Elmore 11
Leonard, "Dutch" Hubert 11, 104
Lexington, North Carolina 20
Liddle, Don 69, 72, 80
Lieb, Frederick Lieb 75
Little League World Series 67
Littlefield, Dick 80
Litz, Marie 103
Lockman, Shirley (wife) 81
Lockman, Whitey 49, 57, 69, 80, 81
Loes, Billy 75
Lolich, Mickey 149, 151
Lollar, Sherman 135
Long Creek High (North Carolina) 16, 17
Lopez, Al 67, 71, 75, 134, 135, 139, 142, 145, 146
Los Angeles Angels (California, Anaheim) 36, 159, 165, 166, 174

Index

Los Angeles Dodgers 38, 129, 134, 152, 163, 166, 175, 176
Los Angeles Memorial Coliseum 38, 106
Los Angeles Times 178
Lou Gehrig Day 11
Louisville 38
Louisville Colonels 4
Luciano, Ron 3, 4, 5
Lumpe, Jerry 89, 91, 92, 93, 101
Lyons, Ted 5, 90, 156, 157

Mack, Connie 29, 30
Macon (Georgia) Peaches 34
Maddux, Greg 91
Maglie, Sal 42, 43, 44, 48, 52, 57, 58, 59, 66, 69, 84
Major League Baseball 1, 3, 5, 19, 24, 29, 31, 58, 66, 99, 130, 149, 178
Major League Baseball Rules Committee 139, 140, 145
Malamud, Bernard 56
Mantle, Mickey 89, 91, 92, 93, 96, 127, 128
Marichal, Juan 130
Maris, Roger 127, 129
Marquard, Rube 90
Marshall, Jim 88
Marshall, Mike 152, 153
Maryland 96
Mathewson, Christy 90
Martin, Billy 33
Martin, J.C. 134, 135, 136, 141, 146
Mathews, Eddie 47, 58, 128, 130
Mays, Carl 118
Mays, Willie 35, 36, 39, 40, 42, 44, 60, 66, 68, 69, 70, 106, 128, 129, 167
McAuliffe, Anthony C. (general) 26, 27
McCall, "Windy" Johnny 65, 180
McCarthy, Joseph (U.S. Senator) 58
McDaniel, Lindy 82, 83
McDaniel, Von 82, 83
McDowell, Sam 149
McGinnity, "Iron Man" Joe 149, 152
McGraw, John 95
McKechnie, Bill 35
McMahon, Don 158
McLain, Denny 149
McLish, Cal 84
McMillan, Roy 64
Mecklenburg County (North Carolina) 8
Melton, Bill 148
Memphis 19
Mikkelson, Pete 175

Miller, Jim 32
Miller, Stu 128, 129
Milwaukee 38, 77
Milwaukee Braves 21, 62, 66, 75, 82
Minneapolis Millers 34, 35, 36, 37, 38, 39, 40, 41, 42, 51, 63, 168
Minneapolis Star Tribune 37
Minnesota 37, 42, 63
Minnesota Twins 36, 130
Minoso, Minnie 155
Miranda, Willy 94, 105
Miss Maryland 103
Mizell, Wilmer (Vinegar Bend) 82
Moeller, Joe 176
Montero, Rafael 90
Montreal Expos 173
Montreal Royals 36
Monzant, Ramon 78
Moon, Wally 106
Moore, Ned C. (Lt. Colonel) 27
Mooresville, North Carolina 20
Mooresville Moors 20, 21, 22, 23, 27, 30, 31, 35, 48
Morgan, Ray 45, 46
Morris, Jack 91
Moss, Les 145
Moyer, Jamie 156
Mueller, Don 57, 66, 71
Murray, Jim 178, 179, 180
Murtaugh, Danny 129
Musburger, Brent 185
Musial, Stan 58, 81

Napp, Larry 116, 117
Narleski, Ray 104
NASCAR 8
National Basketball Association 9, 30
National Football League 9, 30, 68, 99, 102
National League 2, 5, 17, 19, 24, 42, 45, 47, 51, 52, 54, 57, 58, 60, 66, 75, 80, 83, 90, 106, 119, 120, 128, 129, 130, 152, 166, 172, 176, 177, 181
The Natural 56
Nebraska 19
Negro Leagues 36, 39, 47, 66
New Orleans 19
New York 42, 45, 61, 66, 67, 68, 73, 87
New York Daily News 53, 81
New York Giants 2, 18, 20, 32, 34, 35, 39, 40, 41, 42, 43, 44, 47, 48, 49, 51, 53, 54, 55, 57, 59, 60, 61, 62, 63, 65, 66, 67, 68, 69, 70, 72, 73, 74, 75, 76, 78, 79, 80, 81, 100, 106, 117, 137, 168, 183, 186

209

Index

New York Giants (football) 99
New York Highlanders 152
New York Mets 122, 153, 177
New York Post 149
New York Times 167
New York Yankees 5, 11, 18, 19, 21, 24, 30, 43, 46, 49, 58, 60, 66, 67, 75, 76, 78, 88, 90, 91, 92, 93, 94, 96, 101, 102, 106, 118, 120, 122, 125, 127, 128, 153, 154, 171, 177, 179, 180, 184, 186, 189, 192
Newcombe, Don 42, 75
Newhauser, Hal 67
Nicholson, Dave 132, 136
Nicollet Park 36, 38, 39, 40
Niekro, Joe 5, 110, 169, 170, 179
Niekro, Phil 2, 4, 5, 54, 91, 110, 111, 156, 157, 169, 170, 171, 172, 176, 180, 191
Niekro, Phil, Sr. 5, 110, 169
Nieman, Bob 90, 92, 94, 106, 107
Niggeling, Johnny 11, 12
Nixon, Richard (vice president) 106
Nixon, Russ 86
North Carolina 1, 7, 13, 16, 29, 34, 48, 61, 71, 73, 74, 83, 109, 131, 163, 186, 191
North Carolina State League 20, 27, 30, 32, 34
Northwestern League 35
Nunez, Roberto 40

Oakland Athletics 158
Ohio 5, 158, 169
Oklahoma 12, 23
O'Neill, Harry 29
Orient, Iowa 19
The Orioles (poem) 105
Orosco, Jesse 169
Osteen, Claude 172
Owens, Brick 45

Pacific Coast League 126
Paepke, Dennis 165
Page, Joe 46
Paige, Satchel 156, 189
Palmer, Jim 91, 149
Palmolive Rapid Shave 84
Papai, Al 110
Pappas, Milt 125, 132
Paris, Texas 23
Pascual, Camilo 130
Patterson, Floyd 111
Patton, George S. (general) 26
Pearl Harbor 21
Pearson, Albie 105
Perranoski, Ron 176

Perry, Gaylord 91, 156
Peters, Gary 136, 163
Petralli, Geno 64
Philadelphia 13
Philadelphia Athletics 18, 29, 30, 40, 93, 117
Philadelphia Phillies 13, 18, 48, 52, 53, 65, 76, 120, 149, 153
Phoenix 43, 81, 137, 138
Pierce, Billy 58, 139, 184
Pieretti, Marino 12
Piersall, Jim 141
Pittsburgh Pirates 18, 19, 51, 52, 53, 57, 58, 76, 77, 78, 106, 129, 138, 145, 151, 153, 185
Pizarro, Juan 136, 145
Podres, Johnny 75
Poland 21
Polo Grounds 42, 47, 48, 49, 50, 64, 67, 70, 76
Pope, Dave 72
Porter, J.W. (Jay) 85, 86
Post, Wally 63
Powers, Jimmy 70
Presbyterian College 29
Pressly, Ryan 90
Priddy, Bob 165, 168, 169
Pro Football Hall of Fame 122
Pulitzer Prize 178
Purkey, Bob 77, 78, 110

Quinn, Jack 156

Radbourn, Charles 90
Ramsey, Toad 4
Rearden, Jeff 179
Reese, Pee Wee 42, 48, 75
Regan, Phil 176
Reynolds, Allie 58
Reynolds, Debbie 160
Rhodes, Dusty 68, 70, 71
Richards, Paul 83, 84, 88, 93, 94, 97, 98, 101, 102, 106, 112, 114, 117, 118, 120, 121, 123, 124, 125, 126, 127, 128, 129, 130, 131, 134, 139, 140, 145, 146, 161, 162, 166, 186, 187
Richardson, Bobby 89, 91, 94
Richmond Braves 175
Rickey, Branch 17, 78
Ridzik, Steve 78
Rigney, Bill 44, 47, 52, 78
Riverfront Stadium 172
Rivers, Mickey 165
Roberts, Robin 48, 58

210

Index

Robinson, Brooks 90, 94, 98, 99, 128
Robinson, Eddie 83, 84, 116, 117
Robinson, Frank 106, 128, 129
Robinson, Jackie 21, 36, 42, 48, 58, 75, 80
Robinson, Wilbert 95
Rochester Red Wings 177
Roe, Preacher 42
Romano, John 191, 192
Rommel, Ed 5
Roosevelt, Franklin D. 21, 23
Rose, Pete 155
Rosen, Al 67, 69, 72
Rucker, Nap 4
Rusie, Amos 90
Ruth, Babe 24, 45, 46, 127
Ryan, Nolan 54, 90, 131, 156, 160
Ryan, Rosy (Wilfred Patrick Dolan) 38, 39

Sacramento, California 19
Sain, Johnny 153
St. Louis Brown Stockings 90
St. Louis Browns 4, 11, 18, 24, 88, 95, 102
St. Louis Cardinals 17, 18, 24, 31, 46, 58, 62, 75, 80, 82, 83, 87, 100, 102, 119, 125, 128, 159, 168, 182, 185
St. Paul, Minnesota 37, 38
St. Petersburg, Florida 81
Salisbury, North Carolina 20
San Diego Padres 132, 177
Sanford, Florida 40
San Francisco 78, 128
San Francisco Giants 79, 92, 128, 130, 137, 138
San Quentin 120
Sarasota, Florida 131, 157, 163, 164, 189
The Saturday Evening Post 13
Saves (creation of baseball statistic) 45
Schact, Al (Clown Prince of Baseball) 121
Schenectady, New York 67
Schoendienst, Red 80
Schwall, Don 130
Seattle 82
Seattle Rainiers 126
Seaver, Tom 91, 172
Seminick, Andy 64
Shantz, Bobby 93, 94, 95
Shibe Park 52
Shore, Ernie 45, 46
Siebern, Norm 89, 91, 92, 94
Simmons, Curt 58
Simpson, Wallace 103

Skowron, Bill 89, 91, 92, 93, 192
Slaughter, Enos 95, 185
Smith, Al 69, 70, 71, 132
Smith, Hal 82
Smith, Red 64
Snider, Duke 66, 75
South Atlantic League (Sally League) 33, 34
South Carolina 23
Southern League 19
Spahn, Warren 21, 22, 30, 58, 91, 128, 136
Spalding, Albert 119
Spencer, George 48, 52
Spokane Dodgers 175
The Sporting News 46, 75, 121, 132, 145, 166
Sports Illustrated 109, 110, 111, 113, 114
Stanky, Eddie 145, 174, 192
Statesville, North Carolina 20
Steadman, John 180
Stengel, Casey 21, 46, 58, 60, 66, 93, 106, 122
Stevens, Connie 160
Stewart, Tony 8
Stieglitz, Al 138
Stone, George 168, 169
Stoneham, Horace 79, 80, 81
Street, Gabby 156
Superior, Wisconsin 19
Sutherland, Gary 161
Suzuki, Ichiro 156
Syracuse Chiefs 177

Tampa, Florida 157
Tanner, Chuck 148, 150, 152, 153
Tasby Willie 90, 93, 94, 107
Taylor, Elizabeth 160
Tebeau, George 49
Tekulve, Kent 153
Temple, Johnny 63, 64
Terre Haute, Indiana 163
Texas Rangers 64, 180
Thomas, Pinch 45
Thomasville, North Carolina 20
Thompson, Hank 36, 39, 57, 66, 69, 70, 71
Thompson, Sam 156
Thomson, Bobby 42
Throneberry, Marv 89, 93, 94
Tiefenauer, Bobby 139
Tiger Stadium 161
Toledo 38
Tommy John surgery 163, 164

211

Index

Topps (baseball cards) 138
Toronto Blue Jays 171
Torrez, Mike 168
Triandos, Gus 90, 92, 94, 96, 101, 103, 105, 106, 113, 114, 117, 118, 120, 121, 122, 123, 126, 127, 134, 146
Tri-State League 33
Turley, Bob 102

Uecker, Bob 171
United States 21, 25, 30, 56, 106
United States Army 23, 25, 29, 32, 44, 80
United States Marines 56
United States Navy 31
University of North Carolina at Charlotte 8
University of Oklahoma 138

Valentine, Bobby 191
Vance, (Dazzy) Charles 19, 90
Vaughan, Arky 185
Veeck, Bill 155
Verden, Gwen 107
Verlander, Justin 90
Veryzer, Tom 161
Virginia 134

Waddell, Rube 35
Wainright, Adam 49
Wakefield, Tim 5, 156, 157, 176
Walker, Jerry 106, 126
Walsh, "Big" Ed 90, 149
Ward, Pete 132, 136
Washington, D.C. 36, 130
Washington Senators 10, 11, 12, 13, 18, 36, 45, 110, 121, 126, 128, 134, 158
Watts, Ginger 32
Wertz, Vic 69, 70, 71
Western Carolina League 179
Western League 35
West Palm Beach, Florida 167
Westrum, Wes 63, 64, 65, 66, 77
Wetzler, Norman 103
Wheat, Zach 35
White, Bill 49, 80, 130
White, Diane 103
Widger, Chris 192
Wilhelm, Cooper (brother) 18
Wilhelm, Ethel (mother) 7
Wilhelm, James "Hoyt" 1, 2, 3, 5, 6, 7, 8, 9, 10, 11, 12, 14, 15, 17, 18, 19, 20, 22, 23, 24, 25, 27, 28, 29, 30, 31, 32, 33, 34, 35, 36, 37, 39, 40, 42, 43, 44, 46, 47, 48, 49, 50, 51, 52, 54, 55, 56, 57, 58, 59, 60, 61, 62, 63, 64, 65, 66, 68, 69, 71, 72, 73, 74, 75, 76, 77, 78, 79, 80, 81, 82, 83, 84, 85, 86, 87, 88, 90, 91, 92, 93, 94, 95, 96, 97, 98, 99, 100, 101, 102, 103, 104, 105, 106, 107, 108, 109, 110, 111, 112, 113, 114, 116, 117, 120, 122, 123, 125, 127, 128, 129, 130, 131, 132, 133, 134, 136, 138, 139, 140, 141, 142, 143, 144, 145, 146, 147, 148, 150, 153, 154, 155, 157, 158, 159, 161, 163, 164, 165, 166, 167, 168, 170, 172, 173, 174, 175, 176, 177, 178, 179, 180, 181, 182, 183, 185, 186, 188, 189, 190, 191, 192, 193
Wilhelm, James (son) 73, 96, 185
Wilhelm, John (father) 7
Wilhelm, Pam 73, 96, 185
Wilhelm, Patti (daughter) 73, 96, 97, 185
Wilhelm, Reeves Peggy (wife) 73, 81, 88, 95, 96, 97, 131, 157, 185, 186, 189, 193
Williams, Davey 57, 71
Williams, Dick 90, 91, 93, 94
Williams, Ted 21, 22, 29, 30, 31, 35, 56, 57, 58, 100, 101, 180
Wills, Maury 129
Wilson Sporting Goods 121, 146
Wisconsin 58
Wolff, Roger 11, 12
Wood, Sandy (Wilbur wife) 145, 150
Wood, Smokey Joe 111, 112
Wood, Wilbur 5, 114, 134, 135, 143, 145, 146, 147, 148, 149, 150, 151, 152, 153, 155, 158, 160, 161, 162, 163, 180, 184, 193
Wood, Wilbur, Sr. 144, 147
Woodling, Gene 90, 92, 93
World Series 4, 5, 24, 31, 38, 43, 44, 46, 60, 61, 67, 68, 69, 70, 71, 72, 73, 74, 75, 76, 89, 90, 91, 110, 116, 118, 134, 152, 187
World War I 37
World War II 9, 21, 23, 25, 28, 29, 32, 36, 45, 46, 56, 80, 165, 186
Wright, George 118
Wright, Steven 64, 178
Wulf, Bob 84, 85, 86
Wynegar, Butch 171
Wynn, Early 67, 70, 106, 136, 150

Yankee Stadium 11, 30, 121, 153, 185
Yastrzemski, Carl 35
Young, Cy 5, 90, 158, 159, 167

Zimmer, Don 128
Zuverink, George 84

www.ingramcontent.com/pod-product-compliance
Ingram Content Group UK Ltd.
Pitfield, Milton Keynes, MK11 3LW, UK
UKHW041959140426
5217IPUK00015B/886